50 Hikes in West Virginia

50 *Hikes*
In West Virginia
From the Allegheny Mountains to the Ohio River

Second Edition

LEONARD M. ADKINS

THE COUNTRYMAN PRESS
Woodstock, Vermont

AN INVITATION TO THE READER

With time, access points may change, and trails, signs, and landmarks referred to in this book may be altered. If you find that such changes have occurred on the trails described in this book, please let the author and the publisher know so that corrections may be made in future editions. The author and publisher also welcome other comments and suggestions. Address all correspondence to:

The Countryman Press
P.O. Box 748
Woodstock, VT 05091

Note: any water sources are identified for hikers' convenience, but this is not an endorsement of their purity. All water should be treated before consuming.

Maps by Erin Greb Cartography,
© The Countryman Press
Book design by Glenn Suokko
Text composition by Eugenie S. Delaney
Interior photographs by the author

Published by The Countryman Press,
P.O. Box 748, Woodstock, VT 05091
Distributed by W. W. Norton & Company, Inc.,
500 Fifth Avenue, New York, NY 10110

Printed in the United States of America

10 9 8 7 6 5 4 3 2

This world, after all our science and sciences, is still a miracle; wonderful, inscrutable, magical and more, to whosoever will think of it.

—Thomas Carlyle

DEDICATION

Dedicated to the people of West Virginia, who know the trials, tribulations, and hard work it takes to keep the Mountain State wild, wonderful, and full of beauty and majesty.

Acknowledgments

In preparing this book, I relied upon scores of people to point me in the right direction, grant me a place to stay, shuttle me miles out of their way, provide volumes of useful information, and check over manuscripts. Without your unselfish aid, *50 Hikes in West Virginia* would never have become a reality:

Marilyn Aikman, Thomas D. Ambrose, Mathew S. Baker, Steve Bolar, Colby Caldwell, Sam Cowell, Scott Durham, Samuel A. England, Pat Harrison, James E. Harvey, John Hendley, Debbie Keener, Jeffrey D. Layfield, Kenneth Long, Mark Mingele, Paul Minigh, Bert Nolan, Jim Phillips, Michael Smith, J. D. Spencer, Dorinda Taylor, and Jesse Uldrich with the West Virginia Division of Natural Resources; Diane Artale, William J. Cober, Julie Fosbender, Tim Henry, James M. Miller, Janet Miller, and Jack Tribble with the United States Forest Service; Janet Butler with the U.S. Fish and Wildlife Service; Dave Bieri, Scot McElveen, Rebecca Harriett, and Katy Miller with the National Park Service; Tom Raker with Coonskin Park; Craig Pyles with Mountwood Park; Margaret Mary Layne and Rose Rite with the Huntington Museum of Art; and the many others who provided shuttles, hints, information, kindness, and more.

Caryn Gresham with the West Virginia Division of Tourism—Thank you for the hours and days you spent making arrangements.

Dr. Stephen Lewis, Caroline Cheronko, Susie Surfas, and Terry Cumming—Thank you for the many thousands of extra trail miles you have given me.

Nancy Adkins—The foundation you provided me has proved to be strong through the years.

Kathleen, John, Tim, and Jay Yelenic—Thank you for always supporting me, and never saying, "He's doing what?"

Laurie—My love, my life, my all.

50 Hikes in West Virginia at a Glance

HIKE	REGION
1. Harpers Ferry and Virginius Island	Eastern Panhandle
2. Cacapon Resort State Park	Eastern Panhandle
3. Tuscarora Trail	Eastern Panhandle
4. Cranny Crow Overlook	Eastern Panhandle
5. South Branch	Potomac Highlands
6. North Fork Mountain	Potomac Highlands
7. Seneca Rocks	Potomac Highlands
8. Dolly Sods Wilderness	Potomac Highlands
9. Dolly Sods North	Potomac Highlands
10. Flatrock Plains	Potomac Highlands
11. Canaan Valley	Potomac Highlands
12. Blackwater Falls State Park	Potomac Highlands
13. Blackwater to Canaan	Potomac Highlands
14. Laurel Fork Wilderness	Potomac Highlands
15. Allegheny Trail	Potomac Highlands
16. Kennison Mountain and the Cow Pasture Trail	Potomac Highlands
17. Greenbrier River Trail	Potomac Highlands
18. Tea Creek	Potomac Highlands
19. Cranberry Wilderness	Potomac Highlands
20. Cranberry River/Lick Branch	Potomac Highlands
21. Falls of Hills Creek	Potomac Highlands
22. Laurel Creek and Lockridge Mountain	Potomac Highlands
23. Droop Mountain	Potomac Highlands
24. Beartown State Park	Potomac Highlands
25. Lake Sherwood	Potomac Highlands

GOOD FOR KIDS
S   for kids with a bit of stamina

CAMPING
B   backcountry camping
D   developed camping available within
    the park or forest
N   developed camping nearby

DISTANCE (miles)	GOOD FOR KIDS	WATER VIEWS	MOUNTAIN VIEWS	CAMPING	NOTES
2.1	★	★		N	Thomas Jefferson said view "worth a voyage across the Atlantic."
5.6					One of West Virginia's first four state parks
8.8			★	B	Part of a 250-mile multistate long-distance trail
4.1	S		★	N	Moderate ascent to bucolic view of West Virginia and Virginia
1.25	★	★	★	D	Excellent day outing for the entire family
23.9			★	B	Many outstanding views on an easy-to-moderate overnighter
3.0	★		★	N	A 700-foot ascent beside one of the state's famous landmarks
18.8	★		★	B	One of the most popular wilderness areas in the East
12.7			★	B	Plains, barrens, bogs, stunted spruce, and wide vistas
7.5	★		★	B	Landscape similar to previous two hikes, but fewer visitors
8.0	S		★	D	More like New England and Canada than West Virginia
5.5	★	★	★	D	Waterfall on the hike; other falls available via side trips
9.7			★	B	New England–type scenery on a lodge-to-lodge hike
16.0		★		B, D	One of the least visited wilderness areas in the East
44.4		★	★	B	Scenic rivers, virgin spruce, views, and isolated valleys
12.4				B	Gentle grades and obvious routes in lush deciduous forest
25.4				B	Level rail-trail hike with restaurant and lodging options
12.1		★		B	The nine stream fords are easy (except in high water)
22.7	★			B	Moderate grades; many fishing and swimming opportunities
8.7				B	Same beauty and opportunities as previous hike, but shorter
1.5	S	★		N	Three grand waterfalls in one hike
8.8				B	Good choice for a leisurely weekend outing
2.5	★		★		Site of the state's largest Civil War battle
0.5	★				Fairy-tale land of rock formations and narrow crevasses
10.9		★		B, D	A walk along the West Virginia–Virginia border

50 Hikes in West Virginia at a Glance

HIKE	REGION
26. Anthony Creek	Potomac Highlands
27. Kate's Mountain	Southern West Virginia
28. The Appalachian Trail	Southern West Virginia
29. Pipestem State Park	Southern West Virginia
30. Bluestone River	Southern West Virginia
31. Bluestone Lake	Southern West Virginia
32. New River Gorge	Southern West Virginia
33. Grandview	Southern West Virginia
34. Twin Falls Resort State Park	Southern West Virginia
35. Panther Wildlife Management Area	Southern West Virginia
36. Carnifex Ferry Battlefield State Park	Central West Virginia
37. Cedar Creek State Park	Central West Virginia
38. Stonewall Resort State Park	Central West Virginia
39. Lewis Wetzel Wildlife Management Area	Central West Virginia
40. Cooper's Rock State Forest	Central West Virginia
41. Oglebay Park	Northern Panhandle
42. Tomlinson Run State Park	Northern Panhandle
43. Chief Logan State Park	Western West Virginia
44. Beech Fork State Park	Western West Virginia
45. Huntington Museum of Art	Western West Virginia
46. Kanawha State Forest	Western West Virginia
47. Coonskin Park	Western West Virginia
48. North Bend Rail-Trail	Western West Virginia
49. Mountwood Park	Western West Virginia
50. Middle Island/Ohio River	Western West Virginia

GOOD FOR KIDS
S   for kids with a bit of stamina

CAMPING
B   backcountry camping
D   developed camping available within the park or forest
N   developed camping nearby

DISTANCE (miles)	GOOD FOR KIDS	WATER VIEWS	MOUNTAIN VIEWS	CAMPING	NOTES
5.4		★	★	B,D	Can be a combination hiking/fly-fishing outing
8.9			★	D	Site of flora found only on shale barrens
14.9			★	B	Views from two mountain meadows
7.3	★	★	★	D	Views of Bluestone River Canyon, small waterfall, and lake
3.6		★	★	D	Take a tramway to the beginning of the hike
5.0		★		D	Varied landscape of lakeside, streams, forest, and hollow
5.6	★		★		Hike into New River Gorge to old coal mining site
3.6			★	D	Grandview—the name says it all
8.0	★				Two loops that could be done at separate times
5.6	★			D	View of three states
2.0			★	N	Easy family hike at Civil War battle site
2.2				D	Short, but steep ascent and descent; abundant wildlife
1.9	★	★		D	Easy walk to good view of 2,650-acre lake
3.5				D	Rugged hike for experienced hikers on unmarked trails
8.9			★	D	View into gorge, iron furnace ruins, and rock formations
3.9	★			N	Municipal park with many attractions, including a zoo
6.2				D	Two loops that could be done on separate occasions
5.6				D	A spring wildflower-lover's paradise
2.9	★	★		D	Excellent year-round birdwatching
1.6	★				Less than a 10-minute drive from downtown Huntington
11.1				D	Some of the state's most varied flora and fauna
1.1	★				Less than a 15-minute drive from downtown Charleston
22.9				D	Rail-trail hiking with campground or lodging option
3.7				D	An exploration of oil-gas industry history
2.25	★	★			Easy walk on an island in the Ohio River

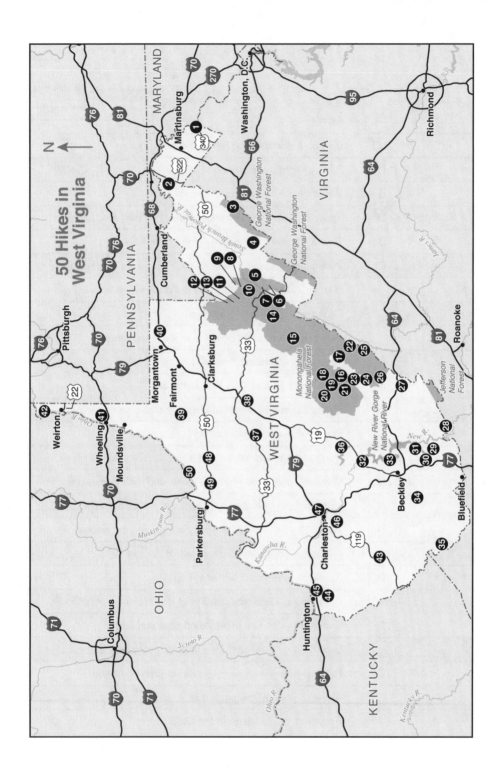

Contents

Introduction

Welcome to this second edition of a hiking tour of my native state, West Virginia. I had more fun doing the field research for this book than a person doing a job should expect to have. I revisited old haunts from high school and college days and tramped around places I had always wanted to visit, but could never find the time. In fact, I had so much fun that I felt like a kid again, set free in a statewide amusement park, excitedly running from attraction to attraction: "Ooh, look at that!" "Wow, can't wait to see what it's like to be on that one!" "Oh yeah, let's go over there!"

This book will take you on your own travels, from West Virginia's lowest point at Harpers Ferry to its loftiest heights more than 4,000 feet above sea level; from its southern border farther south than Roanoke, Virginia, to its Northern Panhandle on the same latitude as Staten Island, New York; from the Ohio River farther west than Columbus, Ohio to the Eastern Panhandle only an hour's drive from downtown Washington, D.C. It is in hiking through these places that you will come to know, and appreciate, the state's human history and the true beauty of its scenery and natural history.

In the Eastern Panhandle, you can walk in the footsteps of Thomas Jefferson and Meriwether Lewis, visit a structure that once protected Lyndon Johnson from the elements, and hike a pathway that was built as an alternate route for the world-famous Appalachian Trail.

Many people hold the belief that the Potomac Highlands possess the state's most spectacular scenery, and, while it may take a great amount of physical energy to negotiate the ups and downs found here, the rewards more than compensate. Your gaze can extend for miles upon wave after wave of Allegheny ridgelines, dozens of waterfalls rush down steep slopes, and the opportunities to camp in the backcountry, well isolated from the modern world, are limitless. Hemlock-lined mountain streams, hidden mountain valleys, and an abundance of deer, black bear, coyotes, and other wildlife are the norm rather than the exception.

Hikes in southern West Virginia will take you by notable wildflowers found only in shale barren environments, into the depths of two spectacular river gorges, and across a land whose natural and human history have been shaped by rich deposits of coal. Water is the focus of several of the outings in central West Virginia, with a large lake, small fishing ponds, and another river gorge providing the scenery.

The Northern Panhandle also leads you beside flowing water, as well as providing an exploration of one of the country's finest municipal parks. Several hikes in the western portion of the Mountain State are within a few minutes' drive of its two largest cities, while other journeys include an overnight outing on a rail-trail and an ambulation of an Ohio River island.

The hardest part of writing *50 Hikes in West Virginia* was deciding which hikes to include and which to exclude. There are certainly more than 50 good hikes in West Virginia, and those of you familiar with the state may wonder why some well-known areas are absent. For example, although there are many nice footpaths around West Virginia's highest point, Spruce Knob, I did not describe any of them because a roadway leads right to the summit, enabling you to enjoy what it has to offer without expending any hiking energy. In addition, places like Otter Creek Wilderness, which is certainly a worthwhile destination, are not included because their scenery and hiking experiences are similar to locations that are included, and I wanted to be able to describe other spots that are unique or not as well traveled.

Although this book contains pages of interpretive information about the human and natural history you will experience, there is certainly much more to be learned than can be presented here. To help you gain an even greater awareness, enjoyment, and understanding of your surroundings, I urge you to read—and possibly carry—some additional books and field guides, and the Suggested Readings and Field Guides list near the end of this Introduction is a good place to start.

Like other guidebooks, this one will direct you to the most popular hikes to be found within a particular region, but it will also open up marvelous, new areas that are too often overlooked. With descriptions of more than 400 miles of trails, this book offers hikes for every degree of physical stamina and time constraint. Mirroring the bounty of outdoor opportunities in West Virginia is the fact that, no matter where you happen to be at any given moment, you will never be much more than a 30-minute drive away from one of the hikes.

Located in the Mid-Atlantic states, West Virginia experiences a wide range of temperatures and weather conditions. Winters can be unpredictably cold or relatively mild, while summers can become hot and humid or may be rather temperate. Spring and autumn can be the most pleasant times of the year to be outdoors, as days warm up to a comfortable degree, nights cool down for easy sleeping, and crowds are fewer. When heat and humidity have taken the joy and fun out of outdoor activities in the lower elevations, the mountains will beckon with temperatures that can be 10 or more degrees lower.

Be willing to visit an area more than once, and do not limit your outings in West Virginia to just one or two seasons. Outdoor adventuring here can be a year-round activity.

In putting this book together, it has been my desire that it will inspire you to visit, appreciate, and learn more about the best that West Virginia has to offer. Happy trails.

HOW TO USE THIS BOOK

The variety of outings in *50 Hikes in West Virginia* ranges from easy walks on level ground to ambitious, multiday backpacking excursions over rugged terrain. No matter your level of fitness or outdoor experience, there are a number of trips that will best fit your abilities, time constraints, or quest for adventure. The headings at the beginning of each hike provide a quick overview of what to expect.

The total distance was determined by walking each hike with a surveyor's measuring wheel. You may notice some differences if you look for additional information from other sources, such as trail signs, brochures from the park or agency, or other books. Many of these merely measure distance from the trailhead and do not take into account how far you must walk to reach it. To be as accurate as possible, I measured the hike from the point where you leave your automobile to where you are able to return to it, and have included the distance of any side trail(s) the hike description tells you to take.

A one-way hike ends at a different point from where you started, necessitating a car shuttle. A round-trip is an out-and-back excursion following the same route in both directions. You will take a circular journey on a circuit hike, rewalking very little, if any, of the same trail or trails.

Keep in mind that the hiking time is the minimum amount of time it would take a person of average ability to do a trip at a leisurely pace. Some of you may go faster, a few of you slower. When planning the hike, remember that the hiking time does not take into account rest breaks or time out for sightseeing and nature study.

The vertical rise provides the best indication of how strenuous a hike will be. It is the sum total of all the uphill hiking you will do, not just the difference in elevation between the lowest and highest points of a hike. This rise was determined by using information on United States Geological Survey (USGS) maps.

The specific USGS maps that contain the topographic features of the hike are included in the map heading. The hike route is traced on these maps and reproduced for you in this book and should be all you need. Of course, you are only getting a partial view, and if you wish to see more, the entire map can help identify various features, such as nearby peaks or waterways, and can help you become proficient in orienteering. They may be obtained through outfitters or from the United States Geological Survey, 1201 Sunrise Valley Drive, Reston, VA 20191, 703-648-5953. You may need several maps to complete just one hike, and the price of each is now in the multiple-dollars range. Of course, there are many map software programs available, and you'll need to decide which one will best suit your needs and hardware. If you do decide to go that way, be sure to first check the USGS website, www.usgs.gov, as some maps are now available free of charge if downloaded.

Most of the other maps identified can be obtained, often free of charge, at the appropriate contact stations, visitors centers, or agency offices.

If you are going to be hiking any of the Forest Service trails, I suggest you purchase the map for the entire Monongahela National Forest. It will not only give you a broad overview of the areas in which you will be hiking, but since it shows almost all of the national forest's trails, it can open up a whole new world of hiking options for you. The map marks the trails with official Forest Service inventory numbers, and to help you orient yourself, I have included them in brackets (for example, {FS 621}) in the hike descriptions. I have used FSR to refer to Forest Service roads (which are usually unpaved). Be aware that trails in the national forest may not be as well maintained or marked as those in the national, state, county, or city parks.

There are, of course, a number of different routes you could take to each hike's trailhead, but the ones described are designed to keep you on four-lane highways as much as possible and, hopefully, take the least amount of driving time.

Do not reject a hike or an area because the length, time, or vertical rise appears to be beyond your abilities. Because of my proclivity to want to experience the outdoors as much as possible, I often depict the most circuitous and longest possible hike available in a particular area. Yet, many places have numerous side trails or alternate routes you could take to shorten a hike. A good example is Hike 46, Kanawha State Forest. I describe a trip of more than 11 miles, but there are so many interconnecting trails that you could take a rewarding circuit hike of only 1.0 or 2.0 miles with very little elevation change. Study maps and my descriptions, and you will find that this is the case in many places.

You do not have to be in the best physical

shape to enjoy a walk, but do take into account the difficulty of the terrain, the weather report, and your conditioning. Allow enough time to complete your outing before dark, and always let someone know where you are hiking.

ADVICE AND PRECAUTIONS

Water

If you are going to be hiking for more than an hour, take along some water. On overnight trips you are going to have to depend on a stream or spring, but the rise in the number of people visiting the natural areas of West Virginia has brought about an increase of giardia, a water-borne parasite. Water can also become tainted by viruses, bacteria, and human pollutants.

Boiling could make these water sources potable, but a portable purifier is more convenient, and possibly more effective. Be aware that a filter only removes bacteria, while a purifier is also capable of eliminating viruses. Since they cost and weigh about the same, be sure to purchase a purifier.

Please note! For your convenience, water sources have been identified in a number of the hike descriptions, but this is not an endorsement of their purity. All sources should be treated before drinking!

Snakes

Only two species of snakes in West Virginia are poisonous. The copperhead and timber rattlesnake are found throughout much of the state, so it would be wise to learn how to identify both of these pit vipers.

Do remember that the outdoors is a snake's natural habitat and that it has as much right, if not more, to be there as you do. Please refrain from killing one; just walk around it, giving it a wide berth, and continue on your way.

Important: All snakebites may contain bacteria, so seek medical attention as soon as possible for any bite.

Black Bears

West Virginia is home to more than 10,000 black bears. Although it is exceedingly rare for a black bear to attack a human, you must remember that they are wild animals and do not like to be approached at close range. Do not try to feed a bear. Not only does this endanger you, it also endangers the bear. Once a bear becomes used to close human contact, it may begin wandering into campsites or housing developments looking for free handouts. This often results in the bear having to be destroyed by the authorities.

Insects

Warm weather brings no-see-ums, gnats, fleas, deerflies, mosquitoes, ticks, and more. Bring repellent on any hike from late spring to mid-fall. (And remember that one of the pleasures of hiking during the colder months is the absence of insects.)

Recent years have seen a rise in the reported cases of Lyme disease, a bacterial infection transmitted by the bite of a deer tick. Check yourself for ticks after each outing, remembering that the thing you are looking for could be as small as the period at the end of this sentence.

Plants

Poison ivy is found just about everywhere in West Virginia. Learn how to identify it, as it can grow in a number of forms. The most common is a woody shrub up to 2 feet high, which will grow in large patches, often lining or overtaking pathways. Just as likely, it will grow as a hairy, root-covered vine that clings to the trunk of a tree, climbing far up into the branches. All parts of the plant contain the poison, and this is true even in winter, when it appears to be dead.

Not as prevalent, but certainly present, poison oak is most often found in sandy soil habitats. As its name suggests, its leaflets resemble the leaves of an oak tree but are fuzzy. Also be on the lookout for poison sumac, considered by some to be one of the most dangerous plants in the United States, poison sumac occurs most notably in the lower portions of the state. Unlike the low-standing poison ivy, it can grow to be 25 feet in height and has compound leaves with an odd number of leaflets. The upper sides of the leaflets are shiny green, while the bottom sides are lighter, with small hairs.

Stinging nettle will grow in large carpets and encroach upon pathways that are not well maintained. Brushing up against the plant may cause your skin to itch for the rest of the day.

Sun

The consensus in the medical community is that you should apply a high-strength sunblock whenever you will be outdoors for extended periods of time—summer or winter.

Hunting

Due to the abundance of wildlife, hunting is extremely popular in West Virginia, even in the more populated counties. The usual season is from early fall into January, with another season in the spring. Dates do vary from year to year and place to place, so check with local authorities. During the season, it may be best to hike in a group; do not venture forth without wearing some kind of blaze-orange clothing. If you are hunting (or fishing), be sure to obtain the proper licenses, and check about local regulations.

Unattended Vehicles

There is always the possibility of theft and vandalism to cars left unattended at trail-heads, so it is wise to leave your valuables at home. Place whatever valuables you do have out of sight, and lock the car. If you are going to leave a car overnight, be sure to give a ranger or the proper authority your vehicle's make and license number, the length of time you will be leaving it, and the name of each person in your party.

One way to avoid a car shuttle on a one-way hike, and the problems associated with leaving an automobile overnight, is to have someone drop you off at the beginning and pick you up when you have finished.

Proper Clothing and Equipment

As with any outdoor pursuit, when hiking you need to be ready for abrupt fluctuations in the weather. Warm and sunny summer days may become cold and rainy in just a matter of minutes. Also, do not be surprised if a pleasant spring or fall day changes to one with sleet or snow.

Because people are caught off guard on days such as this, when the temperature dips into the low 60s and 50s, hypothermia—one of the leading causes of hiker and camper deaths—may strike. Be prepared by carrying raingear and an insulating layer of clothing in your day pack. Layering is a more effective means of keeping warm than wearing one thick garment, so carry several items of clothing for winter travel.

In addition to the above, your pack should include a first aid kit, flashlight, knife, compass, toilet paper, and waterproof matches. Be prepared for possible cool nights, even in the summer.

It is not necessary to subject your feet to the tortures of heavy-duty boots to enjoy hiking in West Virginia. Excluding those who have ankle or foot problems, comfortable tennis, walking, or running shoes would probably suffice for most of the hikes—especially the shorter ones on easier terrain. Lightweight hiking boots or shoes should be sufficient for journeys into the mountains and on overnight trips.

Applying moleskin (available at most pharmacies and outdoors outfitters) immediately at the first sign of a "hot spot" will help prevent blisters from developing.

The above are just the basics you should know about foot travel in areas removed from the mainstream. Obviously it is not the intent of this guidebook to be a hiking or backpacking primer, so I suggest you solicit advice from backpacking acquaintances, trail club members, and outdoors outfitters. I am a firm believer in supporting your neighborhood backpacking shop instead of mail-order companies. Not only will the local folks help fit and adjust your equipment and be there if you have any questions but many shops also rent hiking and camping equipment—enabling you to try something before you decide to buy it.

A number of books are available if you feel the need for further information. Currently, two of the most complete books on the subject of outdoor travel are *Backpacking and Hiking* by Karen Berger and *Hiking and Backpacking: Essential Skills, Equipment, and Safety* by Victoria Logue. *Trail Life: Ray Jardine's Lightweight Backpacking* contains some debatable, yet very innovative information. *The Complete Walker IV* by Colin Fletcher and Chip Rawlins is not only informative but also makes for some entertaining reading.

HIKING AND CAMPING ETIQUETTE

Endorsed by almost every organization connected with the outdoors, the Leave No Trace principles have been developed to protect a fragile natural world from increased usage. (This copyrighted information has been reprinted with permission from the Leave No Trace Center for Outdoor Ethics. For more information or materials, please visit www.LNT.org or call 1-800-332-4100.)

Plan Ahead and Prepare
- Know the regulations and special concerns for the area you'll visit.
- Prepare for extreme weather, hazards, and emergencies.
- Schedule your trip to avoid times of high use.
- Visit in small groups when possible. Consider splitting larger groups into smaller groups.
- Repackage food to minimize waste.
- Use a map and compass to eliminate the use of marking paint, rock cairns, or flagging.

Travel and Camp on Durable Surfaces
- Durable surfaces include established trails and campsites, rock, gravel, dry grasses, or snow.
- Protect riparian areas by camping at least 200 feet from lakes and streams.
- Good campsites are found, not made. Altering a site is not necessary.

In popular areas:
- Concentrate use on existing trails and campsites.
- Walk single file in the middle of the trail, even when wet or muddy.
- Keep campsites small. Focus activity in areas where vegetation is absent.

In pristine areas:
- Disperse use to prevent the creation of campsites and trails.
- Avoid places where impacts are just beginning.

Dispose of Waste Properly
- Pack it in, pack it out. Inspect your campsite and rest areas for trash or spilled foods. Pack out all trash, leftover food, and litter.
- Deposit solid human waste in catholes

dug 6 to 8 inches deep at least 200 feet from water, camp, and trails. Cover and disguise the cathole when finished.
- Pack out toilet paper and hygiene products.
- To wash yourself or your dishes, carry water 200 feet away from streams or lakes and use small amounts of biodegradable soap. Scatter strained dishwater.

Leave What You Find
- Preserve the past: Examine, but do not touch, cultural or historic structures and artifacts.
- Leave rocks, plants, and other natural objects as you find them.
- Avoid introducing or transporting non-native species.
- Do not build structures and furniture, or dig trenches.

Minimize Campfire Impacts
- Campfires can cause lasting impacts to the backcountry. Use a lightweight stove for cooking, and enjoy a candle lantern for light.
- Where fires are permitted, use established fire rings, fire pans, or mound fires.
- Keep fires small. Only use sticks from the ground that can be broken by hand.
- Burn all wood and coals to ash, put out campfires completely, then scatter cool ashes.

Respect Wildlife
- Observe wildlife from a distance. Do not follow or approach them.
- Never feed animals. Feeding wildlife damages their health, alters natural behaviors, and exposes them to predators and other dangers.
- Protect wildlife and your food by storing rations and trash securely.

- Control pets at all times, or leave them at home.
- Avoid wildlife during sensitive times: mating, nesting, raising young, or winter.

Be Considerate of Other Visitors
- Respect other visitors, and protect the quality of their experience.
- Be courteous. Yield to other users on the trail.
- Step to the downhill side of the trail when encountering pack stock.
- Take breaks and camp away from trails and other visitors.
- Let nature's sounds prevail. Avoid loud voices and noises.

Backwoods Ethics: A Guide to Low-Impact Camping and Hiking by Laura and Guy Waterman is an excellent resource, providing details on the "how" and "why" of making little or no impact on the environment.

1

Harpers Ferry and Virginius Island

Total distance (circuit): 2.1 miles

Hiking time: 1 hour

Vertical rise: 120 feet

Maps: USGS 7½' Harpers Ferry; park map

The Hike at a Glance

0.6 Jefferson Rock
0.9 pass under railroad tracks
1.2 bridge to Virginius Island
1.7 remains of Shenandoah Pulp Mill
2.1 end

Harpers Ferry had its beginning in 1733, when Peter Stephens established a ferry service at the confluence of the Potomac and Shenandoah Rivers. Recognizing that passengers and the flow of commercial goods would grow as settlers moved westward, Robert Harper purchased the business in 1747. Soon afterward, he constructed a gristmill on low-lying land, later known as Virginius Island, at the western edge of the Shenandoah River.

Despite those humble origins, Harpers Ferry has been the scene of many major, and pivotal, events throughout the history of the United States.

On his way to Philadelphia to serve as a Virginia delegate to the Continental Congress in 1783, Thomas Jefferson gazed upon the meeting of the Potomac and Shenandoah Rivers and proclaimed the scene to be "worth a voyage across the Atlantic." (You will have a chance to take in the vista from the same vantage point as Jefferson.) In 1794, George Washington convinced the U.S. Congress to establish a federal arsenal and armory on a site close to where Harper had built his gristmill almost 50 years earlier.

Thomas Jefferson and Meriwether Lewis were so impressed with the arsenal's quality munitions that Lewis traveled to Harpers Ferry in 1803 to obtain rifles and related supplies for his upcoming expedition into the newly purchased Louisiana Territory. Around 1820, John Hall opened his Rifle Works, which manufactured rifles with interchangeable parts, a new and innovative feature.

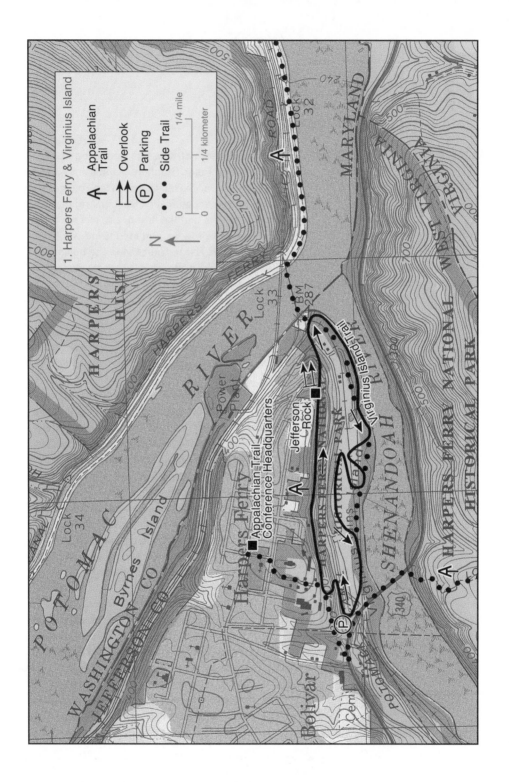

1. Harpers Ferry & Virginius Island

⋀	Appalachian Trail
⇈	Overlook
℗	Parking
••••	Side Trail

0   1/4 kilometer
0   1/4 mile

N ←

Harpers Ferry soon came to be an industrial center, with water power from the Shenandoah attracting mills, machine shops, and various other manufacturers to locate on Virginius Island. By the mid-1800s, the island had close to 40 factories and a population of more than 180.

Yet, the small town's fortunes soon changed. John Brown's short-lived invasion in October 1859 was an attempt to free slaves and destabilize the value of slave property. In what seems like irony to us now, the federal forces ordered by President James Buchanan to Harpers Ferry to capture Brown and his followers were under the command of Lieutenant Colonel Robert E. Lee.

Strategically situated as it was near the border between North and South, the town changed hands eight times during the Civil War. By the time the hostilities ended, much of the town and most of the factories had been burned and the railroad bridge destroyed. Massive floods in 1870 and 1889 damaged almost everything that the war had not. Floods in the 20th century completed the job, and by 1936, Virginius Island was abandoned.

Maple, sycamore, and box elder trees now stand where brick walls once enclosed cotton and flour mills. The songs of wood thrushes, cardinals, and blackbirds have replaced the whine of turbines and saw blades, and ducks float peacefully in the waters of the old canal.

On land that is part of Harpers Ferry National Historical Park, this moderately easy hike—it has only one short, steep ascent—affords the opportunity to relive history while taking in the area's natural beauty.

The hike starts from the small Park Service parking lot located immediately after US340 crosses the Shenandoah River from Virginia into West Virginia. (A larger lot is located 1.0 mile farther up Shoreline Drive at the park's visitors center; shuttle buses will bring you back to town.) There is a parking fee.

Ascend the steps out of the parking lot, cross paved Shoreline Drive, and turn left onto the trail next to the guardrail beside Shenandoah Street. Jewelweed grows in the moist areas to the right. At the end of the guardrail, after 0.1 mile, cross the street diagonally to the left, and climb the steep hillside via a pathway and set of crude steps. There are good winter views of the Shenandoah River as you ascend.

Turn right onto the white-blazed Appalachian Trail (AT) at 0.3 mile and continue to ascend, with money plant growing on both sides of the route. An escapee from cultivated gardens, the plant is a native of Europe that was brought to North America in the time of the Puritans. Its purple flowers are certainly pretty enough, but it is often the seed pods that are most highly prized, as they resemble small coins or coin pouches and turn translucent when dried. Remember that collecting, removing, disturbing, or killing any type of resource (plants or plant parts, animals or animal parts, mineral resources, cultural or archeological resources, and so on) on any national park land is prohibited by federal law.

Less than 200 feet later is a blue-blazed trail to the left that leads 0.3 mile to the national headquarters of the Appalachian Trail Conservancy, the umbrella organization that coordinates the actions of affiliated volunteer clubs, the National Park Service, and U.S. Forest Service. Continue on the AT as it passes below small cliffs, by Asian day flowers, and beside copious amounts of poison ivy.

The trail to the left at 0.5 mile leads to the Park Service's training facility on the campus of what was once Storer College. The school was established soon after the Civil War as one of the country's first institutions dedicated to the education of former slaves.

Stay on the AT, pass a trail to the left at 0.6 mile that leads into Harper Cemetery, and come to Jefferson Rock on your right less than 100 feet later. Sadly, the rock has become unstable, and it is now against federal law to climb on it. Yet, the view is still sweeping enough without getting on it that you can decide if you agree with Jefferson's assessment: "On your right comes up the Shenandoah, having ranged along the foot of the mountain a hundred miles to seek a vent. On your left approaches the Patomac [sic], in quest of a passage also. In the moment of their juncture, they rush together against the mountain, rent it asunder and pass off to the sea . . . This scene is worth a voyage across the Atlantic . . . Perhaps one of the most stupendous scenes in Nature."

Continue on the AT, now descending gradually. At 0.75 mile, pass by the ruins of Saint John's Episcopal Church, built in 1852 and abandoned when the congregation constructed a new church in 1895. As you follow white blazes into town, you will pass the interesting Saint Peter's Roman Catholic Church and the oldest structure in town—the Robert Harper House, constructed between 1775 and 1782. Descend the stone steps that were hand cut out of the hillside near the beginning of the 1800s, and turn right onto High Street. Cross Shenandoah Street and follow the sidewalk (a Park Service visitors center is the first building to the right) as it makes a left turn past the site of the arsenal. Within a few feet is the firehouse that John Brown and his men were forced to use as a fort when federal troops arrived to put an end to their uprising.

Make a turn under the railroad tracks, and enjoy another view, this one much closer, of the confluence of the two rivers. Take steps down to the Shenandoah, and walk upstream. There are a couple of places where the trail splits and comes back together in a few hundred feet. Taking the routes to the left lets you walk closer to the river and pass by the sites of the Market House and the homes of armory workers.

At 1.2 miles, cross the wooden bridge over the old canal and come onto Virginius Island. Near the river is the site of the 1848 cotton factory, which was converted into a flour mill after the Civil War. By 1870, it was producing 80,000 barrels of flour a year but was abandoned after the 1889 flood. Follow the trail as it swings inland, going by the foundation of Lewis Wernag's house. A renowned builder of wooden truss bridges, Wernag also operated a nearby sawmill and machine shop. Little remains to mark where 11 row houses stood just a few feet beyond Wernag's house.

Cross the railroad tracks—first laid in 1836—but be careful, as they are still used by trains carrying freight throughout the eastern United States. Just beyond the tracks is the foundation of the Herr/Child House, which survived the flood of 1870 but succumbed to the 1936 flood. Bear left here to parallel the railroad tracks; do not cross the pedestrian bridge.

You want to swing left again in just a few hundred feet, walk under the railroad tracks, and explore the brick-lined intake archways built in 1848 to control the flow of water into the Inner Basin. Return to the main route and turn left, but within a few yards turn right onto a (possibly) unmarked trail. Follow this through the woods to the right, passing by the site of Abraham Herr's flour mill. In 1861, Confederate soldiers burned the mill to the ground after learning that Herr had helped feed Union forces.

Just before coming to the pedestrian bridge over the canal at 1.6 miles, swing to the left, passing the location of an iron foundry

View from Jefferson Rock

that operated from 1835 to the 1850s. The Shenandoah Canal you are walking beside was constructed in 1806 and 1807 to provide water access to the river for the factories located on the inland side of the island.

The pillars at 1.7 miles are the remains of the Shenandoah Pulp Mill, which operated from 1888 to 1935. When running at full capacity, it produced 40 tons of wood pulp every day. Swing left onto the pathway that reenters the woods, and follow it back to the service road next to the railroad tracks, where you will turn right at 1.9 miles. Snakes are sometimes seen sunning themselves on this dirt road. Most of them are harmless, but be aware that copperheads are among those that live on Virginius Island.

Although there are variations, the copperhead's tan body has darker-colored, hourglass-shaped markings unique to its species. Like rattlesnakes, they have triangular heads, thin necks, and vertical pupils—although, if you can make out the pupils, you are probably too close! Rattlesnakes and copperheads also have heat-sensitive pits on each side of their heads between the eye and nostril that aid in locating warm-blooded prey. Basking during daylight hours in the spring and fall, and having a tendency to become nocturnal in warm summer temperatures, a copperhead can be well camouflaged by leaf litter on the forest floor.

The hike comes to an end when you return to the parking lot at 2.1 miles.

Before leaving this area, you might want to consider two other nearby hikes. One outing goes to fortifications on Maryland Heights overlooking Harpers Ferry and the rivers. Details for it may be obtained in *50 Hikes in Maryland*. The second journey is along the Boliver Heights and Union Skirmish Line Trails on the southern edge of Harpers Ferry. Personnel at the Park Service visitors center can supply information. Be aware that camping is prohibited on these hikes, as they are all on national park property, but a commercial campground is located on US340 between Harpers Ferry and Charles Town, West Virginia.

Other Civil War hikes in West Virginia are Droop Mountain (see Hike 23) and Carnifex Ferry Battlefield State Park (see Hike 36).

2

Cacapon Resort State Park

Total distance (circuit): 5.6 miles

Hiking time: 3 hours, 30 minutes

Vertical rise: 1,380 feet

Maps: USGS 7½' Great Cacapon; USGS 7½' Ridge; park map

The Hike at a Glance

0.4   *cross lower portion of Cabin Loop Trail*
1.6   *cross Middle Fork Indian Run*
2.4   *winter views into Sleepy Creek Valley*
3.2   *trailside shelter*
4.9   *cross North Fork Road*
5.6   *end*

West Virginia has one of the finest and best-managed state park systems in the country. Although some lands had been purchased earlier with the intent of establishing parklands, the system was founded in 1933, when the legislature created the Division of State Parks. The Division was directed to provide outdoor recreational opportunities and protect important natural and cultural sites throughout the state.

Aided by funds appropriated by the federal and state governments, work progressed so quickly that the first four parks—Cacapon, Lost River, Watoga, and Babcock—were dedicated on July 1, 1937. To keep momentum going, the legislature passed a $4 million revenue bond in 1953. The money was used to upgrade existing facilities and to purchase more land for additional parks. It was around this time that the idea to establish "resort" state parks—complete with lodges, modern cabins, and other amenities—began to take hold. Additional moneys in the 1960s, in the form of grants and loans from the federal government, once again permitted the state to upgrade and expand parklands.

One of the state parks' strongest points is that the citizens of West Virginia have always provided firm support. When it became obvious that many of the facilities were in need of maintenance, upgrading, and expanding, voters passed a $44 million aid package in 1997. Today, there are approximately three dozen state parks operated under the auspices of the Division of Natural Resources, which also oversees state forests and wildlife management areas.

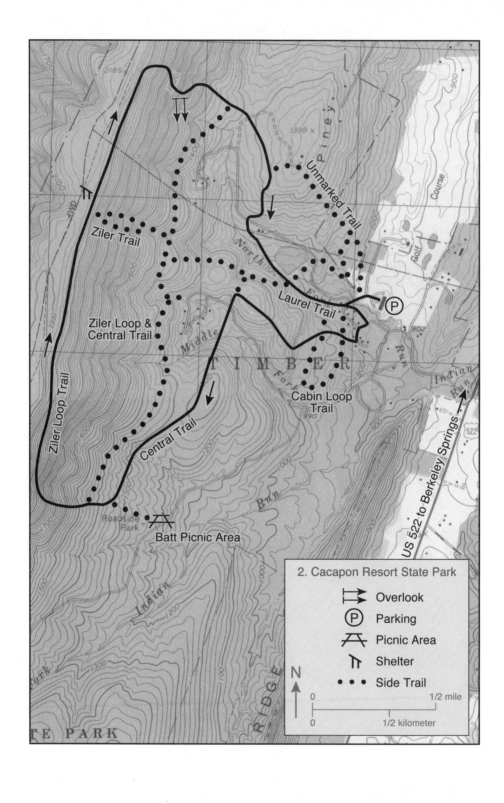

Batt Picnic Area

Roadside Park

Ziler Trail

Ziler Loop & Central Trail

Ziler Loop Trail

Central Trail

Cabin Loop Trail

Laurel Trail

Unmarked Trail

Piney

Northy... Fork

Middle Fork

Indian Run

Run

Indian

Fork

TIMBER

RIDGE

TE PARK

PARK

Golf Course

US 522 to Berkeley Springs

2. Cacapon Resort State Park

Overlook
Ⓟ Parking
Picnic Area
Shelter
•••• Side Trail

N

0   1/2 mile
0   1/2 kilometer

Just as the federal government had purchased land for Shenandoah National Park in Virginia and Catoctin Mountain Park in Maryland, the state of West Virginia obtained land for Cacapon State Park in 1934, in part to demonstrate how parks for recreation and conservation could be created from worn-out lands. Earlier owners and settlers had, for more than a century, clear-cut many acres of forest for timber, stripped oak trees of their bark for tanning, and employed farming practices unsuited to the region's terrain and soil.

Men of the Civilian Conservation Corps (CCC), camped in what is now the main picnic area, busily built trails, shelters, fire roads, and various visitor attractions. Many of the facilities they constructed, such as the Old Inn (check out the hand-wrought iron chandeliers in the lounge to appreciate the quality of CCC craftsmanship), hand-cut stone walls, and a few guest cabins, are still in use.

So many other amenities have been added through the years that the park is now known as Cacapon Resort State Park, complete with a large modern lodge, a restaurant, rental cabins, swimming and boat rentals in a small lake, horseback riding, picnic and playground areas, tennis courts, a nature center, and an 18-hole golf course designed by Robert Trent Jones. There is no campground or backcountry camping permitted. The park does have one of the most active nature and recreation programs I have ever come across in a state or national park. The schedule for just one week during the summer can list as many as 24 different activities. Among other things, you may find yourself wading a stream in search of crayfish and salamanders, identifying bird songs while on a morning stroll, or roasting marshmallows around an evening campfire.

Yet all of the facilities and many of the activities are concentrated on just a few hundred acres, which enables hikers to explore the remainder of the park's 6,115 acres that have been left in a natural and lightly visited state. This hike covers terrain from 825 feet above sea level at the lodge to approximately 2,300 feet on the ridgeline of Cacapon Mountain but has only a few short steep ascents and descents.

Cacapon Resort State Park may be reached by following US522 south from Berkeley Springs for close to 9 miles. Once in the park, follow signs to the main lodge, where you will leave your car in the large parking lot.

Walk back to the main park road and turn left onto it, soon turning right onto the road signed as leading to cabins 24–31. Less than 100 yards later, bear left onto the road to cabins 24–29, and make a right at cabin 25 onto the pathway designated by white, green, and orange markers. Ascend gradually into the woods on the eastern slope of Cacapon Mountain, the highest mountain in West Virginia's Eastern Panhandle. Cacapon (pronounced kuh-KAY-pon) is a derivative of a Shawnee word meaning "medicine water" and refers to the area's many springs, which have long been held by Native Americans and many others to have curative powers.

Cross the lower portion of the white-blazed Cabin Loop Trail at 0.4 mile and the upper portion in another 0.1 mile. Switchback to the right at 0.6 mile, and walk along a shelf on the hillside before turning left to continue the ascent. Drop to a low point at 1.0 mile, turn left to cross the paved Middle Fork Road, and reenter the woods on the red-blazed Central Trail, a narrower pathway than the one you had been following. In fact, it becomes almost indiscernible for a short distance as it passes over a rocky area and through blueberry bushes, whose fruits usually ripen in early August.

At 1.6 miles, cross Middle Fork Indian Run, which may be dry in summer but has

Rock formation along the Ziler Loop Trail

pink lady's slippers blooming close to it in early spring. It is always a joy to see the pouched blossoms of these orchids, but it is an occasion that, sadly, occurs less often that it used to. Habitat loss is one reason the plant is having a hard time surviving, but another is that some people dig them up to transplant into home gardens. Lady's slippers will not grow unless certain fungi are present in the soil, and since these fungi rarely exist in home gardens, the transplanted flowers die within a year or two.

The trail to the left at 1.8 miles leads to the Batt Picnic Area. However, you want to turn right and ascend on a red- and blue-blazed pathway. The Ziler Loop Trail and the Central Trail intersect from the right at 1.9 miles. You want to stay left and follow the blue-blazed Ziler Loop Trail as it continues to ascend. The route steepens after the trail crosses a draw at 2.1 miles, and although it sometimes follows a sidehill trail, it is always going up. Rock formations to the right at 2.4 miles provide good winter views of farmland in the Sleepy Creek Valley beyond the state park boundary. Continue to ascend, and at

2.8 miles, attain the ridgeline in an area of the forest heavily damaged by gypsy moths in the latter part of the 20th century.

The gypsy moth was brought to Massachusetts in 1869 from France for experimental crossbreeding with silkworms. Unfortunately, some escaped and the moth has now spread throughout much of North America, some even being found as far away as California and Washington. It is when they are in the larval, or caterpillar, stage that they feed on the leaves of trees and other foliage, sometimes completely defoliating vast acreages. A healthy tree can usually withstand one or two consecutive years of defoliation, but any more than this and the tree will probably die. Botanists have tried several methods of eradication, but the main hope is that natural forces, such as the nucleopolyhedrosis virus and the gypsy moth fungus, will help bring the moths under control.

The Ziler Trail, which was an important overmountain route in pioneer days, drops steeply to the right at 3.0 miles. Stay left on the Ziler Loop Trail, and begin to descend on the gradually sloping ridgeline. The brown tracks that begin to show up on locust tree leaves as early as late July are the work of leaf miners. Unlike gypsy moths, the miners are native insects and, unless their numbers increase greatly, do little damage to the forest.

The shelter to the left of the trail at 3.2 miles almost appears to be abandoned but is used by the park's horseback riding outfitter to store hay. One side is left clear for you to use for a lunch break or to escape a rain shower. The present condition of this humble structure belies its auspicious origin: It was constructed in the 1960s for President Lyndon Johnson to use at a dedication ceremony in a state park in the southern part of West Virginia and was subsequently moved here.

Begin to descend from the ridgeline at 3.5 miles, encountering mountain laurel for the first time on the hike. A small break in the vegetation at 3.7 miles enables a limited view of the lodge in the valley below. The descent soon quickens, making a couple of switchbacks and providing another limited view of the valley.

The Ziler Loop and Central Trails come in from the right at 4.3 miles. Stay left on the red-blazed Central Trail, cross a gravel road less than 300 feet later, and ascend. There is a T-intersection at 4.6 miles, where an unmarked trail goes off to the left; stay to the right and descend, soon going down rock steps, and make a switchback to the right.

The trail may be a bit hard to distinguish on the ground just a few feet after you cross paved North Fork Road at 4.9 miles. However, simply look for red blazes to mark the way downhill to a pond, whose water is used to keep the park's golf course lush and green. Follow the trail and rise beside the pond at 5.1 miles, but do not take the route that drops left to the dam. Rather, keep to the right, walk under a utility line, and turn left to descend on the green-blazed Laurel Trail at 5.2 miles.

Stay left again at 5.3 miles. Less than 200 feet later, the Cabin Loop Trail comes in from the right, but you want to bear left once more. About 100 yards later, swing left behind the rental cabins, and come to a road beside a couple of the structures. Turn right, but almost immediately make a left to cross the main park road. The hike comes to an end when you return to your car at 5.6 miles.

For a nice diversion before heading home after the hike, drive back to Berkeley Springs, turn left onto WV9 west, and pull into the parking area on top of Cacapon Mountain a few miles later. Local lore claims that George Washington visited this site a number of times to enjoy the spectacular view, which takes in landscapes in West Virginia, Virginia, and Maryland.

3

Tuscarora Trail

Total distance (circuit): 8.8 miles

Hiking time: 5 hours, 45 minutes

Vertical rise: 1,760 feet

Maps: USGS 7½' Wardensville

The Hike at a Glance

0.5	right near top of spur ridge
3.5	open knob with 360-degree view
4.0	Paul Gerhard Shelter
4.6	right onto Forest Service road
5.6	right at T-intersection
5.8	right at second T-intersection
7.7	view of Cove Run and farmland
8.8	end

Concerned that the Appalachian Trail (AT) might become impossible to maintain due to closings by private landowners in the late 1960s, volunteers from Pennsylvania's Keystone Trails Association and the Potomac Appalachian Trail Club (PATC), based in Vienna, Virginia, plotted a route to the west. The aim was to use large portions of public lands in an area not yet rife with development pressures. Leaving the AT in Shenandoah National Park, the Tuscarora Trail runs for 250 miles through Virginia, West Virginia, Maryland (it was originally called the Big Blue Trail in these three states), and into central Pennsylvania, where it rejoins the AT. It was completed in the 1980s, but defoliation of the forest by gypsy moth infestations caused undergrowth to take over much of the route. Thousands of dead trees and branches added to the difficulty of hiking the trail. Those who tried came back with woeful tales, and there were even discussions about forsaking the entire project. Thankfully, members of the PATC did not give up, and they rallied enough volunteers that in the mid-1990s the trail was declared open once again.

Traversing the approximately 50 miles of the Tuscarora Trail in West Virginia is like going back in time to hike the Appalachian Trail before it became world-famous and crowded with people. It can seem as if the forest is yours alone, as you can walk for hours, and sometimes days, without meeting other people.

Like most long-distance pathways, the Tuscarora Trail is a linear route, so there is no way to make a circuit hike using it exclusively.

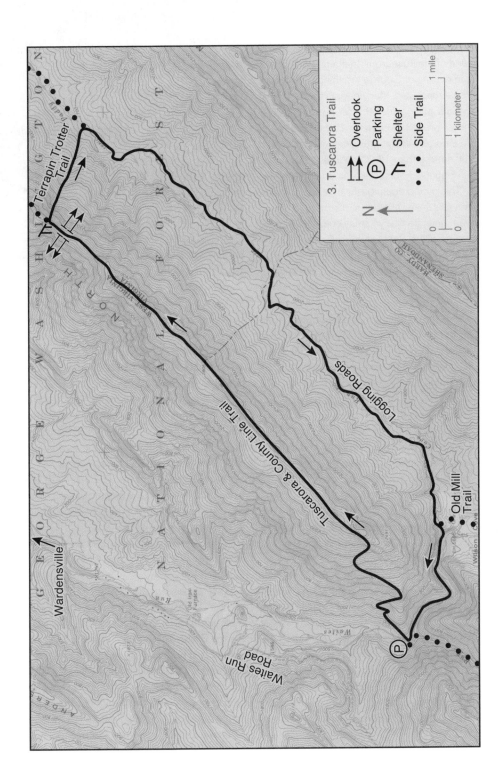

3. Tuscarora Trail

Overlook
Parking
Shelter
Side Trail

N

0   1 kilometer
0   1 mile

GEORGE   WASHINGTON   NATIONAL   FOREST

WEST VIRGINIA
NORTH   VIRGINIA

Terrapin Trotter Trail

Tuscarora & County Line Trail

Logging Roads

Old Mill Trail

Wilson Cove

Waites

Waites Run Road

Wardensville

Old Iron Furnace

Run

HARDY CO
SHENANDOAH

ANDER

The hike described here makes use of 4.0 miles of the Tuscarora Trail and a little more than 4 miles of George Washington National Forest roadways. Many people think of West Virginia having just the Monongahela National Forest, but close to 100,000 acres of the George Washington National Forest and a little more than 18,000 acres of the Jefferson National Forest are located in the state.

This outing could easily be accomplished as a day hike, but consider doing it as an overnighter so that you may enjoy the tranquil setting of the Paul Gerhard Shelter. (Backcountry camping is also permitted throughout the hike.) The journey is a moderately easy one, with just one long uphill at the beginning and a steep downhill in the middle.

The start of the hike may be reached from the intersection of WV259 and WV55 in Wardensville. Drive along WV55 east for less than 0.2 mile, make a right onto WV5/1 (Sanfield Road), go another 0.6 mile, and make a left onto the road signed as leading to the community park. Turn right 0.2 mile later onto a (possibly) unsigned road (Waites Run Road). The pavement ends in 3.6 miles. Continue another 1.7 miles to cross Waites Run for the third time, and park in a small turnout on the side of the road.

Following the blue blazes of the Tuscarora Trail, walk past a gate and ascend a grassy woods road, which is also the national forest's County Line Trail {FS 1013}. A sign notes that you are in the Wilson Cove Deer Study Area, 5,300 acres of national forest land designated by the West Virginia Division of Natural Resources as a place where only muzzleloading rifles may be used during the buck hunting season. One result of this regulation is that, since hunting pressure is less than in other places, some bucks are reaching eight years of age, several years older than most of their counterparts in the rest of the state.

Paul Gerhard Shelter

Be very alert at 0.5 mile! Just before you would top a spur ridge, the trail makes a sudden hard turn to the right that would be easy to miss. Continue to ascend on an older woods road, but less than 200 feet later, turn left onto a rocky footpath. Pinesap, a saprophytic plant that lacks chlorophyll, grows beside the trail. The limited views of the Cacapon River Valley to the left of the route at 1.4 miles are better when the leaves are off the trees during the colder months.

Almost imperceptibly, you will meet up with and turn left onto a very old woods road at 1.8 miles, while the spring to the right at 1.9 miles should only be counted on in wet weather. Leave the deer study area at 3.0 miles, finally attaining the rocky ridgeline at 3.3 miles.

The top of a partially open knob at 3.5 miles presents 360-degree views as you walk along the mountain crest. To the east are the Paddy Run Valley (where you will be walking a short time from now), Paddy Mountain, and Little North Mountain, which hides your view of the Shenandoah Valley beyond it. The vista to the west takes in the landscape of West Virginia's Eastern Panhandle.

If you are here anytime after midsummer,

your gazes to the far horizons may have to be interrupted by glances down to avoid getting scratched by the prickly leaves of tall thistle plants. Close to 20 species of thistle grow in the eastern United States, and all but a few have leaves that you don't want to brush up against.

Descend steeply for just a few hundred feet to come to the Paul Gerhard Shelter at 4.0 miles. Whether you are here for the night or just out for the day, there are only a few more hours of walking to reach the end of the hike, so take a nice long break. Have a snack, watch the antics of the resident squirrels, read a couple of chapters from a favorite book, and maybe take a nap. Awaken from slumber every few minutes and lazily look through the shadows of swaying leaves to enjoy the blue sky above.

When you are finally ready to resume the journey, begin a very steep descent along the Terrapin Trotter Trail (also known as the Gerhard Shelter Trail {FS 900}), which is located to the right (on the east) side of the shelter. You are now hiking in Virginia. The trail to the left at 4.3 miles leads to a spring that, once again, should be counted on only in wet weather. At 4.6 miles, turn right onto a former logging road above Paddy Run that is identified on some maps as the Vances Cove Trail {FS400}. You will be following old roads of one kind or another for the rest of the hike.

Cross a low ridge at 5.0 miles, leave the Paddy Run drainage area, and descend. The wide road you have been hiking upon comes to an end at 5.2 miles. Continue straight into the woods, now following a very old and narrow logging road, which is grassy and lined with ferns and an occasional wintergreen plant. Come to a T-intersection at 5.6 miles, and bear right, now following yellow blazes.

Cross back into West Virginia at 5.8 miles, and come to another T-intersection. Turn right and continue following yellow blazes on a wide and well-used roadway. Star moss and mountain laurel border the route, which is open to traffic during the hunting season from the first Friday in October through January 1.

America's national forests are managed under a philosophy of multiple use, meaning that the extraction of natural resources, as well as recreational uses, is permitted. Therefore, you will pass several logged areas (and maybe even a current logging operation) within the next 2.0 miles. Recently timbered sites may not be the prettiest of places, but their openness does let you look onto the surrounding mountains, and the rocky ridgeline to your right is the one you followed along the Tuscarora Trail.

Yellow blazes may become faint or disappear as you continue to hike, but just stay along the main road, going by fading purple blazes on the left at 7.5 miles that once marked the Peer Trail, closed in 2003 by the owners of the land it crosses. The pink blazes you see on the left mark the Old Mill Trail {FS 1037} that replaced the Peer Trail by going around the private property.

Walk around a gate at 7.7 miles, and come to an eye-pleasing view of Cove Run coursing its way through tended farmland to the left. Be sure to pay attention just 0.2 mile later. To the left is a gated road leading to private land. You want to turn right and walk past boulder fields on the hillside above and next to pretty Cove Run. You might consider going down to the stream to cool your feet if it has been a warm day.

The journey comes to an end when you return to your car at 8.8 miles. If this short jaunt along the Tuscarora Trail has you interested in hiking more of it, you may obtain guidebooks for its entire length by contacting the Potomac Appalachian Trail Club, 118 Park Street S.E., Vienna, VA 22180; 703-242-0693; www.patc.net.

4

Cranny Crow Overlook

Total distance (circuit): 4.1 miles

Hiking time: 2 hours, 30 minutes

Vertical rise: 1,300 feet

Maps: USGS 7½' Lost River; park map

The Hike at a Glance

0.25 switchback left
0.6   right onto White Oak Trail
1.6   right onto Miller's Rock Trail
1.7   Cranny Crow Overlook's stone
       shelter
2.0   left onto Virginia View Trail
2.5   right onto Big Ridge Trail
3.9   left onto gravel road
4.1   end

Bucolic. It's such a mellifluous-sounding word. The dictionary defines it as pastoral, suggesting an idyllic rural life. Taking that into account, there is certainly no better word than bucolic to describe the scenery as seen from the Cranny Crow Overlook.

About 1,000 feet below the mountaintop viewpoint is a narrow valley, with hemlock-bordered Howard's Lick Run flowing down the middle of it. Lush forested slopes gently rise to nearby broad mountain crests covered in green pastures. The lowing of livestock is carried on the wind, as your eyes are drawn to a succession of ridgelines receding to the horizon.

Cranny Crow Overlook is located within 3,712-acre Lost River State Park, which takes its name from the nearby river that disappears underground for about 3 miles and flows under Sandy Ridge to reemerge as the Cacapon River near Wardensville. What is now state park land was once a part of the vast holdings of Lord Fairfax that was later given to "Light Horse Harry" Lee in appreciation for his military service during the Revolutionary War. Lee built a cabin, and, during the early 1800s, his family used it as a summer retreat. The dwelling is now on the National Register of Historic Places and is open as a museum from Memorial Day to Labor Day.

Also in the state park are game courts, riding stables, a swimming pool, an activities building, picnic areas, a gift shop, and rental cabins. A naturalist is on staff from Memorial Day to Labor Day, and you can join in on hikes, stream wadings in search of aquatic

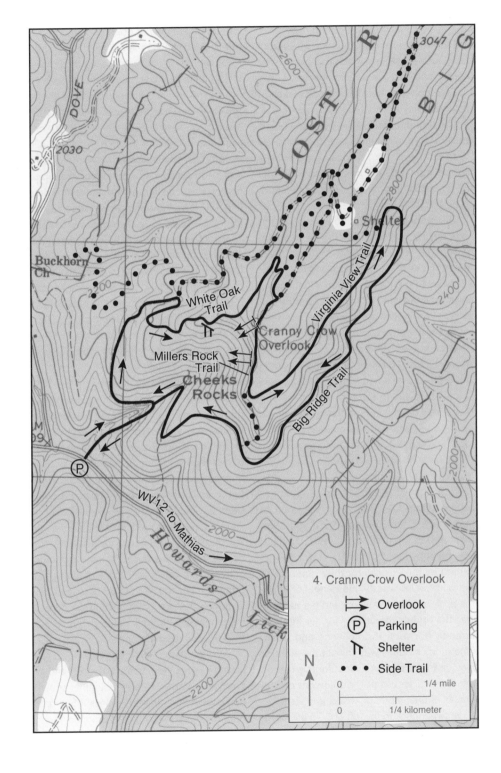

4. Cranny Crow Overlook

	Overlook
P	Parking
	Shelter
•••	Side Trail

N

| 0 | | 1/4 mile |
| 0 | | 1/4 kilometer |

LOST R BIG

3047

Shelter

White Oak Trail

Cranny Crow Overlook

Virginia View Trail

Millers Rock Trail

Cheeks Rocks

Big Ridge Trail

Buckhorn Ch

DOVE

2030

2600

2800

2400

2000

P

WV 12 to Mathias

Howards Lick

2200

2000

life, campfire activities, evening programs, and more. The park has no campground or areas for backcountry camping, but a commercial site, Big Ridge Campground (open May through October), is located just a short distance away on WV14.

The hike described here traverses only a small percentage of the park's approximately 20 miles of trails, but it does take you to its highest point and the best vistas on a relatively moderate route, with just a few short, steep sections.

The state park and the beginning of the hike may be reached from the intersection of WV259 and WV12 in Mathias. Take WV12 (Howard's Lick Road), and drive it for 2.9 miles to the park entrance. Continue an additional 0.4 mile to a gated road bridge leading to a gravel service road. Park here, making sure not to block the gate.

Walk across the bridge, and step over Howard's Lick Run Trail to begin ascending along the gravel service road. At 0.25 mile is a switchback to the left, where the Big Ridge Trail comes in from the right. You will be returning via that route, so stay on the road, walking below interesting rock formations on the hill above you and passing under a utility line at 0.4 mile.

Turn right at 0.6 mile onto the orange-blazed White Oak Trail, which is open to horseback riders—watch where you step. Continue to ascend, and during April and May pass by blooming wild iris, which was named by the Greeks for their goddess of the rainbow. Iris was the messenger of Juno—the protectress of women—and the rainbow was the bridge she utilized for her frequent errands between the heavens and earth. One of Iris's duties was to lead the souls of women to the Elysian Fields; for this reason the Greeks would put iris flowers on the graves of their mothers, wives, and sisters.

A switchback to the left at 0.75 mile is located in a somewhat open area and is colorfully full of flowers, such as thistle, Deptford pink, white snakeroot, and members of the mint family. As you continue to climb on the sidehill trail and a series of switchbacks, breaks in the vegetation show how much elevation you have already gained.

The small shelter to the right at 0.9 mile overlooks a nice eastward view and gives a hint of the vistas to come. Some striped maple trees so large that their bark has begun to lose the stripes grow next to the trail after a switchback to the right at 1.1 miles. There are limited views to the right just as you gain the ridgeline at 1.6 miles. A few hundred feet later is an intersection where you want to swing right onto the yellow-blazed Miller's Rock Trail. Keep right as the route joins a woods road less than 200 feet later.

There is no doubt that all of the uphill effort has been worth it when you come to Cranny Crow Overlook's stone shelter at 1.7 miles. It is time to rest and enjoy the 180-degree view that takes in the mountains and ridgelines of Shenandoah and Rockingham Counties in Virginia, and Pendleton, Grant, and Hardy Counties in West Virginia. The farmsteads on the mountaintop directly in front of you may make you envy the folks who get to enjoy this scenery from their homes every day.

Continue past the shelter along the yellow-blazed trail as it descends a narrow footpath. Every few hundred feet there is another great view, some of which look onto the spur ridge you ascended to reach Cranny Crow Overlook. You are walking along the edge of the mountain, and rock outcrops permit you to look into the valley far below.

Turn left onto the narrow, less-used, red-blazed Virginia View Trail at 2.0 miles, and ascend at a gradual rate. Midsummer growth may crowd in on the trail unless it has been recently maintained. There are also limited

View from Miller's Rock Trail

views through the vegetation of Great North Mountain and other ridgelines near the West–Virginia-Virginia border.

Turn right at 2.5 miles, and descend along yellow-blazed Big Ridge Trail, with wild bleeding heart adding patches of pink to the green understory from late spring to mid-summer. Bees, butterflies, and humming-birds find the flower's nectar to be almost impossible to resist.

There is a nice view through the vegetation as you switchback to the right at 2.7 miles and walk by many lichen-covered rocks. Lichens—those stalwart little plants that are able to grow and survive in some of the most unlikely and harshest of environments—are actually two living entities that have combined into one plant to overcome adversity. The algae are the food producer for the fungus, which is unable make its own nourishment. The fungus, for its part, is able to absorb and hold water, at times even from moist air or fog, keeping the algae alive during hot, dry spells.

A faint trail descends to the left at 2.8 miles; continue right, and ascend for a short distance before resuming the descent through mountain laurel, blueberry, and the vines of greenbrier, which creep over much of the other vegetation.

A break in the tree canopy from a switch-back to the right at 3.7 miles enables you to look back up to the heights you have just de-scended from. At 3.9 miles, turn left onto the gravel road you started the hike on, and re-turn to your automobile at 4.1 miles.

Potomac Highlands

5

South Branch

Total distance (circuit): 1.25 miles

Hiking time: 40 minutes

Vertical rise: 120 feet

Maps: USGS 7½' Petersburg

The Hike at a Glance

0.25   *trail left to campground*
0.45   *begin paralleling the South Branch*
0.8   *trail to river bank*
1.25   *end*

O.K. Let's see if you can keep all of this straight: The Potomac River defines the West Virginia–Maryland and Maryland–Virginia borders as it flows eastward to pass Washington, D.C., and empties into the Chesapeake Bay. The Potomac is formed when the North Branch of the Potomac River meets the South Branch of the Potomac River several miles east of Cumberland, Maryland. The North Branch of the Potomac is considered one stream from its source, which is a spring next to the Fairfax Stone Monument in Tucker County, West Virginia. However, three streams make up the South Branch of the Potomac River. The South Fork of the South Branch of the Potomac River rises in Virginia and flows northward to meet the South Branch of the Potomac River at Moorefield. The South Branch of the Potomac River (which, if it followed form, should really be called the Middle Fork of the South Branch of the Potomac River) also begins in Virginia and flows northward along the eastern side of North Fork Mountain. The North Fork of the South Branch of the Potomac River runs below Seneca Rocks (see Hike 7) and the western side of North Fork Mountain before meeting the South Branch of the Potomac River near Petersburg, West Virginia.

Got it? Well, don't worry. All you need to know is that many people consider the South Branch of the Potomac River to be the prettiest of all these waterways. For more than 20 miles, the river has carved a half-mile-deep gorge, known as Smoke Hole Canyon, between Cave and North Fork Mountains. There are several theories about where the

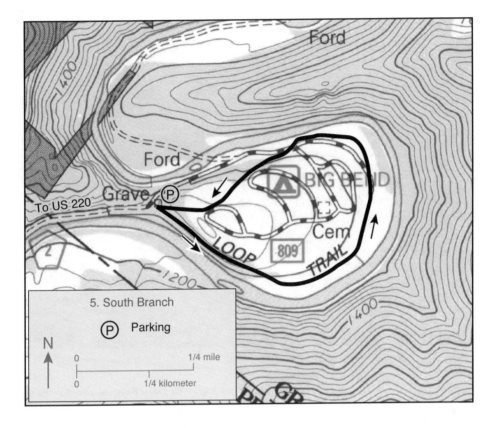

name came from. One says that Native Americans used the many area caves to smoke meat, another claims that smoke rising from moonshine stills gave the canyon its name, and a third alludes to the vaporous fogs that drift up from the cool waters of the river.

Anglers are attracted to the South Branch by the golden and rainbow trout stocked by the state Division of Natural Resources, as well as the abundance of catfish and largemouth and smallmouth bass. You are almost guaranteed to see at least one or two anglers trying their luck. Some local outfitters say it is not uncommon to catch close to a hundred smallmouth bass in just one day. Rafters, canoeists, and kayakers come here to ply the currents, while birdwatchers have hopes of catching glimpses of bald eagles.

All of this makes the area an excellent destination for the entire family. Arrive early in the morning, and let everyone go off to pursue their own activities. Meet back at the campground for lunch, and then spend the afternoon on a group hike along the Big Bend Loop Trail {FS 566}. The first edition of this book described a 3.7-mile hike on the South Branch Loop Trail in this area, but that trail has since been abandoned by the Forest Service. Even though this outing is not as long, it does, at least, provide you with a nice introduction to the South Branch of the Potomac River as the stream makes a major bend, almost doubling back on itself.

The Big Bend Campground (usually open spring to fall) may be reached from the intersection of US220 and WV55/WV28 in

South Branch of the Potomac River

Petersburg. Drive south on US220 and immediately after crossing the South Branch of the Potomac River in 16.6 miles, turn right onto Smoke Hole Road (WV2). Follow this for 5.7 miles, bear right onto FSR 809 (it becomes dirt), and continue for 3.7 miles to the parking area at the entrance to the campground.

Begin the hike by taking the trail that ascends the hillside beside small pawpaw trees, and soon reach the ridgeline via nicely graded switchbacks. Found in many places in West Virginia, the pawpaw tree is usually a large shrub but can grow to 40 feet tall. The best way to enjoy the pawpaw's fruit is fresh off the tree. Cut it open, scoop out the flesh, and be sure to discard the seeds, which are poisonous. Some people say the creamy white-to-orange flesh has the consistency of custard or yogurt and tastes like a very ripe banana with hints of mango and pineapple.

Enjoy, and eat away. Pawpaws contain three times as much vitamin C as an apple, twice as much riboflavin as an orange, about the same amount of potassium as a banana, and lots of amino acids.

The trail to the left at 0.25 mile goes to the campground. Stay to the right along the well-built trail as it switchbacks down, and take in views of the South Branch appearing through the vegetation. Avoid any trails or routes that lead back to the campground or the roadway that you drove in on.

Begin paralleling the river just a few feet above it at 0.45 mile. Once your eyes get adjusted to looking into the clear water, you'll be amazed at how many fish you are able to spot swimming about. The trail widens after passing some interesting rock cliffs at 0.55 mile and swings away from the river to a small wildlife clearing. The open meadow provides views of the surrounding ridgelines, most notably Cave Mountain, showing just how deep a canyon the river has carved into the landscape.

The trail to the left at 0.8 mile goes to the campground; turn right and, for the moment, bypass the pathway that goes left in a few feet, and follow the one that continues to the edge of the river. It's time for a break to sit and watch for bald eagles patrolling the airways above you. The first recorded bald eagle nest in West Virginia was discovered along the South Branch of the Potomac River a few miles north of here in 1981. Bald eagles mate for life, and both male and female share in the incubation of eggs and feeding of the young. Like other birds of prey, eagles were once victims of the cumulative effects of DDT. The insecticide caused some hatchlings to be deformed, but mostly it weakened the shells of the eggs to the point that they simply could not hold together long enough for the eaglets to be born. DDT was banned in the United States several decades ago, and the number of bald eagles is on the rise. It's an inspiring sight to see one soaring through the canyon on a wingspan of 6 feet or more.

Return to, and turn onto, the trail you passed by a little earlier, which will take you by one of the campground's privies off to the left at 1.0 mile. At 1.1 miles is an old cabin site, with just the remains of the fireplace chimney marking the spot. Just beyond this, you will emerge onto the paved campground road, bear right, and return to your car at 1.25 miles.

A short side trail leads to water's edge

All that remains of an old cabin

6

North Fork Mountain

Total distance (one way): 23.9 miles

Hiking time: 15 hours; overnight hike

Vertical rise: 2,200 feet

Maps: USGS 7½' Circleville; USGS 7½' Franklin; USGS 7½' Upper Tract; USGS 7½' Hopeville; USGS 7½' Petersburg West

In one of its articles, *Backpacker* magazine claims that North Fork Mountain possesses "classic Eastern mountain scenery" and is "as good as mountain country gets in the East." The mountain certainly has one of the most distinctive profiles in West Virginia. It rises sharply for more than 1,500 feet from the North Fork of the South Branch of the Potomac River Valley and ends in a ridgeline adorned by miles-long cliffs. Views, of which there are dozens, take in all points of the compass, while the mountain's lower flanks are punctuated by the strikingly upright slabs of sandstone at Judy, Champe, and Seneca Rocks (see Hike 7).

The mountain is a moderate hike if done in the direction described. Your car gets you to the ridgeline, and the trail follows the mountain crest with just minor ups and downs, passing a number of decent campsites along the way. Chickadees, nuthatches, pileated woodpeckers, evening grosbeaks, and northern finches can be found among snow-covered vegetation in winter, and wildflowers are abundant in spring and summer.

The cliffs are the perfect perches from which to watch the fall raptor migration. Heated air from the sun-warmed cliffs and rock outcroppings couples with warm air rising from the lowlands to create forceful drafts, or thermals, that the birds use to soar upward. In addition, by gliding near the crest of the ridges, they are able to take advantage of the northwesterly winds striking the Alleghenies, where air currents are forced across the mountain crests, providing more uplift.

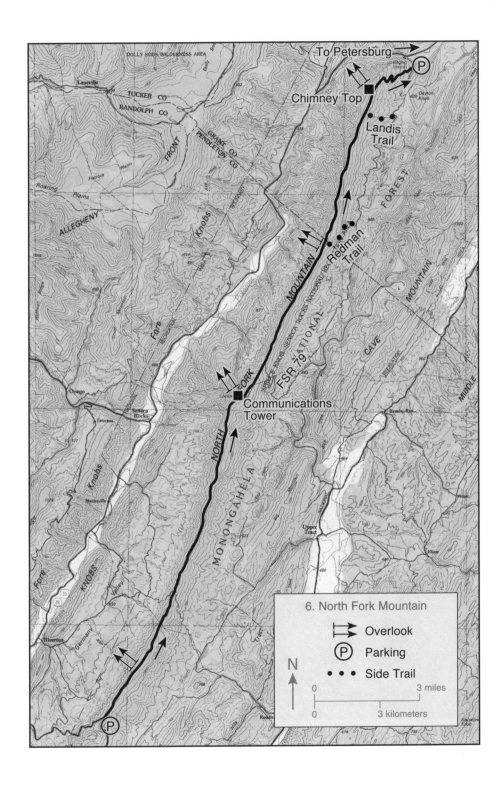

6. North Fork Mountain

Overlook

P Parking

Side Trail

Along the North Fork Mountain Trail

The one downside of this hike is that there may be no water available anywhere along the ridgeline. There is a spring at about the halfway point, but hikers have reported that it may not run well in summer and fall. Therefore, it's probably best to not rely on it. Luckily, there is an option if you don't want to carry the weight of the extra water needed to insure you have enough liquids. A Forest Service road intersects the trip at the halfway point, enabling you to stash some water before beginning the hike.

This is a one-way trek, so a car shuttle—and a long one at that—will be necessary. Drive WV28/WV55 west from Petersburg for 4.0 miles, turn left onto Smoke Hole Road (WV28/11), and leave one car at the trailhead parking on the right in another 0.4 mile. Continue on WV28/11 (which becomes WV2/3 at the Grant County-Pendleton County line) for 11.3 miles to a T-intersection. If you are going to stash water, make a right turn onto FSR79, signed as leading to North Fork Mountain. Ascend this narrow dirt road, and come to a left switchback 3.4 miles later. (The North Fork Mountain Trail takes off to the right here.) Stash water and descend the mountain back to the intersection. Continue on WV2/3 to another intersection in an additional 0.5 mile. Turn right onto WV2 to parallel the beautiful ripples of the South Branch of the Potomac River.

Proceed for 5.5 more miles, turn right onto US220, drive for an additional 11.8 miles, and turn right onto US33 West. Pay attention to your odometer, as the parking for the trailhead—an unmarked small pullout on the right at the very top of the mountain—is 8.4 miles from this intersection. Do not block the gate.

Walk around the gate and ascend the blue-blazed North Fork Mountain Trail {FS501} along a grassy woods road. This is private property, and no hunting or biking is permitted, but it is open to hiking. The road soon fades into a footpath. The rock outcrops to the left at 1.5 miles give you the first of many views into the Germany Valley. (You can take in a view just about anytime you want throughout the hike. Simply rise a few feet from the trail to the mountain's rocky edge.) Enjoy the soft feel of thousands of pine needles on the pathway through mountain laurel, azalea, and blueberry bushes at 1.6 miles, for soon the route will become rough and rocky. Attain a knob at 2.6 miles and descend to pass under utility lines at 3.3 miles.

The woods road you are walking along is bordered by a mixed hardwood forest that is noticeably younger than the woodlands you will be passing through closer to the high point of the hike. Reach the top of a knob at 3.7 miles, descend for a short distance, and resume the climb beside numerous small striped maples. The tree's seedpods are winged, reminiscent of those of the larger maple trees that, when you were a child, you may have thrown in the air so that they would float back down, spinning like helicopter blades.

Cross an old logging road at 4.3 miles that descends 2.0 miles west into Germany Valley and 2.3 miles east to Reeds Creek Road (WV8). A hang glider platform to the left of the trail at 4.5 miles provides another view of Germany Valley, named for the Pennsylvania Dutch settlers of German descent who cleared the forest to farm the rich soil. The humps of the River Knobs separate Germany Valley from the North Fork of the South Branch of the Potomac River Valley. The woods road comes to an end, and the route continues along a footpath lined by spring beauty. A quick rise onto the rocks on the very crest of the mountain at 4.6 miles reveals a quarry in the valley below.

The bit of flat land you descend into at 4.9

miles has a couple of spots where you could set up a tent, while a break in the vegetation at 5.5 miles gives the first good view to the east. The mountains along the West Virginia–Virginia border form a backdrop for the ridgeline farmlands in the foreground.

The trail continues along a gently rising sidehill pathway lined by rattlesnake weed and big, fluffy balls of moss. Mosses can survive in nutrient-poor areas, making them some of the first plants to develop in rocky or disturbed places. As mats get thicker, the bottom layers decay and add to the soil. Seeds from other plants that end up here then have favorable conditions in which to grow and, over time, a full-fledged, diverse forest can become established.

You may be able to find a tent site where the ridgeline is broad and somewhat flat at 6.6 miles. The next 2.0 miles are a series of small ups and downs, until you slab below the summit of High Knob at 8.6 miles and walk along the very crest of the ridge at 8.9 miles. The builders of this trail did a great job of getting many of the large rocks out of the treadway so that you may continue in relative ease. In late spring and summer, tiny spore capsules rise above the small patches of star moss growing between the stones.

You have been protected from the wind because the hike has been on the leeward side of the mountain to this point, but prepare to be buffeted when the trail crosses to the west side at 9.3 miles. Seneca Rocks is visible through the vegetation. Return to the eastern side of the ridge, pass a campsite, and begin to rise on a woods road.

Break out of the trees at 10.2 miles, and bear right onto a service road; the pipeline right-of-way to the left overlooks the valley. A communications tower marks the high point of the journey (3,795 feet) at 10.7 miles, just before the route gradually descends along dirt FSR79 with nice views to

the east. As the road makes a switchback to the right at 12.1 miles, keep left and reenter the woods on a footpath. Be sure to carry your containers out with you if you stashed water here.

Rise to a flat spot at 12.3 miles that may provide a tent site or two, then resume hiking the sidehill trail along the east side of the ridge. Begin a long descent at 13.0 miles and enter an area where laurel, blueberry, and pine crowd the trail. Unless the pathway has been recently maintained, you will find this to be the case sporadically throughout the rest of the hike.

At 14.0 miles, level out a bit for a little over 1,000 feet. Once the trail resumes its descent, you could scramble up the large sloping rock slab for a soaring view of Champe Rocks more than 1,000 feet below. The faint trail coming in from the right at 14.6 miles is the abandoned Kimble Trail. Stay left, ascend, descend, and level out for a short distance on the crest of the ridgeline with views to the east. You may walk by the very small patch of frostweed without noticing it. The yellow blossoms last but a day and only open when the sun is shining bright.

The Redman Trail {FS507} descends right at 16.0 miles, reaching WV28/11 in approximately 1.5 miles. Just beyond is a small shelf in a forest of ash and locust, with possibly the best campsite on the entire trail and a good view of Yellow Rocks to the west. Enter another area of heavy laurel and blueberry growth, which is nothing short of spectacular to walk through when the laurel blooms in early to mid-June.

After a long descent and ascent, regain the crest amid azalea bushes at 17.5 miles. Just as you start dropping again, there is a rock outcrop with another view to the west, where turkey vultures are often spotted soaring just a few feet above the ridgeline. Pass by several small campsites before coming to a cleft in the ridgeline cliff at 18.8 miles. The wind often roars through this opening, wearing away small bits of rock and sand and pelting anyone standing close by.

Be alert when you come to a Y-intersection at 19.9 miles. The Landis Trail {FS501} descends right for 1.5 miles to WV28/11; stay left through a mature oak and maple forest. A level spot on the ridge at 20.0 miles is a possible campsite. A short distance beyond this, you may find a sign indicating that the original route of the trail has been closed to protect peregrine falcons. Like bald eagles, the number of peregrines declined in the mid-20th century, primarily due to the use of DDT (see Hike 5 for a discussion of this). Now that the insecticide has been banned in the United States, breeding the falcons in captivity and then releasing them into the wild has proven somewhat successful. However, when nesting, the birds are easily disturbed, which may result in eggs not hatching. If you find the sign in place, follow the alternate trail, knowing that you have done a small part in helping to reestablish the falcon to its rightful place.

Regain the cliffs of the ridgeline at 20.9 miles for a view of WV28/WV55 snaking through the North Fork Valley. From this vantage point the cars and trucks look like small toys.

Small cairns may be the only things to mark the faint route to Chimney Top at 21.0 miles. You may have decided to pass up other viewpoints, but it would be a mistake to hike North Fork Mountain and not go to Chimney Top. This is one of the best places to gaze upon the mountain's long line of sandstone cliffs. Also, to the north are the impressive talus slopes of New Creek Mountain and the North Fork River flowing through the water gap it has created in the mountains. To the east are a number of small settlements, and to the west is the impressive bulk of the Allegheny Front, on which you could take a number of hikes in this book (see Hikes 8, 9, and 10).

Once you have had enough of this windy aerie, return to the trail and continue on your way. Progress may be slow, though, as you could stop every few feet to enjoy a different panorama. Be alert at 22.0 miles. The trail makes a sudden turn to the right, away from cliffs; do not follow the faint trail to the left that continues along the ridgeline. Descend on switchbacks through splendid growths of mountain laurel. A switchback to the right at 23.7 miles is bordered by the largest colony of rattlesnake weed you may ever come across.

Your journey along what *Outside* magazine once described as West Virginia's "most outstanding foot trail" comes to an end when you reach your shuttled car at 23.9 miles.

7

Seneca Rocks

Total distance (round-trip): 3.0 miles

Hiking time: 1 hour, 45 minutes

Vertical rise: 800 feet

Maps: USGS 7½' Upper Tract

The Hike at a Glance

0.2   *intersection, bear left*
0.9   *first viewpoint*
1.5   *observation platform*
3.0   *end*

What is now West Virginia was at the bottom of a vast inland sea about 500 million years ago. Erosion from a mountain chain to the east, believed by some to be as high as the present-day Andes, washed onto the floor of the sea for millions of years, depositing layer upon layer of sand, rock, and silt thousands of feet thick. The massive weight of these layers compacted and cemented them into various types of rock.

When ancient continents collided a little less than 300 million years ago, the earth folded and buckled upward, creating the Appalachian and Allegheny Mountains. Millions of years of erosion stripped away the softer rock, exposing the harder rock, such as Tuscarora limestone, which Seneca Rocks is made of.

Today, Seneca Rocks rises like a cathedral for close to 900 feet above the North Fork of the South Branch of the Potomac River Valley. Although it is believed that Native Americans climbed the rocks, the first recorded ascent was in the 1930s. Throughout most of the rest of the 20th century, the views that could be obtained from its west-facing wall were available only to rock climbers or those willing to endure the arduously steep and extremely eroded pathway on the eastern side of the rocks.

In the late 1980s, the Forest Service constructed a trail for the rest of us. It won't bring you to the top of the rocks, but it does take you to an observation platform close to North Tower, with a grand view across the river valley and out to some of the state's highest landmasses. The pathway gains al-

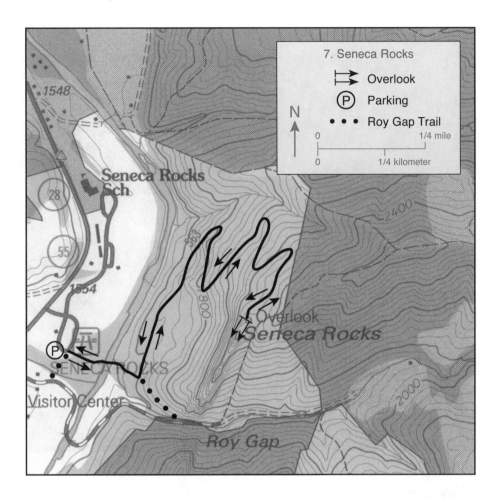

most 700 feet in elevation, but well-graded switchbacks and benches to rest upon make it accessible to just about anyone. Signposts along the way interpret the area's natural history, and the information you learn here will add greatly to future hikes in West Virginia. Camping is not permitted along the trail, but the Forest Service's Seneca Shadows Campground, with hookups and warm showers, is 1.0 mile south on US33/WV28.

Seneca Rocks is located near the junction of US33/WV55 with WV28/WV55. This intersection is a little more than 20 miles west of Petersburg via WV28/WV55 and is close to 30 miles east of Elkins via US33/WV55.

Before beginning the hike, you might want to visit the Forest Service's Seneca Rocks Discovery Center (the entrance is about 0.1 mile south of the intersection) to obtain more background information. Displays depict the geology, Native Americans, natural history, early settlers, and history of climbing in the area. Forest Service employees and volunteers can give advice and information on this and other hikes nearby.

You could start walking from the Discovery Center, but to save a few steps, drive back to the intersection and go 0.1 mile north

Seneca Rocks

on WV28/WV55, and turn right into the Seneca Rocks Picnic Area and parking lot for the Seneca Rocks Hiking Trail {FS563}.

Begin the outing by walking along the wide gravel pathway to the bridge across the North Fork, a popular fly-fishing destination with an abundance of smallmouth bass and stocked trout. Continue on the opposite bank, going by patches of jewelweed and the first of a number of placards that interpret the area's natural history.

Come to a T-intersection at 0.2 mile. The Roy Gap Trail goes off to the right and enables a quick return to the Discovery Center; you want to keep to the left, walking by mayapple, jewelweed, false Solomon's seal, squawroot, ferns, striped maple, and jack-in-the-pulpit growing on and around the huge boulders that have tumbled down the mountainside in years past. The trees of the forest include maple, oak, hickory, and redbud.

Long before the redbud's leaves appear in spring, its branches and twigs become festooned with thick accumulations of dark pink-to-purple blossoms. At one time, the flowers were eaten as part of a salad or fried and mixed with a meat dish. One of the showiest of trees, the redbud is a member of the pea family, which raises an interesting question: Just exactly what is a tree?

We know one when we see it, but it can be hard to define. A reference book may describe a tree as being a woody perennial plant, usually having a single main stem with few or no branches on its lower part. Yet, trees are not a group of plants related to each other, but rather to other types of plants. For example, like the redbud, the black locust is a legume, a member of the pea family. Apple, cherry, and hawthorn trees are roses, and the tulip tree and magnolias are related to buttercups and anemones. Hackberry and the elms have links to nettles and marijuana, while the buckeyes, hollies, and maples are closely related to jewelweed and poison ivy.

Switchback to the right to ascend rock steps at 0.4 mile. Wooden steps at 0.5 mile enable you to gain elevation at a faster rate. Please stay on the main route. Unthinking—or maybe uncaring—people have created unauthorized trails, which cause erosion and loss of vegetation, including plants such as the rattlesnake weed and mountain laurel lining the pathway here. Soon, a break in the forest canopy allows you to look onto the valley floor and see how much elevation you have already gained.

Switchback to the right at 0.75 mile. When you come to the switchback to the left at 0.9 mile, take the short trail to the right for a limited view that reveals where you are—at the base of the Seneca Rocks. Return to the trail and continue to ascend via a series of switchbacks.

The vista that you labored for comes into view when you arrive at the observation platform at 1.5 miles. Almost next to you are the vertical walls of Seneca Rocks, with the North Fork flowing directly below. Spread along the valley floor are the picnic area, Discovery Center, and Seneca Shadows Campground. The humps you see on the first ridgeline to the west are known as the Fore

Knobs. Rising much higher behind them is Spruce Mountain and the state's highest point, Spruce Knob. Since you can go no farther unless you are a rock climber (a sign emphatically states STOP!), it is time to walk back down the trail to return to your car at 3.0 miles.

Spruce Knob is just a short drive away and is certainly worth a visit now that you are in the area. Return to the main highway intersection, continue southward for 10.0 miles on US33/WV28, and turn right onto WV33/4. This is Briery Gap Simoda Road, which is signed as leading to Spruce Knob and Lake. Less than 2 miles later, bear left onto FSR112, follow it for 7.3 miles, turn right onto FSR104, and come to the parking lot in another 2.0 miles.

A short walk through a windswept landscape of blueberry, huckleberry, azalea, and stunted one-sided spruce trees leads you to a stone-and-steel observation tower. You're on top of West Virginia at an elevation of 4,861 feet, so the 360-degree vista is magnificent and far reaching. The 0.5-mile Whispering Spruce Trail encircles the knob, with additional views and interpretive signs explaining the geology, plants, and animals of the area. More than 60 miles of trails meander along the ridgeline, hollows, and creeks of Spruce Mountain. Information on these pathways may be obtained at Seneca Rocks Discovery Center.

There is a hard choice to make on how to end the day. The observation tower is the perfect grandstand seat from which to watch the sun sink into the west. Then again, you might want to drive back to Seneca Rocks. The rays of the setting sun light up the vertical walls, highlighting the limestone with morphing patches of yellow, pink, red, and gold. Maybe you should spend two days here to experience sunsets from both places, the Discovery Center and Spruce Knob.

8

Dolly Sods Wilderness

Total distance (circuit): 18.8 miles

Hiking time: 10.5 hours

Vertical rise: 2,020 feet

Maps: USGS 7½' Hopeville; USGS 7½' Blackbird Knob; USGS 7½' Laneville; USGS 7½' Blackwater Falls

The Hike at a Glance

2.3   views into Red Creek Canyon
3.0   Rohrbaugh Plains and Wildlife
       Trails intersection
3.5   left onto Fisher Spring Run Trail
4.7   right onto Red Creek Trail
5.2   left onto Rocky Point Trail
7.2   right onto Big Stonecoal Trail
7.8   left on Dunkenbarger Trail
9.4   left onto Little Stonecoal Trail
11.9   left onto Red Creek Trail
14.1   return to Fisher Spring Run Trail
       and retrace steps
18.8   end

The trails of the Dolly Sods Wilderness are so popular that it was debated for a long time whether or not they should be included in this guidebook. Many of the pathways are worn from thousands of feet tramping on them, and the crowds at favorite trailheads during weekends can be disconcertingly large. Yet, it would have been gross negligence not to include Dolly Sods Wilderness in a hiking guide to West Virginia, for this is spectacular country. In fact, the Dolly Sods/Canaan Valley area that this and the next 5 hikes (see Hikes 9 through 13) travel through may just have the most sensational scenery in the entire state.

Hiking in the wilderness is akin to being in New England or Canada rather than the southern Appalachians. Red spruce, bogs, and rocky barrens characterize the uplands, while northern hardwood forests and tannin-stained waters are found in the lower elevations. The area was heavily logged in the 19th and 20th centuries, but almost no evidence of human activity is evident today. In all of the East, it may best exemplify what the Wilderness Act of 1964 defined as wilderness: "The area generally appears to have been affected primarily by the forces of nature, with the imprint of man's work substantially unnoticeable."

Be aware that, in accordance with provisions of the Wilderness Act, the Forest Service stopped blazing trails many years ago. Any paint marks that may remain are faded and far between. The act also allows for removal of signs—this has occurred in other wilderness areas—so be prepared for it to

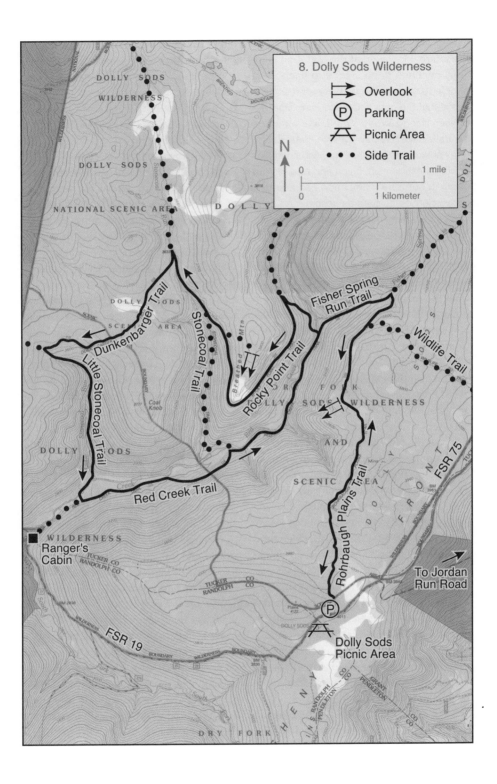

possibly happen in Dolly Sods sometime in the future. However, at present, trail junctions continue to be signed to encourage people to stay on the trail. The primary reason is that the area was used for military exercises during World War II, and although the trails have been swept with metal detectors, most of the land has not, and some live mortar shells remain. If you find one, do not touch it, but note its location and alert the Forest Service as soon as possible.

The beginning of the hike may be reached from the intersection of US220 and WV55/WV28 in Petersburg. Drive westward on WV55/WV28 for 10 miles, and turn right onto what some maps show as WV4, but what the roadway sign says is Jordan Run Road (WV28/7). Make a left in another 0.9 mile onto FSR19, which will soon turn to dirt. Come to the intersection of FSR19 and FSR75 in an additional 6.1 miles, turn left to stay on FSR19, and arrive at the Dolly Sods picnic area in another 0.6 mile. Turn around, go about 150 feet, and park in the small pull-out area.

Enter the New England–type woods of birch, spruce, and ferns on the Rohrbaugh Plains Trail {FS508}. The one thing that may not be so reminiscent of New England are the great rhododendron bushes, which can still be in bloom in late July and early August—weeks after their lowland kin have lost their blossoms. Cross a woods road and a water run at 0.6 mile, where the shamrock-shaped leaves of wood sorrel may make you think you have been transported to Ireland.

The trail swings right and enters a wildlife clearing at 1.0 mile that might provide a campsite with water available from a stream. Pass through a larger clearing at 1.2 miles, and hike through an impressive rhododendron tunnel at 1.4 miles.

Hike out of the woods and onto a vast rocky open area, where several campsites are available, at 2.3 miles. This is just one of the many places on this journey that make it so spectacular. The route takes you along sandstone cliffs on the lip of the precipitous drop into the Red Creek Gorge, with the crooked course of the waterway visible nearly 1,000 feet below you. The boulders of Rocky Point and the flat expanse of Coal Knob, both of which you will traverse within the next few hours, are visible across the canyon. The view to the south is of square mile upon square mile of land that shows not one sign of human activity—a rare thing in the eastern United States.

A number of "renegade" trails go off in different directions, but stay on the main route. If you are here in August, the blossoms of butterfly weed will fill the air with a heady fragrance as you walk through a wildlife clearing at 2.6 miles.

Be alert! At 3.0 miles, the route you have been following continues ahead as the Wildlife Trail {FS560}. You need to bear left to continue on the Rohrbaugh Plains Trail as it descends along an old railroad bed with a very rocky treadway. The number of rhododendron blossoms in July and August is phenomenal.

Cross a stream with small cascades, and come to the end of the Rohrbaugh Plains Trail at 3.5 miles. Turn left onto the Fisher Spring Run Trail {FS510}, and pass a campsite situated on slightly sloping ground. Be very alert at 3.9 miles. The trail leaves the railroad grade and descends to the left. Cross Fisher Spring Run at 4.2 miles, walk upstream a short distance, turn right across some boulders, and resume the descent.

A pathway drops steeply to the right to a campsite at 4.4 miles. Stay on the hillside, and continue to the end of the Fisher Spring Run Trail at its junction with the Red Creek Trail {FS514} at 4.7 miles. To the left, the Red Creek Trail goes 2.8 miles to FSR19.

Red Creek

However, you want to bear right, descend, and ford Red Creek. Some beautiful cascades and large flat spots for camping may cause you to linger here. Even if you had not planned on it, you may want to take a rest break because afterward you will have to negotiate the toughest climb of the journey, gaining hundreds of feet in just 0.5 mile. In rating the difficulty of different hikes as easy, moderate, or difficult, a Forest Service brochure describes this route as "painful."

Continue to ascend, but at a more gradual rate, once you turn left onto the old railroad grade of the Rocky Point Trail {FS554} at 5.2 miles. There are boulders above the rock-crowded pathway as it swings around the southern shoulder of Breathed Mountain at 6.3 miles. Many people climb these rocks to reach the view from Rocky Point, but to avoid the risks associated with this, it is recommended you continue on the Rocky Point Trail for another 0.4 mile. At that juncture, you will find a gently rising pathway to a campsite inside a grove of evergreens. From here, it is an easy walk of a couple of hundred feet across sandstone boulders to the viewpoint.

And what a vista it is. The forested mountain walls drop steeply hundreds of feet into Red Creek Gorge, Coal Knob rises above the narrow gorge of Big Stonecoal Run to the southwest, and to the east are the plains you started the hike on. Looking onto broad Flatrock Plains to the south may entice you to explore it someday (see Hike 10).

Return to the Rocky Point Trail, and continue on your way, coming to a junction at 7.2 miles, where you want to turn right onto Big Stonecoal Trail {FS513}. Following an old railroad bed, pass an excellent 30-foot waterfall at 7.4 miles and several campsites before coming to a junction at 7.8 miles. Turn left onto the Dunkenbarger Trail {FS558}, and begin a pleasant (but often wet and rocky) walk through a spruce forest across the level plateau atop Coal Knob. Cross Dunkenbarger Run at 8.5 miles, and continue to another tail junction at 9.4 miles.

Turn left and descend on Little Stonecoal Trail {FS552}. The pathway, another old railroad bed, drops quickly beside the cascading stream, passing through a forest of birch, poplar, ash, and maple. If you happen to be here as bright sunshine gives way to lengthening shadows, you may hear the songs of (and if very lucky, see) the hermit thrush and veery. Only in the higher elevations of the Appalachian and Allegheny Mountains, which have a climate resembling that found farther

north, will you find either bird during the warmer months. In the poem "When Lilacs Last in the Dooryard Bloom'd," Walt Whitman was so taken by the song of the hermit thrush that he was moved to write:

> Solitary the thrush,
> The hermit withdrawn to himself,
> avoiding the settlements,
> Sings by himself a song.

The trail crosses Little Stonecoal Run just a short distance before the stream empties into Red Creek. You will get wet feet again a few hundred yards later when you ford Red Creek. Ascend the embankment, and, at 11.9 miles, reach the junction with the Red Creek Trail, onto which you want to turn left and follow upstream. (FSR19 is 0.5 mile to the right.) The Red Creek you see today is much different than it was in days past. At one time, it was a slower-moving stream with many deep pools and beaver dams. Hurricane Juan dumped a massive amount of rain on the mountains in 1985, resulting in a flood that washed away the beaver dams and created a swifter waterway filled with rocks, boulders, and crashing cascades.

To avoid a washed-out area, the trail climbs onto the hillside at 12.5 miles before descending back toward the creek. Pass by the intersection with Big Stonecoal Trail at 12.7 miles, only to wander onto the hillside once more, dropping back down again at 13.0 miles.

Something happened here a number of years ago that friends dubbed "The Incident at Red Creek," but which I simply think of as "My First Bear Encounter."

I was on only the second solo backpacking trip of my life and had spent a wonderful day walking Rohrbaugh Plains to Red Creek, where I set up camp. Being a city boy, I was unaccustomed to the sounds of the wilderness, but was enjoying the gurgling of the creek and chirping of birds. However, just as darkness approached, there was a heavy rustling, followed by a sepulchral *haruumph* that echoed off the hillside above. I listened attentively. The rustling got closer, the *haruumphs* louder.

Bear! With that much noise and guttural reverberations, it had to be a bear. The sounds moved from the hillside into the valley. What should I do if it comes out of the woods and into the clearing? I know. I'll climb a tree. (This was before I knew that black bears are excellent tree climbers.) I've never had much upper body strength—I was the kid in high school gym class who couldn't scale the rope—so I don't know what made me think I could climb a tree. Yet, for practice, I grabbed a low-hanging branch, and walking up the trunk with my feet, wrapped by legs around the limb, ending up looking like a dangling sloth. Glancing down, I thought, well, that's just great! My rear end's closer to the ground than if I was standing up, and my body's swaying back and forth as if it were a piñata waiting to be split open by a bear claw.

OK, OK, that won't work. I know. I know. I'll build a fire. That's what they always do in the movies to keep wild animals away. Just as the fire got some good, roaring flames, several loud *haruumphs* erupted in the woods only a few feet behind the tent.

Well, crap! So much for animals being afraid of fire. I'm out of here! After all belongings were hastily thrown in the tent, I took the aluminum polls out of their sleeves and gave the tent one good yank upwards, sending several stakes flying into the darkness. Everything jammed into the pack and fire doused with the contents of my canteen, I was ready to leave.

However, the coals were still smoldering, and wanting to be a good camper, I decided

that, as Smoky says, the fire had to be "dead out." Oh man, what to do, what to do? I need to get out of here now, but I don't have any more water. Wait. Wait. Yes, I do. There's still the liquid inside of me!

So, conscientious camper that I am, I sidled up to the fire ring and relieved myself. Hoooo, weeee! What a lesson I learned! The stench of that serous fluid steaming up from hot embers was unbelievably foul and is an odor that, unfortunately, I can recall to this day.

Fire finally out, I grabbed the flashlight and walked the 3 miles out to the forest road where my car was parked. It was 2 AM by that time, so I dropped off into a fitful sleep curled up in the backseat of my Volkswagen Beetle.

The rays of the early morning sun had just hit the car when, *haruumph, haruumph.* In my slumber I thought, Oh man, is that sound going to haunt me in my dreams, too? *Haruumph*, again. Crap. It's not in my dreams. Can it really be? Did that thing follow me all of the way out here? Slowly, I open one eye. All I can see through the back window, blocking out any scenery, is a huge patch of fur. Oh, man. It really did. It really did. It followed me. OK. OK. So, let's at least get a good look at it. I opened the other eye, and there . . . just on the other side of the glass and looking in at me . . . there . . . there was the biggest buck deer I've ever seen in my life.

To continue on your journey, cross a side stream at 13.2 miles, and pass by a steep side trail that goes a short distance to a pretty waterfall at 13.6 miles.

Return to the junction with the Fisher Spring Run Trail at 14.1 miles. From here it's a simple matter of regaining elevation and retracing your steps along this and the Rohrbaugh Plains Trail to return to your car at 18.8 miles.

Dolly Sods Wilderness

9

Dolly Sods North

Total distance (circuit): 12.7 miles

Hiking time: 7 hours

Vertical rise: 1,040 feet

Maps: USGS 7½' Blackbird Knob; USGS 7½' Blackwater Falls

The Hike at a Glance

1.0 left onto Dobbin Grade Trail
3.5 cross low ridgeline
5.6 Harmon Knob
8.2 Red Creek Trail junction
10.2 left onto FSR75
12.7 end

The land that came to be called Dolly Sods first appears in literature in the diaries of Thomas Lewis, who explored the region as a surveyor for Lord Fairfax, who owned a large portion of land in northern Virginia, in 1746. One of his diaries' entries states:

> *The fallen trees, of which there was great numbers and naturally large, were vastly improved in bulk with their coats of moss. The Spruce pines, of which there are a great plenty, their roots grow out on all sides from the trunk a considerable height above the surface, covered over and joined together in such a manner as makes their roots appear like slimey [sic] globs. The Laurel and Ivy as thick as they can grow whose branches growing of an extraordinary length are so well woven together that without it cut away it would be impossible to force through them.*

Why is it, then, that most of the photographs you see of the sods show a windswept landscape of rocky plains, heath barrens, sphagnum bogs, stunted spruce trees with limbs growing on just one side, and wide vistas in all directions? The answer is loggers, who, from the mid-1800s to the early 1900s, cut almost all the trees (which averaged 4 feet in diameter) growing on the mountain's broad plateau. The amount of slash left behind, along with the dried-out soil, was perfect tinder, and massive fires

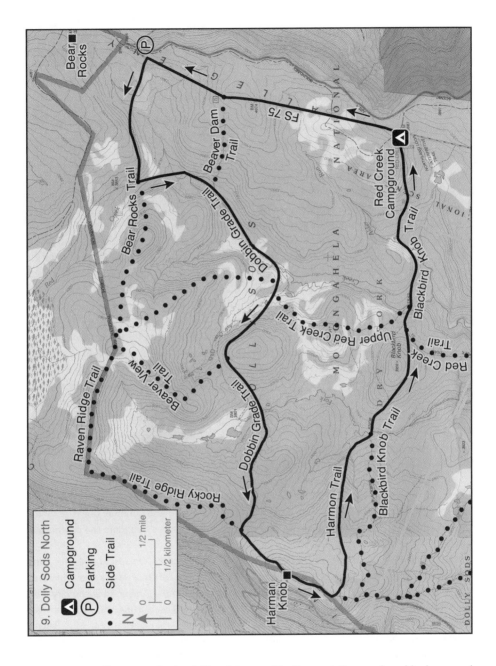

swept repeatedly across the land. The rich humus layer, which some sources say was more than 6 feet deep, was completely burned away.

Heath vegetation, such as blueberry and teaberry, tolerate such poor soil and soon thrived. In addition, it is theorized that, with no large trees to draw moisture, the water table rose, thereby restricting the growth of new forests and expanding the bogs.

This eerily beautiful landscape was in private hands until the 1990s, when it was added to the national forest through the efforts of dedicated conservationists; it was designated a continuous part of the Dolly Sods Wilderness in 2009. The Forest Service has named many of the previously unnamed old routes, enhanced and slightly altered the course of some of them, and erected trail signs at major junctions. However, you should be aware that there are no bridges over streams or aids to help you climb some very high banks. Off-road vehicles (ORVs), which are not permitted in the area but have easy access from adjacent private lands, are creating new tracks that may become more discernible on the ground than the route of the official pathway. Because of these conditions, it is suggested that you save this hike until you have confidence in your outdoor travel skills.

Also, be aware that the area was used for military exercises during World War II, and some live mortar shells remain. If you find one, do not touch it, but note its location and alert the Forest Service as soon as possible.

For those up to these challenges, this can be one of the most magnificent hiking experiences in the Mountain State.

The outing may be reached from the intersection of US220 and WV55/WV28 in Petersburg. Drive westward on WV55/WV28 for 10.0 miles, and turn right onto what some maps show as WV4, but what the roadway sign says is Jordan Run Road (WV28/7). Make a left after another 7.9 miles onto FSR75, which soon turns to dirt. Reach the top of the mountain 4.8 miles farther on, and leave your car in the large parking area on the right.

Before beginning the actual hike, you might want to take a short walk to Bear Rocks, the huge boulders on the edge of the cliff north of the parking area. You were able to arrive by car, but once you are a standing on these rocks, you will understand why Thomas Lewis was moved to write:

. . . we had very difficult access to the top of the Allegheny mountains where was a precipice 16 feet high and were hard set to get a place where there was any probability of our ascending.

This is the Allegheny Front, the eastern rampart of the Allegheny Plateau, and also a part of the so-called Eastern Continental Divide. Raindrops that happen to fall on the eastern side of the divide will flow onward to the Atlantic Ocean, while those that fall to the west will eventually reach the Gulf of Mexico. Something to ponder as you stand upon this windswept topography: It is possible that a small grain of sand that is washed into a stream on top of this mountain may one day add just a bit more mass to the delta at the mouth of the Mississippi River.

Start the hike by walking FSR75 along the top of the mountain for 0.2 mile, and turn right onto the Bear Rocks Trail {FS522}, an old roadway leading into the plains. The blueberry bushes will be full of fruit if you are here in midsummer, and you may come across a number of families spending the day picking berries.

Enter a partial woods at 0.4 mile, and swing to the left of a low knob. This was once a part of the American Discovery Trail, which stretches across the country from Cape Henlopen, Delaware to Point Reyes, California. Liability concerns about the unexploded mortar shells caused the oversight organization to move the trail onto FSR75.

Top the knob at 0.6 mile, and descend into deeper woods. At 1.0 mile, turn left onto the Dobbin Grade Trail {FS526}, a wet,

Stunted spruce in the fog

grassy logging grade. The open meadows to the left are especially scenic as you pass huge anthills built by Allegheny mound-builder ants. Scientists speculate that the mounds help protect the colony from heat and loss of moisture.

Cross a small stream at 1.2 miles, and begin paralleling Red Creek, which at this point is a slow-moving waterway, not the crashing, rushing stream it becomes once it drops into the Dolly Sods Wilderness (see Hike 8) a couple of miles to the south. Soon pass by the Beaver Dam Trail {FS520} coming in from the left. By now you have probably decided that, even though it appears, at least from a distance, the ground you are walking upon should be solid, it is not, and you are going to have wet feet throughout most of this journey.

You can blame sphagnum moss for this. Unlike most other plants in the world, it grows from the top and dies at the bottom. Through the years, these layers of moss become ever-thickening masses, which eventually meet deposits of organic material, or peat, to close off the open water of a pond. Yet, it still "floats" upon what has now become subsurface water. Providing an ever drier, partially solid base, the moss permits other, somewhat less water-tolerant plants to begin to grow upon the surface of the bog.

Some of the most interesting of these plants are carnivorous (or insectivorous, as some botanists now call them). In the sods, be on the lookout for sundews that rise above hummocks of sphagnum mosses. Glandular hairs—coated with a glistening, sweet, sticky fluid on rosettes of small leaves—are attractive to insects, which become entangled in some of the longer outer hairs. In a unique occurrence, the hairs begin a spurt of fast growth, adding cells that enable them to "fold" over the insect and draw it into more intimate contact with the leaf,

where shorter hairs secrete digestive enzymes. If the prey is quite active, the hairs respond quickly and can encircle the victim in less than 20 minutes. If the prey is already dead, the plant seems to recognize that there is no urgent need to ensnare it and will take up to several days to complete the process.

Enter the head of a wide valley at 1.8 miles, where the hike and the scenery seem to get better with every step taken. To give you an idea of how special this spot is, my notes from scouting this hike read "Open! Views, gorgeous! Wonderful!"

Ford a branch of Red Creek at 2.4 miles, pass by the Raven Ridge Trail {FS521} coming in from the right, and pay attention when you come to the junction at 2.6 miles. You want to stay to the right on the Dobbin Grade Trail and not cross the creek onto the Upper Red Creek Trail {FS509}. The shade of a forest of birch, beech, and striped maple that you enter at 2.9 miles may provide welcome relief on a sunny summer day. Attain a low ridgeline at 3.5 miles, and say hello to a whole new world. Gone is the Red Creek Valley you have been walking in; different meadows now stretch out before you, while Harmon Knob, the highest point of this journey, rises off to the left.

At 3.7 miles, pass by a small pond that may have been abandoned by the beavers by the time you hike here. Be alert less than 500 feet later. You need to swing to the left to cross the Left Fork of Red Creek and begin a long, gradual ascent through the open meadows. Attain the ridgeline at 5.0 miles, and bear left onto the Rocky Ridge Trail {FS524}.

The views from Harmon Knob at 5.6 miles are some of the best of the day. Cabin Mountain drops quickly to Canaan Valley, where the rays of the sun highlight the widespread wetlands of the Canaan Valley National Wildlife Refuge. The prominent outcrop on the western horizon is Chimney Rock on Canaan Mountain. Backbone Mountain to the northwest sports a squadron of tall windmills, whose spinning blades provide an alternative to coal in the production of electricity.

Rest, relax, and enjoy. With open meadows providing 360-degree views and cool mountain air blowing across your face, hiking just doesn't get much better than this. Once you do continue on your way, be very alert at 5.9 miles. Turn left, leave the ridgeline, and begin following the Harmon Trail {FS525}. Your gaze takes in much of the country you have walked through as you descend along this route, which comes to an end at 7.3 miles.

Bear left onto the Blackbird Knob Trail {FS511} in a landscape that gives a supreme feeling of isolation. Ford the Left Fork of Red Creek at 7.5 miles, and gradually rise into a small patch of red spruce trees. Break out into open country at 7.6 miles, and find spectacular views once again. Skirt the southern side of Blackbird Knob, and stay to the left at 8.2 miles, where the Red Creek Trail {FS514} descends to the right.

Continue along the rocky route of the Blackbird Knob Trail, which descends to a large campsite (popular and often occupied) next to Red Creek at 8.8 miles. Be cautious in fording the creek here. There have been times when I could rock-hop it, only to come back after a rainstorm and find that it had risen so much that it was impossible to cross. Ascend from the creek on a wet and muddy trail, pass by more mound-builder anthills, cross Alder Run at 9.3 miles, and climb into semi-open areas. The trail makes a sudden turn to the right at 10.0 miles and descends through a grove of evergreens. Cross a boardwalk and turn left onto FSR75 at 10.3 miles. Red Creek Campground, with outhouses, is a few feet to the right.

The final portion of the hike is a road walk, but the scenery is so magnificent that you won't care. You can look onto the open meadows you hiked through earlier in the day. Near the end of the logging era, settlers, including the Dahle family, burned the land to create open meadows, or "sods," on which to graze livestock. They obtained a good grass cover by doing this, but it didn't last long, as the soil was too nutrient-poor to support such luxuriant growth. Disillusioned, the Dahles moved on, but the land has borne the Anglicized version of their name ever since.

You should also take the time to examine the characteristics of the heath communities. The patches beside the road may be small, but it's still possible to find seven or more species of the family growing here. Look for mountain laurel, rhododendron, huckleberry, azalea, trailing arbutus, teaberry, and blueberry. Many people use the names huckleberry and blueberry interchangeably, but they are two distinct plants. The branches of blueberries always have small warts, and each berry will have more than 100 seeds. A huckleberry contains fewer than a dozen seeds, and its twigs are wart-free.

The hike comes to an end when you return to your car at 12.7 miles.

10

Flatrock Plains

Total distance (circuit): 7.5 miles

Hiking time: 4 hours, 30 minutes

Vertical rise: 1,360 feet

Maps: USGS 7½' Laneville; USGS 7½' Hopeville

The Hike at a Glance

0.7	first ford of the South Fork of Red Creek
3.2	right onto FSR70
4.8	right onto Boars Nest Trail
5.3	view of Dolly Sods and Red Creek Valley
7.5	end

Like Dolly Sods (see Hikes 8 and 9), the Flatrock Plains area is located atop the Allegheny Front. The name has evidently caused some confusion, as many people, and even a few resource books, maintain that the massif is the eastern edge of the Allegheny Mountains. Part of the mix-up may come from the fact that geologists often refer to the land that stretches from where the Alleghenies do rise on the western edge of the Shenandoah Valley in Virginia to the Allegheny Front as the "Ridge and Valley Province," and not the Allegheny Mountains.

The Allegheny Front does have the distinction of being the eastern rampart of the Allegheny Plateau. Unlike the Blue Ridge region far to the east, which attained its appearance through pressure and heat, or the Ridge and Valley Province, which was shaped by being folded and angled, the entire Allegheny Plateau was lifted up as one continuous mass. Once the floor of an ancient ocean, the land was raised to new heights when Africa collided with North America 250 million years ago. Through time, water and wind have cut valleys and eroded softer rock, yet the plateau has remained essentially a mountain tableland.

The hike to Flatrock Plains is both easy and difficult. Although the trip gains more than 1,200 feet, it does so at a fairly moderate grade as it courses for a little more than 5 miles to the top of the plateau. However, all of that elevation is lost quickly during the next 2 miles of steep and rugged trail. Also, be aware that the numerous fords of the South Fork of Red Creek are easy when the water

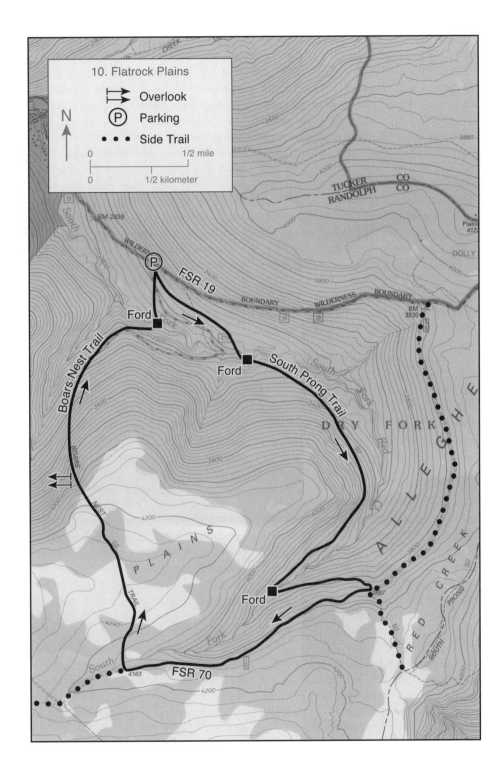

10. Flatrock Plains

is low, but can be dangerous and impassable during times of high water.

Unlike the pathways of the Dolly Sods Wilderness, all the trails in the Flatrock Plains area are signed and blazed, welcome assurances for those just beginning to hone their outdoor abilities. It is also a good place to escape the large numbers of people drawn to Dolly Sods. The Forest Service says that hiker traffic in Flatrock Plains is on the rise, yet I have seen few people each time I have been here. In fact, on an overnight journey I took here on a beautiful Labor Day weekend, I did not see anyone on the pathways.

The trailhead may be reached from the intersection of US220 and WV55/WV28 in Petersburg. Drive westward on WV55/WV28 for 10 miles, turn right onto what some maps show as WV4, but what the roadway sign says is Jordan Run Road (WV28/7). Make a left in another 0.9 mile onto FSR19, which will soon turn to dirt. Come to the intersection of FSR19 and FSR75 in an additional 6.1 miles, turn left to stay on FSR19, and drive another 2.8 miles to turn left onto FSR479. Leave your car on the small pullout on the left, but do not block the gate.

Walk around the barrier, and follow the South Prong Trail {FS 517} as it descends on a grassy woods road. Ford the South Fork of Red Creek at 0.75 mile, follow the trail upstream for 200 feet, then swing right, and begin to ascend through rhododendron, birch, and thousands of fern. Swing left onto an old railroad bed at 1.0 mile. Before bulldozers cut roads and large trucks drove on them, railroads were the most economical way of transporting timber out of the mountains. You will find evidence of this during many of your hikes in West Virginia.

Just about the time you get used to the easy grade of the railroad bed, the trail leaves it at 1.2 miles by turning right onto a rising footpath. However, the rate of ascent is not

that bad, and anyway, you get to turn left onto another old railroad bed at 1.5 miles.

It is a good bet that by now you have come across at least one pile of bear scat. Although black bears have to cope with numerous kills during hunting season and loss of habitat, West Virginia has a well-established bear population. Female black bears give birth in winter to a litter of (usually) two to four cubs once every two years. Amazingly, for an animal that can grow to be more than 500 pounds, a newborn cub weighs less than a pound and is smaller than a squirrel. They are born toothless and bald but already have claws. Getting nourishment from their mother's milk, they will emerge from the den in springtime fully furred, toothed, and weighing about 8 pounds.

At 1.6 miles, there is a spring close to the old stonework that allowed the railroad to cross this small dip in the land. If you need water, a better spring is less than 150 feet beyond this one. Rhododendron and striped maple begin to crowd the trail at 2.0 miles, and the sound of the creek becomes audible again. A break in the vegetation a few feet later lets you look into the narrow valley carved by the stream.

A good spring with sweet-tasting water, surrounded by moss and ferns and dripping from underneath boulders, is located at 2.2 miles. Nearby, you may see rusting iron implements left over from the logging days. The railroad bed is wide enough to be used as a campsite at 2.5 miles, and it is at this spot that the trail turns left, fords the creek, and continues to rise.

Intersect and turn right onto wide FSR70 at 3.2 miles. (The South Prong Trail crosses the road and continues to ascend through the forest.) Birch, rhododendron, and striped maple vie for space on top of the ridge, while a lone apple tree is a bit of a mystery. Did the tree sprout from the discarded lunch of a

Flatrock Plains along the Boars Nest Trail

hiker or forest employee a half century ago? Was the seed secreted away by a squirrel and then forgotten? Or is the tree the remnant of some valley dweller's mountaintop orchard? Spruce trees become a part of the forest beside the road at 4.6 miles.

Just after an overgrown road goes off to the left at 4.8 miles, you want to turn right and enter the spruce forest on the Boars Nest Trail {FS518}. Within a few feet, cross the South Fork of Red Creek, now not much more than a trickle compared to the roaring stream you forded near the beginning of the hike. Rise onto level Flatrock Plains, with some of the low-growing vegetation allowing you to look out to the spruce-covered slope of the Allegheny Front. This is a colorful place to be in the fall, when the blueberry leaves turn a deep crimson and the small maple trees become a vibrant fiery red.

Thank the trail workers who have placed thousands of rocks in the pathway, permitting you to proceed without getting your wet feet while also protecting the fragile environment. If you are here from late August into fall, watch for the blossoms of bottle gentian as you look down to see where to place your feet. The purple petals provide a wonderful illustration of the intricate workings of the natural world. Because the flowers remain closed, it takes a lot of effort for an insect to work its way to the nectar. As a result, they are usually visited by only the largest and strongest of bees, but even they are hesitant to expend the energy unless they know they will be amply rewarded. Botanists have

discovered that the flower has developed a coding system: Blossoms whose nectar has already been harvested turn purple around their tips, while those that still have nectar are marked with a bit of white to alert bees that the sweet payoff still remains.

The trail passes through another small spruce grove before breaking out into the open again. The route soon begins to descend and, at 5.3 miles, comes to a most spectacular view of the mountains of the Dolly Sods Wilderness and the dramatic cut in the landscape that Red Creek has made as it flows to the west. This scene is certainly as thrilling as any found in the Mahoosuc Mountains of Maine along the Appalachian Trail. In fact, the hike takes on the aspects of the section of the AT that passes through those mountains, as the next section of the Boars Nest Trail descends steeply, sometimes going down rock faces and over huge boulders—which may force you to use hands as well as feet to continue on your way.

Enter a rhododendron tunnel at 5.9 miles. When these plants are in bloom, it is easy to see how they came to be named. *Rhodo* is Greek for "rose" and *dendron* translates as "tree." Negotiate several switchbacks and cross a railroad grade at 6.7 miles. You might be tempted to cool your feet in the small wading pool below a waterfall at 7.1 miles. Then again, your feet are going to get wet anyway when you ford the South Fork of Red Creek just a few feet later.

Climb up the steep bank, swing to the right to ascend the rocky hillside, and return to your car at 7.5 miles.

11

Canaan Valley

Total distance (circuit): 8.0 miles

Hiking time: 4 hours, 15 minutes

Vertical rise: 740 feet

Maps: USGS 7½' Blackwater Falls; park handout map

The Hike at a Glance

0.4	left on Middle Ridge Trail
2.4	right on Ridge Top Trail
3.75	right on Back Hollow Trail
6.1	left on Deer Run Trail
8.0	end

When glaciers advanced from the Arctic during the last Ice Age, the only way many plants and animals were able to survive was to "migrate" southward. Once the ice floes receded, some of these plants and animals were able to take up permanent residence by clinging to the Allegheny Mountains' higher elevations, where conditions closely resemble those of their original habitats much farther north.

Canaan Valley is one such place. At an elevation of 3,200 feet and above, it receives 150–200 inches of snow annually and looks more like New England and Canada than West Virginia. In this highest large valley in the East, which is close to 14 miles long, grow spruce, balsam fir, bigtooth aspen, sphagnum moss, snowberry, and cranberry trees. Here is the land of the snowshoe hare, beavers, mink, and the endangered West Virginia flying squirrel. About 9,500 acres of wetlands, the largest such complex in West Virginia, attract shorebirds not often found anywhere else in the state. Solitary and spotted sandpipers are often seen darting about in the bogs, muskegs, spirea thickets, and shrub swamps. Bobolink and Savannah sparrows wing their way through the swaying vegetation of extensive grasslands.

Canaan Valley State Park occupies more than 6,000 acres of this grand scenery. One of West Virginia's resort parks, it has an 18-hole championship golf course, tennis courts, a heated outdoor pool as well an indoor pool, a restaurant and lodge, rental cabins, and a campground. The park's abundant snowfall makes it an obvious choice for skiing, and

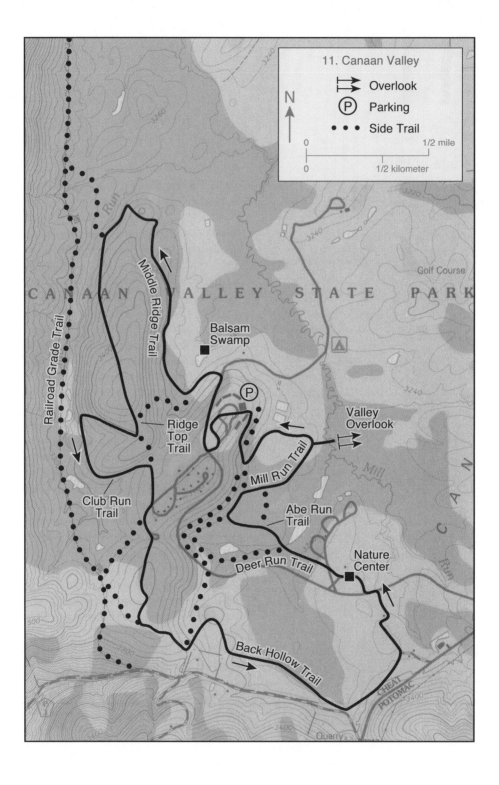

11. Canaan Valley

Overlook
P Parking
• • • Side Trail

N

0   1/2 mile
0   1/2 kilometer

Golf Course

C A N A A N   V A L L E Y   S T A T E   P A R K

Railroad Grade Trail

Middle Ridge Trail

Balsam Swamp

P

Ridge Top Trail

Valley Overlook

Club Run Trail

Mill Run Trail

Abe Run Trail

Nature Center

Deer Run Trail

C

Mill

Run

Back Hollow Trail

CHEAT
POTOMAC

Quarry

more than 20 trails provide an 850-foot drop from atop 4,250-foot Bald Knob. The park also rents equipment for cross-country skiing. (Nearby, Timberline Resort offers additional downhill opportunities, and White Grass Touring Center has multiple miles of cross-country trails.)

The park's hiking trails wind through many of the valley's different environments, and the outing described below takes you from wet swamp and bog to thick upland forest to open meadow. It is a moderate trip with just a few short uphills.

The start of the hike may be reached from the intersection of US219 and US33 in Elkins. Drive north on US219 for 35.0 miles and turn right onto WV32. Continue for another 12.9 miles, passing through Thomas and Davis (and by the turnoff to Blackwater Falls State Park—see Hike 12) before turning right into Canaan Valley State Park. Follow the main park road for an additional 1.9 miles to the lodge, where you may pick up a trail map. *Please note:* The lodge was undergoing major new construction as this book went to press. You may find the beginning and end of the hike to be slightly altered but easy to follow.

From the lodge, walk to the far end of all of the parking lots, turn left onto the exit road, and turn right onto the next road. Make another right at 0.2 mile onto the roadway to the golf course. The road walking comes to an end when you swing left onto the green-blazed Middle Ridge Trail at 0.4 mile. Skirt the edge of Balsam Swamp before entering a forest of cherry, birch, and maple, and crossing a pretty hemlock-lined stream. A swamp is different from a bog in that it contains some open water in which trees and other vegetation grow, while a bog is wet, spongy ground composed primarily of decayed matter. Although there are none in West Virginia, some people use the word *marsh* to describe a swamp or bog. Marshes have no trees and are most often associated with brackish water.

Come to a (possibly) unsigned intersection at 0.6 mile. Stay to the right, walking in a maple and beech woodland that often echoes with the sounds of woodpeckers hard at work. The trail swings to the left at 1.2 miles and begins a gentle descent in an area where ferns and running cedar cover the forest floor.

The wonderfully isolated valley you walk into at 1.5 miles is so typical of Canaan: moist trail, stream running down the middle of the valley, evidence of beavers, ferns, running cedar growing on bumpy hummocks, and mountainsides rising up to meet the sky. There are many stories about how Canaan Valley was named. The most widely circulated one says that an early explorer in the mid-1700s was so moved by the scene he saw from a mountain overlook that, in reference to Biblical passages, he proclaimed "Behold, The Land of Canaan!" Be sure to pronounce this as Kuh-NANE or locals will immediately recognize you as a visitor.

The Railroad Grade Trail comes in from the right at 1.6 miles. Swing left, and ascend to stay on the Middle Ridge Trail, which is now a part of the American Discovery Trail, a route that runs more than 6,800 miles from the Atlantic Ocean to the Pacific shore.

Hemlocks at the top of the rise at 2.0 miles can provide some welcome shade on hot summer days. Descend and come to an intersection at 2.4 miles, where the Middle Ridge Trail stays to the left. You want to turn right onto the white-blazed Ridge Top Trail, going just a few hundred feet to make another right, this time onto the red-blazed Club Run Trail.

Descend into Club Run Valley, another place that feels so isolated it can be hard to believe that a developed golf course is just a short distance away. Violets, trout lilies, and dwarf ginseng dot the edges of the valley, which opens into a wider bowl before you gradually rise to a (possibly) unsigned intersection at 3.3 miles. Turn right, walk several hundred yards, and turn right again onto a paved roadway to pass by several rental cabins.

Bypass the entrance to the Railroad Grade Trail at 3.6 miles, but at 3.75 miles, turn right onto the Back Hollow Trail, which starts out as a white-blazed service road. The road splits at 3.9 miles, with the right fork going into a meadow. Stay left, soon walking by old fruit trees and along the edge of the meadow whose lack of tall trees lets you gaze up to the great expanse of sky and surrounding ridgelines. Beyond the meadow, descend through the woods and into an overgrown orchard, with views of Cabin Mountain forming the eastern edge of the valley.

The trail to the left at 4.3 miles goes to the main park road and then to the lodge. Stay to the right on the pathway going through a field, and signed as leading to the nature center. Swing left onto paved WV45 at 5.1 miles, but be alert just 500 feet later. The trail turns left into the meadow and onto on old country lane bordered on one side by hawthorn trees. Hawthorns were planted as hedgerows because their sharp thorns kept cattle from wandering from one field into another. Small birds use the trees as a place to escape predators. Continue to follow blazed posts through the field.

Merge onto a service road at 5.8 miles. About 300 feet later, make a left onto the paved park road, only to make an almost immediate right onto the road signed as leading to the nature center. Walk by the nature center (restrooms and water are available when it's open), and turn right onto the road to the campground.

At 6.1 miles, turn left onto the red-blazed Deer Run Trail, constructed by members of the Youth Conservation Corps in the late 1970s. Make a right onto the blue-blazed Abe Run Trail about 500 feet later. The maniacal call of a pileated woodpecker is often heard in these lowlands of swamps, bogs, hardwoods, and hemlocks. It may be time to take a break on the boardwalk at 6.25 miles so that you can study the wetland you are walking through. The false hellebore and cattails are natives, but they are being crowded out by an invasive plant, the yellow flag iris.

The pretty yellow flag was imported from Europe to be cultivated in backyard gardens but has escaped into the wild. Invasives often take over an area, eliminating the diversity of a plant community, while providing little or no food for birds and animals that had fed upon the native vegetation. Unfortunately, yellow flag iris is becoming well established in the Canaan Valley and in other wetlands throughout West Virginia. This one plant may end up changing the landscape of thousands of acres in the state.

One of the park's naturalists calls the deep, dark hemlock grove you enter at 6.4 miles the "enchanted forest" on her walks that introduce children to the valley's many different environments. Some of the enchantment comes from the nurse logs seen along the trail. As a fallen tree decays, it provides a nutrient-rich environment for seeds to take hold, and it is not an uncommon sight to see a row of new trees sprouting along the full length of the rotting log.

There is a rapid succession of intersections in the next 0.5 mile. Stay left on the Abe Run Trail at the first one, but in a mixed forest of hemlock and hardwoods just 100 feet later, make a right onto the red-blazed Deer Run Trail. Several hundred yards later, bear right onto the green-blazed Mill Run Trail, staying to the left on that pathway in a forest

Looking across Canaan Valley to Cabin Mountain

once again dominated by hemlocks when you come to the next intersection in another 0.1 mile.

Break out of the woods into an open meadow at 7.3 miles, and make a right turn at a T-intersection to arrive at an overlook into the heart of the valley. Stay here for a few moments, and you might catch one or more of the local inhabitants going about their daily lives. Muskrats, beavers, herons, frogs, green-winged teal and other ducks, turtles, and mink all live here.

Mink share numerous traits with other members of their family tree. Like skunks, they possess anal glands that secrete a fetid discharge that many people find more offensive than that of the skunks, although mink do not spray the discharge. Being ferocious hunters, mink, like weasels, kill by biting their prey's neck. Their diet includes fish, frogs, snakes, crayfish, birds, turtles, rabbits, and other small mammals. Their preferred food appears to be muskrats, as evidence of that animal is found more often in mink scat than the remains of any other living thing.

Return to the intersection, and continue on your way to a somewhat confusing junction at 7.5 miles. Do not go left downhill; rather, cross under utility lines and follow the gradually rising Deer Run Trail. The small pond at 7.7 miles was constructed to provide water for the livestock of a farm now long gone.

Pass below a couple of lodge buildings at 7.8 miles, swing left at the swimming pool, and walk through the lodge causeway. The return to the parking lot at 8.0 miles marks the end of this exploration of the Canaan Valley.

The Canaan Valley National Wildlife Refuge, established in 1994 as the nation's 500th such sanctuary, is just a short distance north of the state park. A stop at its headquarters on WV32 will provide you with information on other pathways that will enable you to further investigate the beauties and wonders of the area.

12

Blackwater Falls State Park

Total distance (circuit): 5.5 miles

Hiking time: 3 hours, 10 minutes

Vertical rise: 535 feet

*Maps: USGS 7½' Blackwater Falls;
USGS 7½' Mozark Mountain; park map*

The Hike at a Glance

1.0	right onto the petting zoo road
2.5	Balanced Rock
3.1	begin following Cherry Lane Trail
4.8	overlook of Falls of Pendleton Run
5.3	Elakala Falls
5.5	end

Blackwater Falls State Park was established in 1937 to highlight and protect the falls and the land around it. Depending on what source you consult, the falls drop 63 feet, 5 stories, 57 feet, almost 6 stories, 65 feet, or 59 feet. No matter the actual height, the falls are an inspiring sight. Throughout much of the year, it is split into three. A jutting rock sends one part of the river down the precipice as a long cascade, another portion seeks various paths as it washes over dozens of layers of rock, and a third runnel tumbles straight down for close to 30 feet before breaking apart near the base of the falls. In April and May, the swell from spring rains overwhelms the jutting rock, and water roars down the falls in one crashing stream, wider than the length of the drop. The scene can become suspended in time when the falls freeze solid in winter.

Two trails lead to views of the falls. The paved 0.25-mile Gentle Trail stays high above the falls. The slightly longer trail from the park's trading post descends into the gorge to an observation deck so close to the falls that visitors often get soaked from spray. The hike described below follows other pathways in the park that meander above the Blackwater Canyon and into forestlands reminiscent of Maine, New Hampshire, and Vermont.

Within the state park are rental cabins, more than 50 guest rooms in the lodge, a campground, a restaurant, game courts, and an indoor pool. Boating (rentals available) is permitted in Pendleton Lake, and bicycles are rented from Memorial Day to Labor Day. Nature programs, such as the Astronomy

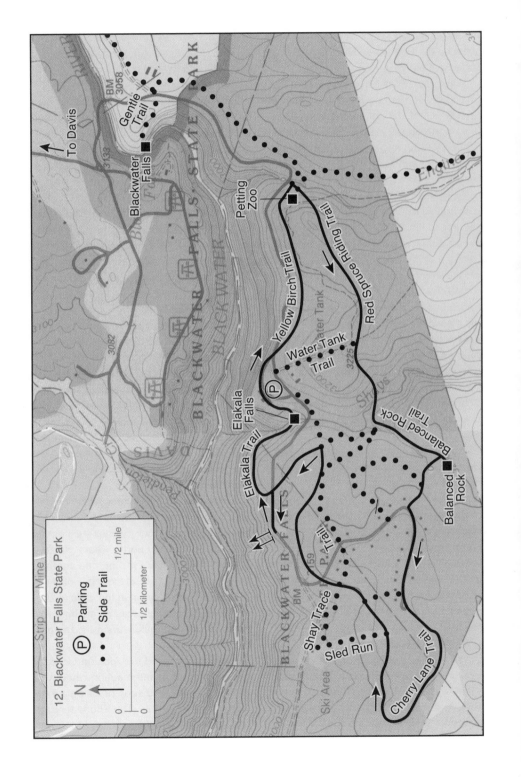

12. Blackwater Falls State Park

N

P Parking
•••• Side Trail

0 ____ 1/2 mile
0 ____ 1/2 kilometer

To Davis

RIVER

BM 3058

Gentle Trail

Blackwater Falls

BLACKWATER FALLS STATE PARK

Petting Zoo

Yellow Birch Trail

Red Spruce Riding Trail

Water Tank Trail

Elakala Falls

Elakala Trail

P

Balanced Rock Trail

Balanced Rock

Shay Trace

Sled Run

Cherry Lane Trail

BLACKWATER FALLS

BM 3159

Ski Area

DAVIS

Strip Mine

Pendleton

Weekend, Wildflower Pilgrimage, or Walk between the Parks (see Hike 13), are held throughout the year.

Blackwater Falls State Park and the beginning of the hike may be reached from the intersection of US219 and US33 in Elkins. Drive north on US219 for 35.0 miles, turn right on WV32, and pass through Thomas. Continue for another 2.4 miles to the northern edge of Davis, turn right onto Blackwater Falls Road (WV29), and enter the park in an additional 0.9 mile. Turn left in 0.3 mile (the trail to the falls from the trading post is a short distance straight ahead), pass by the Gentle Trail in a few hundred yards, and pull into the lodge parking area about a mile later.

Walk back out on the parking lot entrance road, turn right, and within a few feet bear left into the woods on the Yellow Birch Trail. The sunlight immediately fades, and you walk into deep shade created by the heavily needled branches of the hemlock trees. Rise out of the hemlocks at 0.25 mile and into a forest of rhododendron and birch, where young hemlock trees vie with running cedar for space from which to grow in the soil. Be alert, as the trail makes many twists and turns. A red squirrel may run across the path in its search for food or may scold you from an upper branch for daring to walk through its home.

Red squirrels are very territorial and are quick to show their anger at any intruder by stamping feet, jerking tails, and releasing a series of loud chucks, barks, squeaks, spits, growls, and chatter. Although protective of its own domain, a red squirrel is not above raiding others' property to obtain bird eggs or a hiker's snack foods.

You get to do a few feet of rock scrambling when you negotiate the cleft at 0.8 mile. Upon reaching the petting zoo road at 1.0 mile, turn right, ascend the road, walk to the left of the building, and make another right onto the Red Spruce Riding Trail, located behind the building. Ascend on the woods road, lined with rhododendron and red spruce, and soon level out.

The hike passes under a utility line at 1.7 miles, where a turn to the right would lead back to the lodge. You want to continue straight on the Red Spruce Riding Trail and descend, crossing a tributary of Shay Run on a footbridge at 1.9 miles. The stream's dark color is produced by tannin, a chemical released by the leaves, needles, and bark of some trees and plants. The spruce and hemlock trees are the largest contributors of tannin in this area. Although you shouldn't drink the water—or any other surface water anywhere—without treating it, tannin retards the growth of bacteria and was used for centuries as an astringent.

At 2.0 miles, turn left onto the Balanced Rock Trail, a footpath through heavy growths of vegetation. (The Red Spruce Riding Trail continues straight and, within a few feet, intersects a portion of the Balanced Rock Trail that descends to the right.) Unlike most rhododendron thickets that block out any view, the plants here only grow 5–7 feet high, letting you see much of the forest around you. Stay to the left when you come to the next intersection at 2.4 miles.

Less than 400 feet later, arrive at Balanced Rock, a large sandstone boulder sitting atop a smaller rock. Scenes such as this are common farther north, where glaciers pushed many rocks over top one another. Yet, the ice floes stopped moving southward in central Pennsylvania. In the case of Balanced Rock, erosion wore away the lower part of a fissured rock, leaving the top part untouched.

Continue beyond the rock on the spur trail, coming to an intersection where you want to turn left and soon crossing a footbridge over Shay Run. The Rhododendron Trail comes in from the right; stay to the left

Blackwater Falls

on the Balanced Rock Trail. Swing left onto the paved cabin road at 2.75 miles, and, at the top of the cul-de-sac circle, reenter the woods on the Cherry Lane Trail at 3.1 miles. Crows foot covers much of the ground, with the low growing vegetation making for open forest views.

Rhododendron closes in on the trail for a short distance as the trail swings to the right at 3.4 miles. The Sled Run Trail descends quickly to the left at 3.8 miles; continue with a gradual descent on the Cherry Lane Trail. A faint trail ascends to the cabins at 4.0 miles. Cross the Shay Trace Trail at 4.1 miles, and continue on the Cherry Lane Trail in a forest populated by birch, maple, hemlock, cherry, and many beech trees.

Diagonally cross the paved cabin road to the left at 4.4 miles, and reenter the woods on the Red Spruce Riding Trail, but turn left onto the Shay Trace Trail at 4.5 miles. Make another left to descend along the Balanced Rock Trail at 4.6 miles.

Turn left onto the paved park road at 4.7 miles for a short side excursion to an overlook into the Blackwater Canyon. On the far side of the canyon are the Falls of Pendleton Run, dropping hundreds of feet from Pendleton Lake into the Blackwater River. You are standing close to the canyon rim, where dozens of turkey vultures may be soaring just a few feet away.

Retrace your steps along the paved road, and turn left onto the Elakala Trail. Within a few feet is a junction whose right fork goes back to the road. Stay left and descend to Elakala Falls. This lovely spot, with the falls dropping 20 feet through a green forest of moss, rhododendron, and hemlock, is less than a 10-minute walk from the lodge, yet most park visitors never go there. You even get to walk directly over the falls as the trail continues across a footbridge and rises to return you to the lodge. You should walk behind the building in order to obtain one more magnificent view into the Blackwater Canyon before returning to your car at 5.5 miles.

If the hike has been a warm one, you could cool off in the lodge restaurant with a scoop of ice cream. A cup of coffee or hot chocolate may be in order if the temperatures have been low.

13

Blackwater to Canaan

Total distance (one way): 9.7 miles

Hiking time: 5 hours

Vertical rise: 860 feet

Maps: USGS 7½' Blackwater Falls

The Hike at a Glance

1.5	intersection with Stemwinder Trail
2.7	shelter
3.5	right onto FSR13
5.1	left off of FSR13
6.3	enter Canaan Valley State Park
8.1	left onto Middle Ridge Trail
9.7	end

The hike from Blackwater Falls State Park to Canaan Valley State Park is such a good one that the parks and affiliated organizations sponsor at least four Walks Between the Parks every year that are attended by scores of locals and visitors. However, there is no need for you to wait for an official walk, as the trails are open to everyone year-round.

Gradually rising from the Blackwater Falls Lodge onto the flat plateau of Canaan Mountain, the pathways take you through a wet and boggy landscape of spruce, beech, birch, and fir trees that grow above an understory of lush rhododendron thickets, blueberry bushes, and mossy rocks. The hike drops off the mountain and passes through a wonderfully isolated valley and by a balsam swamp before delivering you to the lodge in Canaan Valley State Park. The list of animals that make their homes along different portions of the outing reads like a who's who of West Virginia wildlife. Among the many you may see, hear, or notice evidence of are bear, deer, beavers, red and gray fox, skunks, owls, snakes, grouse, hawks, squirrels, frogs, box turtles, salamanders, snowshoe hares, cottontail rabbits, fisher cats, mink, muskrats, turkeys, raccoons, and bobcats.

You have the choice of doing this as a day trip or making it an overnighter by staying in the trailside shelter 2.7 miles into the journey. Camping is permitted at other places on Monongahela National Forest land, but good, dry sites are hard to find. (Backcountry camping is not permitted in the state parks.) For a bit of luxury, consider doing this as a lodge-to-lodge hike by staying at Blackwater

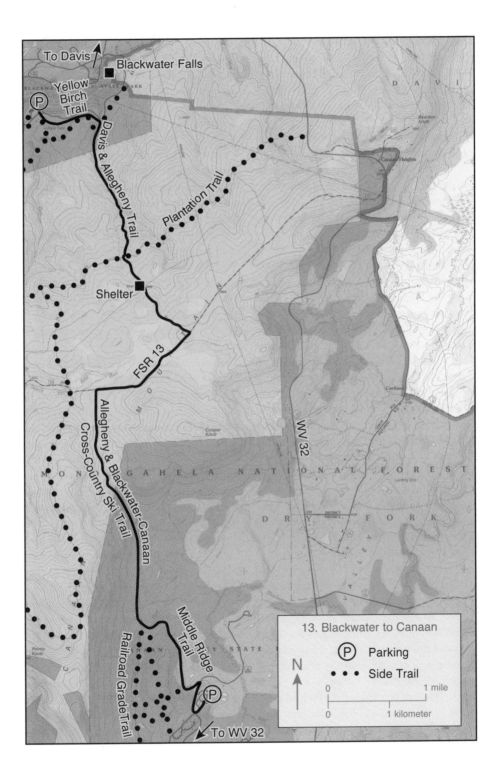

To Davis

Blackwater Falls

Yellow Birch Trail

P

Davis & Allegheny Trail

Plantation Trail

Shelter

FSR 13

Allegheny & Blackwater-Canaan Cross-Country Ski Trail

WV 32

MONONGAHELA NATIONAL FOREST

DRY FORK

Middle Ridge Trail

Railroad Grade Trail

P

To WV 32

13. Blackwater to Canaan

P Parking

N

• • • Side Trail

0   1 mile

0   1 kilometer

Falls on the night you arrive and spending the evening after the hike in Canaan Valley. Background information on both parks may be found in Hikes 11 and 12. Reservations for the lodges can be made by calling 800-225-5982.

Whatever option you choose, expect to have wet feet almost from start to finish.

This is a one-way trek, so a shuttle will be necessary. The parks may be reached from the intersection of US219 and US33 in Elkins. Drive north on US219 for 35.0 miles and turn right on WV32. Continue for another 12.9 miles, passing through Thomas and Davis (and by the turnoff to Blackwater Falls State Park on WV29) before turning right into Canaan Valley State Park. Follow the main park road for an additional 1.9 miles to the lodge, where you may leave one car. Return to Davis, turn left onto Blackwater Falls Road (WV29), and enter the park in an additional 0.9 mile. Turn left in another 0.3 mile, and pull into the lodge parking lot 1.6 miles later.(In order to avoid driving two cars, you may be able to hire a shuttle. Call the Tucker County Visitors Center, 800-782-2775 or 304-259-5315, to see if anyone is currently offering the service.)

Walk back out the parking lot entrance road, turn right, and within a few feet make a left into a grove of hemlocks on the yellow-blazed Yellow Birch Trail. Rise out of the hemlocks and into a forest of rhododendron and yellow birch.

The yellow birch survives in West Virginia by growing at elevations of 3,000 feet and above, where the climate resembles that found farther north. The tree has a peeling bark like the paper birch, but it has more of a shiny-yellow-to-silvery-gray color as opposed to the creamy white of the paper birch. The bark on older yellow birches often turns reddish brown. The tree produces large amounts of seeds in small, winged cap-sules that may be transported for miles by the wind. At the end of its life, the decaying wood was considered by Native Americans to be excellent tinder to start a fire.

Pass through a narrow cleft between two boulders, where rhododendron and young hemlock trees crowd the trail, at 0.75 mile. Cross the road to the petting zoo at 1.0 mile, continue on the Yellow Birch Trail for just a few more feet to use a footbridge over Engine Run, and turn right onto an old, unblazed railroad grade, now part of the park's bicycle trail system. A few hundred yards later, join up with the yellow-blazed Allegheny {FS701} and Davis Trails. The Allegheny Trail (see Hike 15) runs for more than 300 miles, from the West Virginia–Virginia border near Lindside, West Virginia to the West Virginia–Pennsylvania line a few miles east of Morgantown.

Leave Blackwater Falls State Park at 1.5 miles, and enter Monongahela National Forest, where backcountry camping is permitted. Cross Engine Run on a footbridge at 1.6 miles, and continue along a picturesque and narrow pathway hemmed in by towering rhododendron bushes. The "soap suds" you see in the water are not from human pollution but are a product of the tannin that has leached into the water. (See Hike 12 for a discussion about tannin.)

Cross a small water run at 2.2 miles, and rise at a bit stiffer rate than what you have experienced so far. Turn right onto the access trail at 2.7 miles, and come to your "home" if you're spending the evening. If not, take a well-deserved break in the shelter, reveling in the fact that the wind passing through the trees and the songs of birds may be the only sounds you hear. To pass the time, read the register and learn about the exploits of Allegheny Trail thru-hikers. Whereas hundreds of people traverse the Appalachian Trail in one hiking season, the Allegheny Trail usually

Cardinal flower

plays host to fewer than 10 people a year walking its full length. Entries in the register—some humorous, some axiomatic, and some full of disillusionment—provide insight into what they experience.

Return to the trail, continue on your way, and cross the Plantation Trail {FS101} at 2.8 miles. The large stone slab you walk upon at 3.0 miles is reminiscent of those in the Adirondack Mountains of New York or the Barren Mountains in Maine. These may be the few muck-free steps you get to take on the entire hike. The faint, almost nonexistent trail you cross at 3.2 miles is an old fire lane that the Forest Service has permitted to be reclaimed by nature.

Turn right onto FSR13 at 3.5 miles, and if it's springtime descend by patches of bluets; at any time of year, nearly constant winds blow. Bogs line both sides of the road as you begin a gentle rise at 4.3 miles.

There are many different types of bogs and names for them—relict, quaking, glacial, sphagnum, level, flat, raised, domed, slope, geogenous, mineritrophic, ombrogenous, ombrotrophic, transitional, oligotrophic, kettlehole, and others. The differences are subtle, having to do with the original topographic feature, where the bog is situated, how it was created, what the predominant plants are that grow in it, or how it receives its water and nutrients. In the scientific community there are even discussions and distinctions as to what truly constitutes a bog. Some boglike areas could actually be fens or peatlands, not bogs.

If you are desperate for a campsite, there is a poor one on the left at 4.6 miles. Begin a gradual descent, with abundant spruce and hemlock growing beside the road, but be alert at 5.1 miles. Turn left onto the trail signed as the BLACKWATER–CANAAN X-COUNTRY SKI TRAIL. (On most maps it is identified as the Allegheny Trail.) The roots and muck you have walked on so far were nothing compared to this next mile of pathway working its way through the moist landscape of this mountaintop bog. Your feet *will* get wet. The makeup of the forest changes—for just a little while—at 5.9 miles, as ferns, club mosses, and blueberry bushes make up the underbrush, and birch and other deciduous trees replace the evergreens.

Step over a stream on a small footbridge at 6.25 miles, and descend past large patches of striped maple for the first time on the hike. You will soon enter Canaan Valley State Park (see Hike 11), where backcountry camping is prohibited. The pathway goes over a series of small bridges before coming to an intersection at 7.8 miles.

Bear left onto the Railroad Grade Trail, signed as leading to the lodge. Cross a water run on a footbridge, and walk along the edge of a wonderfully isolated mountain valley in which it is obvious that beaver have been at work.

When beavers dam a stream, it slows the flow of water and floods the area. Snags—trees that die because they are accustomed to dry land and cannot tolerate the extra moisture—provide homes for woodpeckers and other creatures. Around the pond, new trees grow where beavers had cut others, and water plants grow along the edges. This new wetland becomes a habitat for frogs, turtles, salamanders, muskrats, ducks, and other birds.

A footbridge takes the pathway across Club Run, just before coming to an intersection at 8.1 miles. Bear left onto the Middle Ridge Trail (signed as leading to the lodge). It provides another chance for you to walk along the edge of the valley before swinging right and ascending beside beech trees. Enter an open forest with towering maple trees, and gradually descend to an intersection at 9.1 miles.

Go left (not right uphill), cross a stream, and ascend along the edge of Balsam Swamp. Turn right onto a paved road, and make a left at 9.5 miles onto the road that leads to the lodge. Return to your shuttled car at 9.7 miles.

If you have used a little foresight, your room at the lodge is waiting for you. Shower off the dirt and grime of the trail, have dinner in the restaurant, and spend the evening watching the sun drop behind the landscape you traversed earlier in the day.

14

Laurel Fork Wilderness

Total distance (one way): 16.0 miles

Hiking time: 8 hours, 45 minutes

Vertical rise: 840 feet

Maps: USGS 7½' Glady; USGS 7½' Sinks of Gandy; USGS 7½' Whitman

The Hike at a Glance

1.6	left onto Laurel River Trail
4.3	junction with Beulah Trail
5.4	junction with Forks Trail
6.0	Laurel Fork Campground
8.6	cross Adamson Run
10.9	cross Scale Lot Run
12.9	cross Mud Run
16.0	end

The years around the turn of the 20th century were boom times for logging in West Virginia—so much so that many mountain crests, hillsides, and valleys had been cleared by the 1920s, and the land around the Laurel Fork of the Cheat River was no exception. At first, horses were employed to drag timber from the higher elevations before it was floated downstream. Later, railroad tracks snaked along the river and into side valleys, enabling loggers to use powerful locomotives to carry out larger loads.

Logging continued in the Laurel Fork drainage system—some trees carried out by rail, others along haul roads—for several years after the Forest Service purchased the land in the mid-1920s. Yet, by the time the area was designated the Laurel Fork South Wilderness and Laurel Fork North Wilderness by Congress in 1983, almost all evidence of logging had disappeared. The railroad grades and roadbeds have now become pathways to explore an isolated valley once again covered by a dense Appalachian forest.

This hike along Laurel Fork is for experienced hikers looking for a challenge. Trail signs and blazes are virtually nonexistent—the only ones still around were installed decades ago, before the area became a designated wilderness, where management guidelines don't permit the use of paint or plastic blazes. Those that do remain are quickly rotting and fading; you may find an occasional rock cairn marking the way.

Nevertheless, the rewards are many if you are willing to face these hardships. This is the

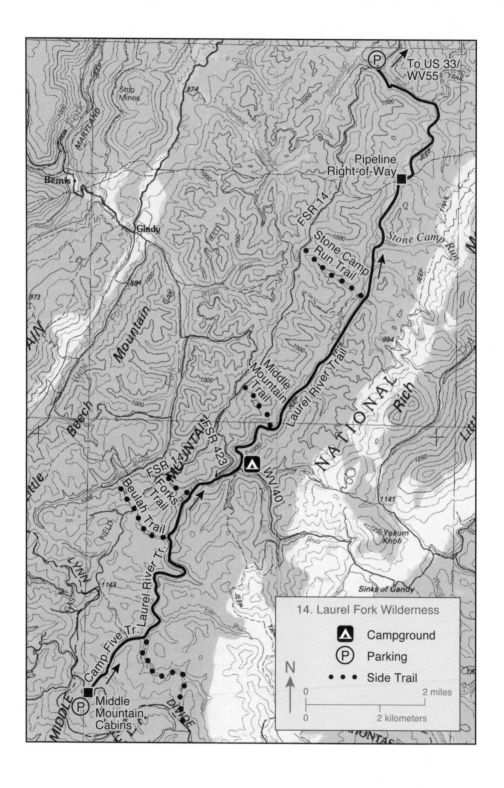

Strip Mines

874

MARYLAND

Bemis

Glady

884

973

1000

Mountain

Beech

FSR 14

Stone Camp
Run Trail

1000

Middle
Mountain
Trail

Laurel River Trail

994

Stone Camp Run

Pipeline
Right-of-Way

To US 33/
WV55

NATIONAL

Rich

FSR 423

FSR
Forks
Trail

Beulah Trail

WV.40

1250

1141

Yokum
Knob

Sinks of Gandy

LYNN

1143

Camp Five Tr. Laurel-River Tr.

Middle
Mountain
Cabins

DIVIDE

MIDDLE

14. Laurel Fork Wilderness

🔺 Campground

Ⓟ Parking

• • • Side Trail

N

0 ——— 2 miles

0 ——— 2 kilometers

least visited designated wilderness in the state, so you may not run into anyone else throughout the hike, which just adds to the overall sense of seclusion. Wildflowers abound within the confines of the valley and on the hillsides of bordering Rich and Middle Mountains. It's possible that you may see blue cohosh, Indian cucumber root, wood sorrel, lady's slipper, trillium, Canada mayflower, partridgeberry, cinquefoil, and skunk cabbage all on the same hike. Keep an eye out for the rare glade spurge in midsummer. Wildlife includes black bear, bobcats, deer, turkeys, mink, squirrels, and an active beaver population. Sharp-shinned and red-shouldered hawks have been seen flying overhead, and you should consider bringing along a fly rod, as the river contains native brook and stocked trout.

A journey of 16.0 miles may be a nice day hike in other areas, but because of the difficulty of negotiating the Laurel River Trail, it is recommended that you make this an overnighter. Campsites abound along the river, or you have the option of using the Forest Service's Laurel Fork Campground. If you set up the tent in the campground beforehand, you could turn the trip into day hikes of 6.0 and 10.0 miles. Just be aware that the campground is popular and can fill up quickly in nice weather.

This is a one-way trek, so you will need to shuttle cars. The trailheads may be reached from the intersection of US219/US250/WV55 and US33/WV55 in Elkins. Drive eastward on US33/WV55 for 15.1 miles, turn right onto Middle Mountain Road (FSR14), and stay right in another 2.9 miles at an intersection with a private road. Leave one car in the small parking area (do not block the gate) in an additional 2.1 miles. Continue on your way, stay on FSR14 at the intersection with FSR422 in 7.0 miles, and again at the intersection with FSR423 in an-

other 0.3 mile. (Turning left on FSR423 would bring you to the Laurel Fork Campground within a few minutes.) Continue on FSR14 for another 1.5 miles, and park at the entrance to the Middle Mountain Cabins. Do not block the road or the gate.

Walk around the gate, and follow the gravel road past the cabins and a small pond to enter the woods on the Camp Five Trail {FS315}. Within a short distance, the road narrows, and the trail follows the route of an old railroad grade. Rock-hop across Camp Five Run to the left side of the stream at 0.6 mile; do not stay right on what may look like the more obvious route. Within the next mile, you will cross the water three more times and follow a sidehill trail above the stream a couple times. The quiet of the narrow valley may be broken if a great blue heron takes flight on its 70-inch wingspan.

Be alert at 1.6 miles. When the trail you have been following swings to the right around the hillside, you need to take the faint, descending route and turn left onto the Laurel River Trail {FS306}. Several nice campsites are located among the evergreens just before you ford Camp Five Run and head downstream along Laurel Fork.

Ascend the side of the hill at 2.1 miles, soon walking through a virgin stand of spruce. Descend back to the stream at 2.4 miles, only to rise once again, this time on a thread-thin pathway through a forest of ferns and birch trees. A wide variety of ferns are abundant on this hike, so be sure to bring along an identification guide. You may find Christmas, New York, cinnamon, bracken, hay-scented, interrupted, silvery glade, cut-leaf grape, and sensitive ferns growing on both hillside and bottomland.

You may not immediately recognize the sensitive as a fern. Unlike most of its kin, it has expansive, flat leaves that are veined, like those of a flowering plant. Come Septem-

Laurel River

ber or October, it may seem that it has disappeared from the forest, as it is sensitive to frost—hence its name. If you look closely, though, you will find that it is still there, but all that remains are upright stems and small branches tipped by tiny spore dots.

A steep pathway to the right at 3.6 miles drops to a campsite amid a plethora of running cedar. Once you are back close to the creek and railroad grade at 4.3 miles, the Beulah Trail {FS310} rises to the left and goes 0.9 mile to FSR14. Stay right, and cross a side stream. The trail may be hard to follow for the next stretch—it officially stays to the left above Laurel Fork, but it may be hard to locate. If you lose it, you can follow its former route by fording Laurel Fork several times before coming to a meadow at 5.3 miles. Here the trail curves left around the overgrown vegetation to ascend onto the hillside.

The faint Forks Trail {FS323} rises to the left at 5.4 miles to reach FSR14 in 0.6 mile. Stay right and continue downstream on an old woods road. At 5.8 miles, because there is no water available at the Laurel Fork Campground, stop to fill up at the piped spring, a remnant of a 1930s Civilian Conservation Corps camp. Less than 300 feet later, walk through a portion of the Laurel Fork Campground (toilets in season). Turn right onto FSR423/WV40 at 6.0 miles, cross Laurel Fork on the road bridge, and turn left into another section of the campground.

If you set your tent up earlier, you are home for the night. Hopefully, you also stashed some binoculars to observe the plentiful and varied birdlife around the campground. At the forest edge, look for goldfinches, indigo buntings, chipping sparrows, and yellow-billed cuckoos. In the woods you might spy scarlet tanagers, juncos, black-capped chickadees, and white-breasted nuthatches. Flying about in the field may be common flickers, phoebes, and ravens. As evening comes on, you might hear the wail of a screech owl but may never know that the saw-whet owl is also here, as it remains silent much of the time.

Continue the hike by walking to the bulletin board at the far edge of the field. Enter the woods a few feet to the left of the bulletin board on an obvious old railroad grade. Cross several side streams, and emerge into an open meadow full of Queen Anne's lace, butter-and-eggs, and several different varieties of mint at 6.4 miles. Turn left, and ford Five Lick Run at 6.5 miles. The crossing may be easier if you go a few feet upstream.

Birch trees populate the hillside at 7.0 miles, where you rise along an old logging road, putting a short distance between you and Laurel Fork. There are two routes you could follow from here until milepoint 12.0. Because the railroad grade that stays in the valley is harder to follow, can be wet and muddy, and is washed out in some areas, this hike description follows the route of the old logging road.

Soon ascend high above Laurel Fork, only to drop back down and join the railroad grade on soggy ground at 8.0 miles. Beaver dams and the stumps of trees these animals have felled can be seen on the opposite shore. Beavers were once abundant in West Virginia, but trapping nearly wiped them out by the early 1800s. A reintroduction program in the 1930s released 64 beavers, and they are now becoming more numerous throughout the state.

The trail may be faint (or completely overgrown in late summer and fall) when you enter a meadow at 8.6 miles. Continue straight ahead and cross Adamson Run. It may seem as if you have lost the trail once you are on the other side, but continue along the edge of the field closest to the hillside, and you will come to the defined railroad grade in a few hundred feet. The valley is wide and sunny here, with many potential campsites.

Cross Bill White Run at 9.3 miles, and swing slightly to the right to rise on the old logging road. Drop back to Laurel Run at 9.6 miles, where bear scat and paw prints are often seen in the mud. Instead of crashing through the vegetation of the meadow at 10.4 miles, stay close to the hillside on the right, and go upstream along Three Bear Run before crossing it. Then find the old logging road and continue downstream along Laurel

Fork. There may be no sign or foot tread to indicate the Stone Camp Run Trail {FS305} that goes off to the left at this point and rises 1.5 miles to FSR14. The open meadows may make it hard to follow the trail, but the hundreds of bellflowers, ironweed, golden Alexanders, and asters growing in them are pleasing to the eye.

Rejoin the railroad grade at 10.9 miles, cross Scale Lot Run, and soon leave the grade for the old logging road. At 11.6 miles, walk downhill through an overgrown field (there may be no obvious trail), cross Stone Camp Run, and stay close to the hillside so that you may once again find the old logging road. Return to the railroad grade one more time before staying right on the logging road at 12.0 miles and rising high above Laurel Fork.

Cross under an old telegraph line (which may have fallen down by the time you hike here) at 12.8 miles. Swing right onto a pipeline right-of-way through a field where swallowtail butterflies flit from one thistle to another. Butterflies are a favorite food of birds, lizards, and other animals, especially during the caterpillar stage. Evolution has provided them with several adaptations to help increase their chances of survival. Giant swallowtail caterpillars look like bird droppings, while other caterpillars have scent glands that give off unpleasant odors. The pipevine swallowtail is poisonous, both as a caterpillar and as a butterfly, because it feeds on toxic birthworts. The female tiger swallowtail gains some protection from predators by mimicking the look of the pipevine.

Cross Mud Run on the pipeline culvert at 12.9 miles, and swing left (do not continue on the right-of-way) to return to a railroad grade and Laurel Fork. Leave the grade at 13.3 miles, but return to it less than 600 feet later. The route may be faint, but once again stay close to the hillside.

Walk into an open field at 13.9 miles. There may be no discernible route, but stay along the left side, and pick up a faint pathway once you reenter the woods. If you become disoriented in the field, just continue downstream along Laurel Fork and you will be headed in the right direction.

However, at 14.5 miles, you must be very, very alert! The trail to the left that you want to take may not be very obvious. (When I was here one time, a tree had fallen across it, completely obliterating the turnoff. Another time, a horse party had trampled the ground, again obscuring the pathway.) Look for several large boulders on the left side of the trail, just a few feet before the turnoff. If you miss this, you will soon come to a dead end at Laurel Creek, with no apparent way to continue. If this happens, turn around to find the trail.

The pathway soon ascends along Beaver Dam Run, but makes a sudden sharp left steeply uphill at 15.3 miles. Swing right onto a woods road above Beaver Dam Run Valley at 15.4 miles, with ninebark, meadowsweet, fireweed, and cinnamon fern growing in the open area around the creek. Turn right onto FSR14 at 15.8 miles, and return to your car at 16.0 miles.

After having successfully faced the rigors and possible confusions of the Laurel River Trail, you may reach the same conclusion I have: Sometimes it is more interesting and gratifying to hike a route that requires you to use a bit of your own navigational skills, rather than one that coddles you with groomed treadways and manicured foliage.

15

Allegheny Trail

Total distance (one way): 44.4 miles

Hiking time: 4 days

Vertical rise: 6,960 feet

Maps: USGS 7½' Glady; USGS 7½' Beverly East; USGS 7½' Wildell; USGS 7½' Durbin; USGS 7½' Green Bank; USGS 7½' Cass

First Day's Hike at a Glance

3.2	right onto High Falls Trail
4.5	left in gap
5.6	Wildell Shelter
7.1	pass former Camp 48 Trail
12.5	Johns Camp Shelter

Second Day's Hike at a Glance

3.1	Gaudineer Knob Scenic Area
6.5	high-water alternate goes right
8.1	ford of West Fork of the Greenbrier River and right turn onto the West Fork Trail
11.7	wooden bridge over side stream
13.6	Durbin

Third Day's Hike at a Glance

1.4	cross Spillman Run
4.4	cross Brush Run
5.7	left at Y-intersection
8.7	campsite

Fourth Day's Hike at a Glance

2.4	Slavin Hollow–Hosterman Road
7.6	Greenbrier River becomes visible
9.6	end

For approximately 300 miles, the Allegheny Trail traverses some of eastern West Virginia's most inspiring scenery. Stretching from the state's southeastern border with Virginia to the Pennsylvania line near Morgantown, it passes through national forests, numerous state parks and forests, and—with owner cooperation—across an assortment of private lands.

Nick Lozano, Bob Tabor, and Charley Carlson, all from the Charleston area, are generally acknowledged as having advanced the idea of a long-distance hiking trail through the state. Along with Dr. Bob Urban, Fred Bird, Shirley Schweizer, and Doug Wood, they established the West Virginia Scenic Trails Association (WVSTA) in the early 1970s. The association is a grassroots organization, with the trail route being identified, built, and maintained almost exclusively by volunteers.

A number of years ago, my future wife, Laurie Messick, and I were recognized by the WVSTA as being the first people to walk the trail's entire length. We repeated the trip a couple years later.

By design, the Allegheny Trail can be a rugged hike. Do not expect Appalachian Trail–level maintenance. There are a number of places where there is no dug treadway to delineate the route, and the yellow blazes that mark the way may be faded or have disappeared. Many miles are across steep, rocky terrain where footing is unsure and vegetation may have overtaken the pathway despite the best efforts of volunteers. Yet, the rewards are many. Scenic rivers, a virgin

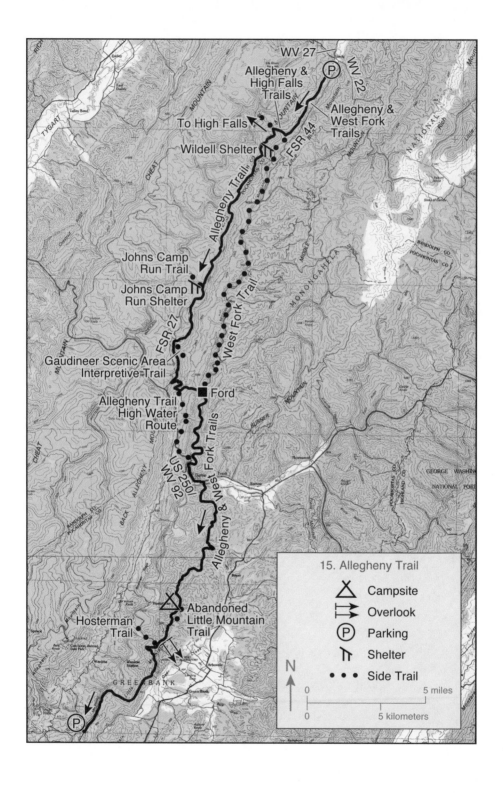

WV 27

Allegheny &
High Falls
Trails

P

WV 22

Allegheny &
West Fork
Trails

To High Falls

Wildell Shelter

FSR 44

Allegheny Trail

West Fork Trail

Johns Camp
Run Trail

Johns Camp
Run Shelter

FSR 27

Gaudineer Scenic Area
Interpretive Trail

Ford

Allegheny Trail
High Water
Route

US 250/
WV 92

Allegheny & West Fork Trails

Hosterman
Trail

Abandoned
Little Mountain
Trail

GREENBANK

15. Allegheny Trail

△ Campsite

Overlook

P Parking

Shelter

• • • Side Trail

N

0   5 miles

0   5 kilometers

red spruce forest, pleasing views, and isolated mountain valleys are only a few of the reasons why this particular four-day stretch was selected. Water is abundant, possible campsites are many, and there is the opportunity to spend a night in an inn and two opportunities for side excursions on scenic railroads.

Be prepared for a long car shuttle before the hike. Leave one car in the scenic railroad parking lot in Cass after asking permission at the station. From Cass, follow WV7 eastward for several miles, turn left on WV92/WV28, travel 12.0 miles, turn left onto US250/WV92, and come into Durbin in 4.0 miles. At the far side of town, turn right onto Highland Street, go 0.2 mile, and turn left onto FSR44. Follow this dirt road for approximately 20 miles, turn left on WV22, go a few hundred yards, turn left on WV 27, and come to the trailhead parking area.

FIRST DAY

Total distance (one way): 12.5 miles
Hiking time: 7 hours, 45 minutes

Follow the combined Allegheny {FS701} and West Fork {FS312} Trails south through a rural countryside of meadows and grazing cattle. Running for a little more than 22 miles from Glady to Durbin, the rail-trail is open to hikers, bikers, and horseback riders. The Allegheny Trail was moved onto a portion of it after being displaced from the northern end of Shaver's Mountain by a private landowner near the turn of the 21st century.

Rise very gradually, but be alert at 3.2 miles. It is time to leave the easy walking behind by turning right onto the High Falls Trail {FS345} and negotiating the 500-foot ascent of Shaver's Mountain. Rise through an overgrown field with an abundance of thorn bushes before entering the forest to follow a series of switchbacks.

Attain the ridgeline at 4.5 miles, where the flat land in the gap contains a number of good campsites and the Allegheny Trail continues by turning left and ascending. (The High Falls Trail drops down the other side of the mountain for 1.5 miles to the spectacular High Falls of Cheat, one of the state's best waterfalls. This is a highly recommended side trip if you have the time.)

An abundance of ferns line the Allegheny Trail and, in fact, will be almost constant companions throughout this hike. Be ready for many ups and downs as the trail crosses more than 10 peaks and knobs in the next 11.0 miles. The side route to the left at 5.6 miles goes about 200 feet to Wildell Shelter (no water), named for a former town at the base of the mountain. At 6.2 miles, cross a woods road that some older maps identify as the Camp 57 Trail; it was abandoned by the Forest Service due to access problems through private land.

Cross another woods road at 6.8 miles, and pass the faint blue blazes of the former Camp 48 Trail on the right at 7.1 miles. That route has been abandoned for so long that you might not even notice it, but you might be able to find a tent site or two in the gap at 7.6 miles before the trail begins to rise at a steady rate. At 8.1 miles, descend along a woods road that is relatively newer than the ones you crossed earlier. Its construction has opened up good views of the West Fork Valley below and the ridgelines of the Allegheny Plateau to the east.

Be alert at 8.5 miles. The trail turns right off the woods road and onto a narrow pathway, which swings below the side of the knob directly ahead, gradually ascends back to the ridgeline at 9.4 miles, and enters a spruce forest. The knob at 11.0 miles has large boulders on the left side of the trail that some people say offer views if you scramble to the top of them. I could never find a place that got higher than the surrounding trees; you may have better luck.

Johns Camp Shelter is to the right of the trail at 12.5 miles. A spring in front of the shelter provides water, while the blue-blazed Johns Camp Run Trail takes off from behind the shelter and goes 0.8 mile to FSR317.

SECOND DAY

Total distance (one way): 13.6 miles
Hiking time: 7 hours, 45 minutes

Awaken early and welcome the mountain morning! There are miles to cover and many things to discover.

One of those discoveries is the extensive growth of rock tripe just 0.2 mile from the shelter. While tripe may not look appealing, stories abound of people lost or trapped in alpine areas who have survived for days by eating nothing but lichen such as this. Richardson and Franklin, famous explorers of the far reaches of North America, lived on it for months, according to Ernest Thompson Seton, a founder of the Boy Scouts of America. Seton says to wash it very thoroughly, remove the roots, and roast in a pan until crisp. After this, it should be boiled for at least an hour. He also states that it tastes like tapioca with licorice, but that it must be carefully cooked or it produces cramps. Do be aware that some deaths are thought to have been related to the ingestion of rock tripe.

Cross a small water run at 1.2 miles. Although the land is a bit soft and damp in most places, you might be able to find a small campsite on dry, level ground if you look hard enough. Turn left onto FSR27 at 3.1 miles, go less than 300 feet, make another left, and enter the Gaudineer Knob Scenic Area's virgin spruce forest on a blue- and yellow-blazed interpretive trail.

Slow down and enjoy this magical place. The spruces and moss-covered logs and rocks keep the area looking richly green throughout the year and provide the feel of a forest primeval. This small woodland is the lucky recipient of a surveying error that spared it from logging in the early 20th century. Some of the towering trees are 250–300 years old, while others are young and are sprouting upon the fallen trunks of their ancestors.

Be alert at 3.4 miles. The interpretive trail swings to the left and descends. You want to go right and gradually ascend on the less-used, yellow-blazed Allegheny Trail, lined by mats of club moss. Breaks in the vegetation provide an occasional limited view to the east, but be alert at 5.4 miles. The Allegheny Trail makes a sudden hard turn to the left on a very faint pathway and soon begins to descend. The blue-blazed trail to the right goes 0.5 mile to FSR27.

Unless the Allegheny Trail has been reworked by the time you hike here, it will be slippery and rocky, with no real discernible treadway. Watch carefully for blazes (which may be faint) as the route makes several switchbacks. The rough footing and luxuriant growths of stinging nettle (put on long pants or gaiters so that your legs won't itch and burn for hours) make this possibly one of the least pleasurable stretches of trail I have ever been on. Watch for those blazes!

It is time to make a decision when the trail splits at 6.5 miles. The blue-blazed trail to the right is the high-water alternate that should be used in the spring or at other times of heavy rain when the ford of the West Fork of the Greenbrier River would be dangerous. It is 4.4 miles long and rejoins the yellow-blazed route in Glady.

Because it is more scenic and does not involve a fear-inspiring walk of approximately 2 miles on heavily traveled, narrow-shouldered US250/WV92 (which overlaps with the blue-blazed route), follow the yellow-

In the Gaudineer Knob Scenic Area

scending grassy road, pass under utility lines, and follow a woods road that parallels and crosses Baucher Run. This serene, narrow valley—with its isolated feel, towering hemlocks, green ferns, and crow's-foot—makes up for the earlier trials and tribulations.

The trail rises onto the hillside at 7.7 miles, intersects and turns right onto another woods road, and arrives at the West Fork of the Greenbrier River at 8.1 miles. Some say you should go upstream for the ford; I like going downstream, crossing Baucher Run, and fording at a bit shallower spot. Actually, on a hot summer day the river can be quite an inviting place for swimming and wading. A number of flat rocks make nice sunbathing spots and platforms from which to look for hellbenders, one of the world's largest salamanders. They can grow to be 29 inches long and are usually found only in water that drains into the Mississippi.

Once across the river, crash through tall vegetation, climb the bank, and turn right onto the West Fork Trail. The rail-trail once again enables carefree, easy walking so that you may enjoy looking at the river, which is sometimes wide, sometimes narrow, and sometimes like the glacier-melt streams of the Rocky Mountains. Fall flowers such as Queen Anne's lace, milkweed, mint, pokeberry, joe-pye weed, and thistle grow in fields along the bank. If you don't want to spend the night in Durbin, start looking for a campsite. They are harder to find the closer you get to town.

A wooden bridge takes the trail over a side stream at 11.7 miles, while the piped spring on the left is easy to miss just before you walk under US250 at 12.5 miles. Turn onto US250 at 12.9 miles, enter Durbin, and come to the Durbin Rocket depot in the center of town at 13.6 miles. The scenic train rides into the surrounding countryside are a worthwhile diversion if you have the time and

blazed route. Stay left, descend, and bear right onto a very old woods road, but be alert at 6.7 miles. It may appear that you should continue for a few more feet to make a right turn onto another descending road. Instead, the trail makes a sudden left, goes a few feet, crosses a woods road, and descends onto a route that is hard to follow and may have only a few sparse, faded blazes to show the way. Be alert and watch for them as the trail zigzags this way and that before turning left onto dirt Simmons Road (WV250/1) at 7.0 miles. (If you lose the trail through all of this, simply go downhill, and you will find the road.)

Be alert at 7.1 miles. Turn right onto a demoney. The East Fork Campground (304-456-3101) is in a field beside the river, while the Greenbrier Suites (304-456-5409) sits across the street from the depot. Its furnishings are sparse, but the rooms are clean. There's also a small restaurant that is open year-round.

THIRD DAY

Total distance (one way): 8.7 miles
Hiking time: 6 hours, 30 minutes

There are fewer than 9 miles in today's hike, so, if you wish, you have time to linger over breakfast in the inn or town restaurant. Just remember: There will be many rugged ups and downs, so progress may be slow.

Leave Durbin by following yellow blazes onto River Road (WV 250/2) and the bridge across the river. Turn right immediately after the bridge, go 300 feet, and turn left onto an ascending dirt road. Be alert about 250 feet later; you need to follow the trail as it makes a sudden right and ascends at a rapid rate, first through rhododendron tunnels and then into an old forest with large hemlock trees.

Attain a ridgeline at 0.8 mile, cross a woods road, descend quickly, cross Spillman Run at 1.4 miles (possible campsites), and ascend to a sidehill pathway through hemlocks and an extensive network of rhododendron tunnels. The trail builders must have worked long and hard to cut this route for you out of the jumble and tangle of roots and branches.

Reach another ridgeline at 2.6 miles and descend. The pattern is now set as you rise and descend twice more before crossing a side creek at 4.0 miles and Brush Run at 4.4 miles. The going may be steep and tiresome on these ups and downs, but the narrow valleys you're passing through give the impression that you may be the only person to have passed this way in years. Being able to feel this isolated in eastern America is a privilege hard to come by in our modern world.

Watch where your feet land when you ford Brush Run; you may see a crayfish or two scurry away under the water. The compound eyes of a crayfish, which are composed of many small eyes, like those of an insect, are placed at the ends of stalks and look for danger by being extended, retracted, and moved in any direction. The crustacean's two long, flexible antennae extend from the head and explore behind and ahead, often thrusting themselves into streambed mud in search of a tasty morsel.

Ascend steeply, descend, cross a stream, and ascend again before merging onto a woods road at 4.9 miles. Stay left when a faint road comes in from the right at 5.4 miles, and go left again at 5.5 miles, where the Brush Run Trail goes off to the right. There may or may not be a sign at this intersection, but be aware that route is no longer listed as a Forest Service trail. Follow the left fork when you come to a Y-intersection at 5.7 miles, but stay right when another road comes in from the left at 6.3 miles. The faded blue blazes you see along this stretch are from the former Little Mountain Trail, which was abandoned with the establishment of the Allegheny Trail.

Pass a couple of wildlife clearings that could provide tent sites in this ridgeline forest of chestnut, white, and northern red oaks. The death of American chestnuts from the chestnut blight of the 1930s liberated the oaks to become a dominant species in the Allegheny Mountain forests. White-tailed deer, wild turkeys, chipmunks, squirrels, and black bear are just a few of the woodland creatures that feast upon the oaks' abundant acorns.

Cross a woods road at 7.1 miles, and, at 8.1 miles, begin a steep descent, made only slightly less steep with a couple of switchbacks. Enter the Laurel Run Valley at 8.5

miles, and come to a trail junction that may or may not be readily apparent. The faded blue blazes of the abandoned Little Mountain Trail go off to the left. Continue to follow the yellow blazes, and come to your evening's destination when the trail drops to the flat bottomland close to Laurel Run at 8.7 miles. Please practice no-trace camping and use your stove to cook. There are few signs of camping on the Allegheny Trail, and it would be nice to keep it this way.

FOURTH DAY

Total distance (one way): 9.6 miles
Hiking time: 5 hours, 45 minutes

While wandering around last night, you may have found that the Allegheny Trail leaves the bottomland just a few feet from the campsite and ascends onto the hillside. Follow it and drop to cross Laurel Run in 0.3 mile before crossing a smaller stream and ascending to the ridgeline of Little Mountain at 1.0 mile, where you may once again see the blue blazes of the old Little Mountain Trail.

Top a knob with a view of the telescopes of the National Radio Astronomy Observatory (NRAO), which studies the universe through radio waves emanating from distant stars, planets, and galaxies. Make a quick descent onto a woods road, and come to the Slavin Hollow–Hosterman Road at 2.4 miles. Turn right, go about 70 feet, and make a sudden left to ascend along an old woods road. The Slavin Hollow–Hosterman Road was once used by locals to deliver livestock and other agricultural goods to trains running along the Greenbrier River on the western side of the mountain. It is now a part of the Hosterman Trail {FS337}.

Be alert at 2.8 miles! Just before you would reach the high point of a gap, make a sudden left onto an even older woods road. This turn would be easy to miss if you are not paying attention. Continue to ascend to the ridgeline, where you will begin a series of small ups and downs.

Visible through the vegetation are the facilities of the NRAO, which includes the world's largest radio telescope. In contrast to this place, which looks for future discoveries, is the sound of the steam whistle from the Cass Scenic Railroad that harkens to days gone by.

The footpath can become very faint at 5.6 miles, so pay attention to the blazes as the trail descends to the right. Campsites and water are available when you cross a creek amid hemlock and rhododendron at 6.4 miles. Continue downstream, sometimes close to it, other times on the hillside above.

Soon after the Greenbrier River becomes visible through the vegetation at 7.6 miles, pass by a private home and a couple cabins as you walk along a dirt road. Turn right onto paved WV66 at 9.4 miles, cross the river, and return to your automobile at 9.6 miles.

A ride on the Cass Scenic Railroad, which chugs its way to the second highest point in the state, would be the perfect ending to this journey. If these four days on the Allegheny Trail have you interested in hiking more of it, you may obtain a guidebook and information from the West Virginia Scenic Trails Association, P. O. Box 4042, Charleston, WV 25364; www.wvscenictrails.org.

16

Kennison Mountain and the Cow Pasture Trail

Total distance (one way): 12.4 miles

Hiking time: 7.5 hours

Vertical rise: 1,220 feet

Maps: USGS 7½' Lobelia; USGS 7½' Hillsboro

The Hike at a Glance

1.5   possible campsites
2.4   right onto Kennison Mountain Trail
3.6   cross WV55/WV39
4.0   right onto South Fork Trail
6.4   cross FSR102
9.3   cross second arching footbridge
11.6 site of Mill Point Federal Prison
12.1 right onto Highlands Scenic Highway
12.4 end

Gifford Pinchot, appointed America's first chief forester by President Theodore Roosevelt, piloted the fledgling U.S. Forest Service with his concept of multiple use. The idea, which still guides much of what forestry is considered to be, states "Conservation is the foresighted utilization, preservation, and renewal of forests, waters, lands, and minerals for the greatest good of the greatest number of people for the longest time." In prosaic terms, it is the belief that public lands can be used simultaneously and sustainably for recreation, timber, mining, and wildlife habitat.

If descriptions of some of the previous hikes in this book make you apprehensive about trying to follow undefined courses across rugged terrain and steep grades, you might want to thank Pinchot for the ease with which you can do this hike. For most of its length, it follows former logging roads and railroad grades with gentle ascents and descents along obvious routes through a forest that, decades after being timbered, has regenerated and renewed itself. There are no grand sweeping vistas, but that should matter little as you can immerse yourself in a green world of deciduous trees, tall spruce and pine, and mountain streams rippling over moss-covered rocks. The hike begins on a ridgeline and descends to encircle the botanically interesting Cranberry Glades (see Hike 21). There is an abundance of possible campsites, except on the sidehill descent of Kennison Mountain on the South Fork Trail. However, be aware that you are not permitted to wander off-trail into the

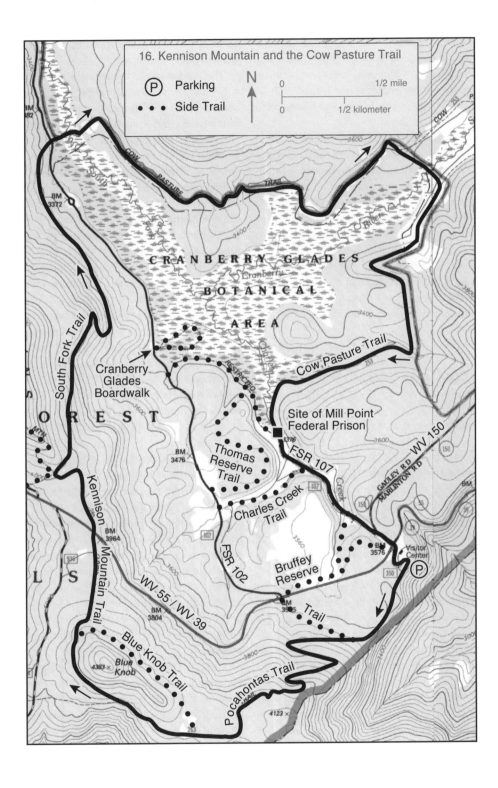

16. Kennison Mountain and the Cow Pasture Trail

Ⓟ Parking
••• Side Trail

N

0 ———————— 1/2 mile
0 ———————— 1/2 kilometer

CRANBERRY GLADES

BOTANICAL

AREA

Cranberry

South Fork Trail

FOREST

Cranberry Glades Boardwalk

RESTRICTED

Cow Pasture Trail

Site of Mill Point Federal Prison

FSR 107

Thomas Reserve Trail

BM 3476

Kennison Mountain Trail

BM 3964

Charles Creek Trail

FSR 102

Bruffey Reserve

Trail

BM 3576

Visitor Center

Ⓟ

WV 150

GAULEY RD

MARLINTON RD

WV 55 / WV 39

BM 3804

Blue Knob Trail

Blue Knob 4383 ×

Pocahontas Trail

4123 ×

glades because of the fragile environment. Black bear, deer, red squirrels, grouse, owls, chipmunks, raccoons, beavers, skunks, snakes, other reptiles, and birds, such as turkeys, live in this forest, and hikers often see signs of them.

In some places you may find scratchings that mark where wild turkeys have been digging for beetles and other insects; searching for their favorite nuts, such as acorns, leaves large areas of the forest floor cleared of decaying leaves and other small deadfall. It's easy to determine the sex of a wild turkey. The male, also called a tom or gobbler, is large, has spurs on the rear of each leg, and has a red wattle (or beard) that hangs in folds. The smaller female (or hen) lacks the spurs and has only a hint of red along her neck.

The trailhead may be reached by taking exit 169 off I-64 at Lewisburg, driving US219 North for almost 32 miles, and turning left onto WV55/WV39 West. Make a left into the Cranberry Mountain Nature Center parking area in an additional 6.5 miles.

Begin by taking the trail from the upper end of the parking lot and turning right onto the Pocahontas Trail {FS 263}, soon bypassing the Cranberry Mountain Nature Center Interpretive Trail that goes off to the right at 0.15 mile. This is a nice place to be in the fall, as the trail, beginning to ascend at 0.4 mile, passes through the changing leaves of a beech, birch, cherry, and maple forest. Soon come to a fork, and stay to the right. Stay to the left on a narrowing pathway where the Bruffey Reserve Trail {FS 280} goes off to the right at 0.6 mile. Three switchbacks, one at 1.0 mile, another at 1.25 miles, and the third at 1.35 miles, bring you to possible campsites on the ridgeline. (The trail to the left leads to the Cranberry Lodge, a guest house whose electricity comes exclusively from solar power.) Spruce trees become more numerous as you continue to gradually gain elevation.

The easiest way to tell a spruce tree from a fir tree is to shake hands with their branches: The fir will feel soft and welcoming to the touch, and while the spruce's sharp, stiff needles won't puncture your skin, you certainly will not want to give it a firm handshake. Another way to distinguish the two is by looking at their needles. The spruce's extend out from all sides of the branch, while the fir's needles have two white stripes on the bottom and grow with only two rows, one on each side of the branch.

The Blue Knob Trail {FS 255} comes in from the right at 2.3 miles. Stay left on the Pocahontas Trail, but be alert just 0.1 mile later. The Pocahontas Trail continues to the left, but you want to bear right onto the ascending Kennison Mountain Trail {FS 244}, an obvious old woods road. Also pay attention when, from the right, the Blue Knob Trail again intersects your route at 3.0 miles. Stay left on the Kennison Mountain Trail, making an easy descent to cross WV55/WV39 at 3.6 miles. Reenter the woods, still following the Kennison Mountain Trail, but be alert when you come to an intersection at 4.0 miles. You want to turn right to begin following the South Fork Trail {FS 243}.

There are some good wintertime views of the Cranberry Glades where the route makes a switchback to the right at 5.0 miles. From here, you may need to watch closely for the trail's blue blazes as the obvious route you have been following begins to fade away and makes a number of twists and turns while becoming narrower, less distinct, and rockier.

Cross FSR102 at 6.4 miles, and begin following the railroad grade of the Cow Pasture Trail {FS 253}, going over the elaborate and arching footbridge across the Cranberry River at 6.5 miles. The trail is a favorite of

One of the elaborate footbridges over the Cranberry River

mountain bikers, but by late summer and early fall, vegetation has overgrown much of the trail (you will experience this in a number of places, especially the open areas where goldenrod grows tall), discouraging most riders.

Frogs' eggs are often seen in springtime in the puddles on the old logging roads, rail beds you follow, or pools of the water runs you cross. The mass of jellylike substance in the water contains thousands of eggs, often looking like small black dots when first laid.

Within a few days, tiny tadpoles can be seen wriggling inside their individual pouches. Only a day or two later, they will work their way out and swim into the water in search of something to eat. A tiny upper jaw moves back and forth, while the lower jaw drops down to open the mouth and scoop in food. In nature's scheme of things, though, many of them will never live much longer than this, as they are a favorite food of other woodland creatures.

Come to a trail to the right at 7.0 miles that may or may not be signed. Regardless, turn right onto it, and arrive at an observation deck in a little more than 300 feet, with views of a small tributary of the Cranberry River and the surrounding ridgelines, including Kennison Mountain, which you recently traversed. Return to the main trail, and turn right to continue the hike.

In fall, ladies tresses grow on the low ridge you begin to rise over at 7.4 miles. For those who admire and study orchids, it seems that members of this family almost always have ingenious and interesting methods of becoming fertilized, and the ladies tresses are no exceptions. When a flower develops, the first insect to visit it (which, in this case, will probably be a bumblebee) breaks apart a small fascia that releases a glue, thereby insuring that any pollen that comes in contact with the insect will stick to it and travel on to the next flower.

Descending from the low ridge, walk along the very edge of the glades at 8.3 miles, remembering that you are required to stay on the trail and not wander into the more open areas. Cross another arching footbridge at 9.3 miles, and soon begin following a wide and obvious route, where at 10.9 miles rhododendron becomes very conspicuous for the first time on the hike. The broad way comes to an end as the trail narrows at 11.4 miles and skirts the left side of a meadow, where the activity of beavers may have dammed a stream and flooded the wide valley. From where you are standing, it may be possible to make out the individual sticks of the beavers' dome house. Although beaver ponds can be a nuisance to humans by flooding agricultural fields or blocking the route of a pathway, they also provide a place for insects to lay eggs, supporting a fish population that feeds on the insect larvae. In turn, the fish provide nourishment for osprey, mink, bear, and other birds and mammals.

Interpretive signs at 11.6 miles mark the site of the Mill Point Federal Prison that operated from 1938–1959. More than 6,000 prisoners (about 300 at a time) went through this prison without walls. Although the signs say that most of the prisoners were conscientious objectors or moonshiners, some of them, such as movie director Edward Dmytryk, were victims of the Red Scare during the McCarthy era of the 1950s. Dmytryk spent 12 months in the prison before being released and, later, denouncing the Communist Party and providing the names of other Hollywood insiders to the House Un-American Activities Committee. In order to get a better understanding of what life was like in the prison, take the time to read all of the plaques before heading uphill on an old road (FSR107, with small patches of pavement still visible in places). A short distance later, the Charles Creek Trail {FS 260} comes in from the right, with another portion of that pathway also coming in from the right at 12.0 miles.

Turn right onto the Highlands Scenic Highway (WV150) at 12.1 miles, cross WV55/WV39, ascend the nature center's driveway, and return to your car at 12.4 miles.

17

Greenbrier River Trail

Total distance (one way): 25.4 miles

Hiking time: 12 hours, 30 minutes; overnight hike

Vertical rise: 160 feet

Maps: USGS 7½' Clover Lick; USGS 7½' Edray; USGS 7½' Marlinton; USGS 7½' Hillsboro

The Hike at a Glance

1.6   campsite
4.1   Big Run
5.6   Sharp's Tunnel
7.5   campsite
11.8 Halfway Run
15.1 Marlinton Depot
16.1 Stillwell Park (camping)
19.8 campsite
21.9 mouth of Beaver Creek campsite
23.3 Watoga bridge
25.4 end

At one time, railroads wound into nearly every valley and hollow of the Allegheny Mountains, carrying out the riches of timber, coal, and iron ore. They were also like the metropolitan bus systems of today, running on a scheduled basis several times a day to transport passengers and goods between small settlements and commercial centers.

Construction of a line of the C&O Railroad along the Greenbrier River began in 1899, with the first train chugging into Marlinton in the fall of 1900. Mirroring the experiences of most small rail lines, this one was profitable for many decades but fell into disfavor as Americans turned to highways for their transportation needs. Soon after the line was abandoned in 1978, the company donated the right-of-way to the state to develop as a rail-trail.

The Greenbrier River Trail runs for more than 70 miles between Cass and North Caldwell. The 25.4-mile stretch described below is almost always within sight of the river as it passes by open farmland and natural meadows, through lush forests and rural landscapes, and into historic communities dating from the railroad's heyday.

Never far from civilization, yet with long periods of detachment from the humanized world, this is a great place to introduce someone to the joys of outdoor walking without subjecting them to the rigors, and fear, of a harsh or isolated terrain. The pathway is level (even with a slight downhill trend if walked in the direction described), while the historic aspects of the railroad are an added bonus. Mile markers help keep track of your

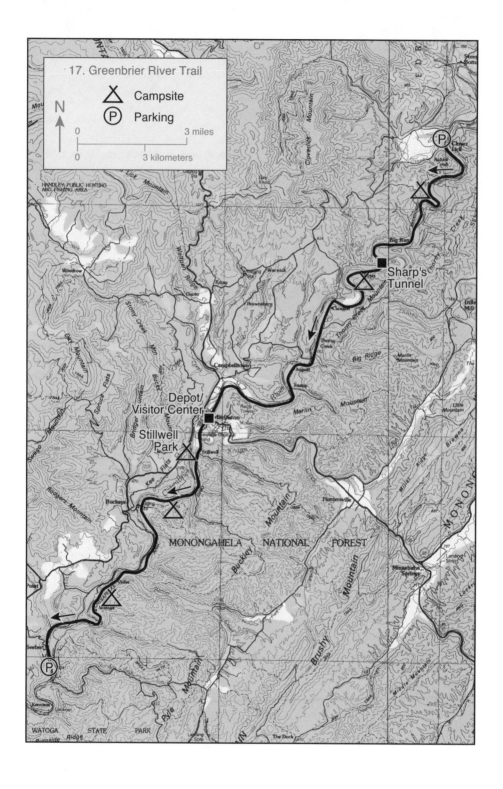

progress. (The W you'll see on some posts reminded the train engineer to blow the whistle as he approached road crossings.) Camping is permitted at designated sites, which often include a water source and pit toilets. Marlinton, where you can obtain a restaurant meal and/or stay in a B&B instead of camping out, is located 15.1 miles into the hike. This is a multiuse trail, also open to bicyclists and equestrians, so be ready for possible frequent encounters.

Since the hike is one way, a car shuttle will be necessary. Take exit 169 off I-64 at Lewisburg, drive US219 North for 30.7 miles, turn right onto Seebert Road (WV27), and leave one car in the parking area beside the bridge in another 2.0 miles. Return to US219, turn right, drive 11.6 miles, and make another right onto WV39 in Marlinton. Continue for an additional 5.6 miles, bear left onto WV28, go another 13.1 miles, turn left onto Laurel Run Road, and follow it to the parking area at the Clover Lick Depot. Built near the turn the 20th century, the depot and small settlement are named for a nearby farm whose salt lick stood in a field of clover. The pilings in the river are all that remain of a bridge that serviced a lumber mill from 1913 to 1929.

Gentian and lyre-leaved sage, a member of the mint family, grow below the rock walls as you begin the hike by following the trail downstream. Ferns and hemlocks line the trail at 1.2 miles, while mayapples adorn the forest beside the campsite (which has a water pump, table, pit toilet, and fire ring) at 1.6 miles. The yellow flag iris in the water of the ditch beside the trail at 3.7 miles is certainly pretty to look at, but it is an invasive plant that is crowding out native vegetation. (See Hike 11 for a discussion about invasive plants.)

If the day has been warm, you may want to soak your feet in the pool below the small waterfall on the right just before crossing the

bridge over Big Run at 4.1 miles. Although the train line has been abandoned for decades now, the smell of creosote, the substance used to preserve railroad ties, still permeates the air as you get close to Sharp's Tunnel at 5.6 miles. The 511-foot tunnel (you may need a flashlight, as it gets dark less than halfway through) was cut through the mountain in 1900 to avoid a long horseshoe curve in the river. Echoes resound well in here, and they are always fun, so go ahead and shout—no one will care. After going through the tunnel, cross the 229-foot bridge, also built in 1900, that takes you to the east side of the river. The short path at its far end can deliver you to the river's edge for some fishing. *The Mountain Highlands Outdoor Sportsman's Guide* says "The smallmouth bass are plentiful, and when they slow down, the rock bass always bite."

The campsite in the open field to the right at 7.5 miles has a water pump, pit toilet, and picnic table, while the remnants of an old farm at 9.2 miles are a reminder that even here, in this rural valley, the agrarian life is disappearing from the American landscape. About 0.2 mile south of the crossing of Halfway Run at 11.8 miles is an exceptionally large patch of columbine, one of springtime's most beautiful and ornate flowers. Some sources say that its five long, curving spurs resemble an eagle's talons and resulted in the plant's genus name *Aquilegia*, derived from Latin for "eagle." Others claim the name comes from *aqua* for "water" and *legere* for "collect," which refers to the sweet liquid nectar that collects in the spurs.

The trail becomes paved and wheelchair accessible just about a mile before you reach the center of Marlinton at 15.1 miles, the site of the 1901 railroad depot, which, unfortunately, was destroyed by fire in 2008. The Pocahontas County Convention and Visitors Bureau (1-800-336-7009; restrooms and

Greenbrier River Bridge

water) is located a few blocks toward the river (plans are to move the bureau back to the railroad station once renovations are completed), and the people there can steer you in the right direction for lodging, dining, and other services within easy walking distance. If you contact them before beginning the hike, they may be able to suggest someone to provide a shuttle, saving you the hassle of dealing with two cars.

Continuing southward, at 15.4 miles you reach the Knapps Creek Bridge, built in 1929 to replace the original bridge constructed in 1900. Just 0.7 mile beyond this, hikers are permitted to camp in Stillwell Park, giving you another option for overnighting close to town. Be sure to pick up water here; it is the last readily available source on the hike. The pavement comes to an end at 17.1 miles, close to where the Greenbrier River flows around several small islands. Alders, river birch, and sycamores (all moisture-loving trees) grow on the islands and along the riverbanks.

If you need supplies or a cold drink, a right turn onto WV219/15 at 19.0 miles will deliver you to several businesses in Buckeye along US219 in about a mile.

Continuing along the Greenbrier River Trail, you find beardtongue, geranium, serviceberry, viper's bugloss, New Jersey tea, and St. John's wort springing from the ground around the campsite (no water pump or pit toilet) at 19.8 miles. Don't be frustrated if you can't tell what species of beardtongue grows here. Roger Tory Peterson, possibly America's most famous naturalist, claims that there are well over a dozen different beardtongues in the eastern part of the United States and that even experts may have trouble identifying the individual species.

A pit toilet near the mouth of Beaver Creek at 21.9 miles marks the final designated campsite of the hike. Now that the trip is drawing to a close, this is an appealing spot to rest and reflect on what you have been privileged to walk through. The trail may be in a river valley, but the scenery has been constantly changing. At times, the trail has been forced by the presence of steep cliffs to go close to the river. In other places, the valley was wide with meadows full of daisies, buttonbush, asters, milkweed, and goldenrod. And always there has been the river, sparkling in the sunshine or rolling over rocks darkened by mountain shadows. You may want to return to it someday for a canoe or kayak trip. Its long flat stretches broken by short class I–II rapids make it an ideal place for those just learning the art of reading the water.

The Watoga Bridge, whose original structure had to be replaced after a train wreck in 1924, returns the trail to the west bank of the river at 23.3 miles. Nearby was the logging town of Watoga, a bustling place in the early 1900s, but little remains of it today except for a few rusting items surrounded by a regenerated forest.

The small general store, visible through a meadow to the right, is located just a few hundred feet before the journey concludes at 25.4 miles by returning you to the car you left here many hours ago.

If you enjoyed your hike, there are many more miles of the Greenbrier River Trail to explore. Wildflowers abound in spring, the river is perfect for wading and swimming in summer, vibrant colors adorn hillsides in the fall, and cold weather brings long icicles clinging to overhanging rocks and winter snows for cross-country skiing. If you find you like a rail-trail's ease of travel, you should be heartened to know that there are more than a dozen additional such pathways in the state. Some of the best are the Allegheny Highlands, West Fork (see Hike 15), North Bend (see Hike 48), and Caperton/Mon River/Decker's Creek Rail-Trails.

18

Tea Creek

Total distance (circuit): 12.1 miles

Hiking time: 7 hours

Vertical rise: 1,560 feet

Maps: USGS 7½' Woodrow; USGS 7½' Sharp Knob; U.S. Forest Service Tea Creek Area handout map

The Hike at a Glance

2.7   *trailside shelter*
4.3   *left onto the Boundary Trail*
6.8   *intersection with the Saddle Loop Trail*
7.75 *left onto Bannock Shoals Run Trail; immediately another left onto Saddle Loop Trail*
9.3   *left onto Turkey Point Trail*
10.0 *left onto Turkey Point Connector Trail*
12.1 *end*

There are some places that are so special that it takes more than a cursory weekend trip to thoroughly appreciate and enjoy them. Two such places are the Cranberry Wilderness (see Hikes 19 and 20) and Tea Creek Area. There are so many good spots to explore that you should plan on spending your entire two-week vacation here. Within an hour's drive of both places are Beartown State Park (see Hike 24), where you can follow a boardwalk into a fairy tale landscape of huge boulders and towering hemlock trees; pathways wandering by trenches built during the state's largest Civil War battle (see Hike 23); and more than 70 miles of the Greenbrier River Trail (see Hike 17) running beside its namesake. The not-to-be-missed Falls of Hills Creek and Cranberry Glades (see Hike 21) are short walks into grand and uncommon scenery.

Five Forest Service campgrounds can be low-cost places to pitch the tent or park the RV if you decide not to spend the evening along one of the area's longer pathways. If you get too lazy to hike, you can always drive the 22-mile Parkway section of the Highland Scenic Highway (WV150), stopping at overlooks to enjoy the vistas of Allegheny Mountain ridgelines. In addition to sightseeing and hiking, there are many opportunities for fishing, paddling, mountain biking, wildlife watching, and plant and wildflower hunting.

In fact, whether you are a professional or an amateur botanist, the hike into the Tea Creek Area can be a plant lover's dream. With the trip rising from 3,000 feet in elevation at the Williams River to over 4,000 feet

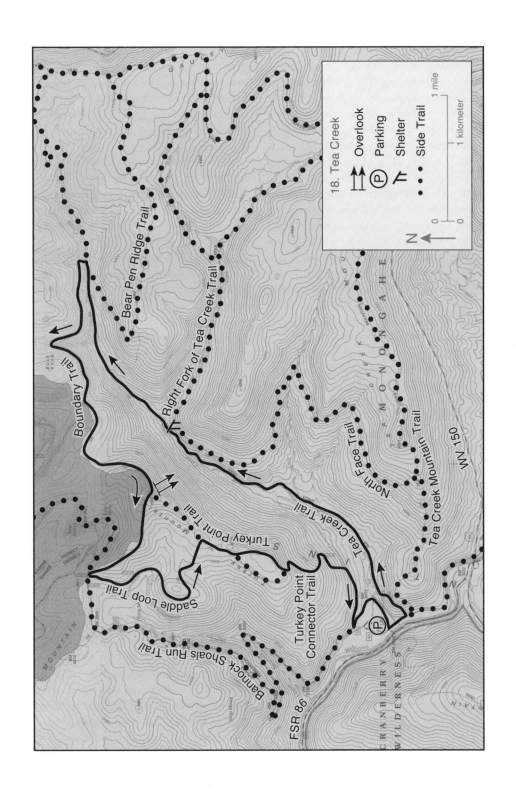

18. Tea Creek

Overlook
Parking
Shelter
Side Trail

N

0   1 mile
0   1 kilometer

Bear Pen Ridge Trail

Right Fork of Tea Creek Trail

Boundary Trail

Buck Knob

North Face Trail

Tea Creek Trail

Tea Creek Mountain Trail

Turkey Point Trail

Saddle Loop Trail

Turkey Point Connector Trail

Bannock Shoals Run Trail

FSR 86

Williams

WV 150

CRANBERRY WILDERNESS

MONONGAHE

GAULEY

MOUNTAIN

above sea level along the crest of Turkey Mountain, you will pass through several different environments. The lower elevations contain maple, beech, birch, oak, locust, basswood, cherry, ash, and more. Witch hazel, hobblebush, and a variety of berry bushes make up a part of the understory. A quick glance at the ground right where you begin the hike will reveal more than a dozen wildflowers, including monkshood, wood sorrel, goldenrod, white snakeroot, asters, phlox, chickweed, and wood betony. In the moist areas around the streams look for jewelweed, black snakeroot, joe-pye weed, and buttercup. What's more, the Tea Creek drainage receives 60 inches of rain annually, making it the ideal habitat for more than a dozen different mosses, well over 30 species of fungi, and luxuriant growths of ferns.

All that precipitation can be rough on the trails, and the area's main pathway has been flooded and washed out many times through the years. Be prepared for wet feet, as you will ford Tea Creek at least nine times—maybe more, depending upon any other floods that occur before you hike here. However, take heart. Except in times of high water, most crossings are easily accomplished, all trails are well blazed, and the ascent of 1,300 feet is done along gradually rising old railroad beds and logging roads.

In droves, mountain bikers have discovered the Tea Creek Area. Although the rough terrain keeps most from venturing onto the trail next to the creek, you should be prepared to possibly have groups of them zip by you on any of the other pathways. Backcountry camping is permitted anywhere along the hike, or you may choose to stay in the trailside shelter at 2.7 miles.

It is recommended that you visit the Cranberry Mountain Nature Center before beginning the hike (see directions below). Not only can you obtain free trail maps and information on the Forest Service campgrounds, but exhibits about local history, wildlife, plants, forestry, and mining will provide knowledge that will add depth to your hikes. Best of all, a diorama gives an excellent three-dimensional image of the terrain you are about to immerse yourself in.

The trailhead may be reached by taking exit 169 off I-64 at Lewisburg, driving US219 North for almost 32 miles, and turning left onto WV55/WV39 West. Make a right turn onto WV150/Highland Scenic Highway in an additional 6.5 miles (the nature center is on the left), and continue for another 13.2 miles. Turn downstream along the Williams River on FSR86, and go an additional 1.0 mile to park in the Tea Creek Campground.

Enter the woods on the Williams River Trail {FS487}, and cross the footbridge over Tea Creek. (Enjoy it because this is the one and only time a bridge will help you cross the stream.) Do not turn left onto the unmarked trail along the creek, but continue straight for several yards to turn left onto the Tea Creek Mountain Trail {FS452}. Less than 100 feet later, turn left onto the Tea Creek Trail {FS454}, and begin to ascend via a series of short switchbacks. Descend at 0.5 mile, and turn right to walk upstream on an old railroad grade. Already there are plants that were not found in any abundance at the campground. Look for ironwood, purple fringed orchids, yellowroot, running cedar, crow's foot, and other club mosses.

Yellowroot is a small, deciduous shrub that grows well along moist streambanks. Its drooping racemes of tiny purple flowers appear at about the same time the heat of summer really starts to kick in. Years ago, its bright yellow roots and inner bark were brewed with honey and liberal amounts of whiskey to relieve stomach cramps. Most likely, it was the effects of the alcohol that made users think their pain had gone away. A dye obtained from the entire plant is still used by basket weavers to color their white oak baskets.

There's a nice wading pool at 0.7 mile, where the bedrock juts into the creek beside copious growths of bee balm and jewelweed. By midsummer, you may have to push your way through the tall vegetation that overtakes the trail at 1.0 mile, but it is stinging nettle you will have to contend with at 2.0 miles, when the trail is forced dozens of feet above the creek by the narrowing valley. The swimming and wading pools where the trail drops back down to the stream are nice enough, but before you take a dip, you might want to wait until you get to the shelter at 2.7 miles. Here, a small falls slides down smooth rocks and into some great wading pools.

Less than 200 feet beyond the shelter, the North Face {FS450} and Right Fork {FS453} Trails come in from the right. Stay left on the Tea Creek Trail, and cross Right Fork just a few feet above its confluence with Tea Creek. (The crossing may be a bit easier if you go a few feet upstream.)

Ford Tea Creek for the first time at 2.8 miles. You will cross it again at 3.1 miles, and six more times before coming to the intersection with the Bear Pen Ridge Trail {FS440} at 4.3 miles. Stay left, but less than 100 feet later the Tea Creek Trail turns to the right, where you want to swing left onto the Boundary Trail {FS449} and ford Tea Creek for the ninth and final time.

Cross a small stream at 4.4 miles, ascend gradually along an old woods road, and pass a small campsite to the left of the trail just before you cross a small creek at 5.0 miles. More than one hiker has had his or her heart skip a beat when a grouse, or two, or three suddenly bursts upward and flies within a few feet of startled faces. This scene may become less common in the future as the forest matures and the undergrowth needed by grouse gradually disappears. Often when this happens, wild turkeys may move in and take the place of the grouse.

Be alert at 5.6 miles. The trail suddenly leaves the road and ascends to the left through a New England–type red spruce forest. There is no sign warning you of this, and if blazes happen to be absent, it would be easy to miss this turn. (The red paint blazes you see mark the national forest boundary and not a trail.) You have now been walking for several hours, so take a break and enjoy the view of the deep Tea Creek valley at 6.8 miles, where the Turkey Point Trail {FS447} comes in from the left. Stay right on the Boundary Trail. (You could shorten the hike by about 2 miles by staying left on the Turkey Point Trail and rejoining this hike description at the 9.3 milepoint.)

The rhododendron tunnels you walk through at 7.3 miles are punctuated by thousands of blossoms in early to midsummer. At 7.75 miles, turn left onto the Bannock Shoals Run Trail {FS446}, a gravel Forest Service road, but almost immediately make another left onto the Saddle Loop Trail, which starts out as a descending old logging road. Butterflies and bumblebees flit from one blossom to another along the overgrown route.

Just before you would cross a stream at 8.25 miles, the trail turns left into the woods, ascends a few feet, crosses the stream, and returns to the old road to bear left. However, be very alert just a few feet later. The trail turns left off the road again and ascends along a narrow footpath. You are on the western side of the mountain, which receives the bulk of the rainfall, and vegetation is lush, with ferns and vibrant green moss growing upon everything, including rocks, boulders, and even tree roots.

At 9.3 miles, turn right onto the Turkey

Tea Creek

Point Trail {FS447}, and walk along the nearly level crest of Turkey Mountain. The pathway that goes off to the right at 9.8 miles is also signed as the Turkey Point Trail, but it is just a loop off the main route you are following and rejoins the trail in a few hundred yards. Stay left and come to a second intersection at 10.0 miles, where you want to bear left again, now following the Turkey Point Connector Trail {FS 410}.

The trail swings to the right at 10.3 miles and joins a very quickly descending old road.

Another road comes in from the right at 10.5 miles; stay left, continue the quick descent, and swing right onto a more level old road at 10.9 miles.

The Bannock Shoals Run Trail (which may or may not be signed) comes in from the right at 11.5 miles. Turn left, descend the woods road, and do not take the unauthorized trail that drops to the right a few hundred feet later. Walk around a gate at 11.8 miles, and follow the gravel road through the campground to return to your car at 12.1 miles.

19

Cranberry Wilderness

Total distance (circuit): 22.7 miles

Hiking time: 12 hours

Vertical rise: 2,740 feet

Maps: USGS 7½' Webster Springs, SE; USGS 7½' Woodrow; U.S. Forest Service Recreation Guide for the Gauley District and Cranberry Wilderness hand-out maps

The Hike at a Glance

0.4	left onto the North Fork Trail
6.8	right onto FSR102
8.9	right onto Birchlog Trail
11.1	right onto North-South Trail
12.0	left on Laurelly Branch Trail
15.0	ford Middle Fork of the Williams River
16.8	second ford
17.5	third ford
21.1	right onto North Fork Trail
21.2	left onto North-South Trail
22.7	end

Designated a wilderness by Congress in 1983, and expanded in 2009, the Cranberry Wilderness encompasses more than 47,000 acres, making it the largest such preserve in West Virginia. That's close to 75 square miles of land on which no natural resource extraction or motorized vehicles are permitted.

Situated near the southern end of the Allegheny Plateau, the land is broken up by deep and narrow stream valleys. The elevation ranges from 2,400 feet to 4,600 feet, with red spruce dominating the higher places and hardwood trees such as black cherry and yellow birch growing on the middle and lower elevations. Protected from the transgressions of the modern world, wildlife is varied and abundant. Whitetail deer, mink, bobcats, foxes, snowshoe hares, cottontail rabbits, wild turkeys, grouse, and several species of squirrels have all been seen by hikers at one time or another. This large expanse of land is also one of the best places in the state to possibly catch glimpses of black bears.

Although trails in the wilderness are not blazed, most of them are signed at junctions and follow old logging roads, so route finding is usually not a problem. However, the area receives 60 inches of rain annually, so be aware that there are no bridges across the streams and that fording them can be dangerously difficult, if not impossible, in times of high water. Also, be prepared for temperatures that could be many degrees cooler than they were when you left home. Storms that are dropping rain just a few miles away

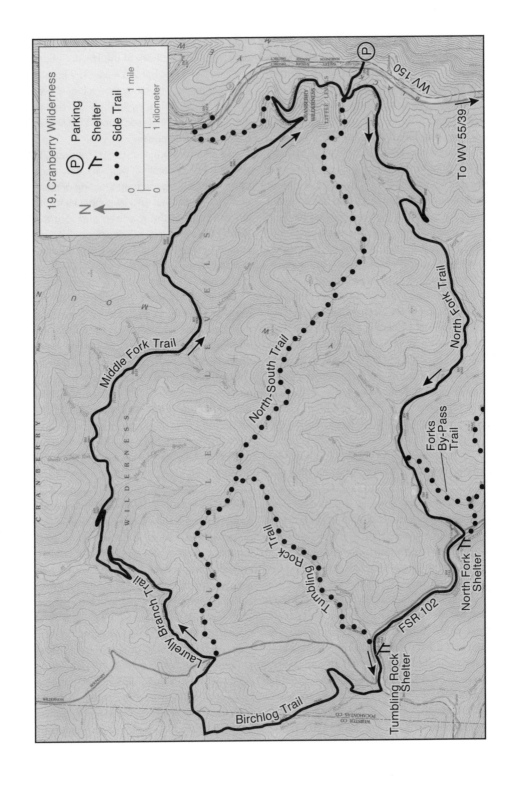

19. Cranberry Wilderness

Parking Ⓟ
Shelter 🏠
Side Trail ••••

N ←

0 — 1 mile
0 — 1 kilometer

Ⓟ

WV 150

To WV 55/39

CRANBERRY WILDERNESS
LITTLE LEVELS

North Fork Trail

Forks By-Pass Trail

Middle Fork Trail

North-South Trail

CRANBERRY WILDERNESS

SNOW MOUNTAIN

LITTLE LEVELS

Tumbling Rock Trail

Laurelly Branch Trail

North Fork Trail Shelter

FSR 102

Tumbling Rock Shelter

Birchlog Trail

WEBSTER CO
POCAHONTAS CO

may be depositing a deep covering of snow on the wilderness. The attraction of this place is that it is wild and remote, but remember that you are responsible for your own safety. Many people hike here, but they are spread out over a large area, and you may see very few, if any, of them.

The hike described here is more than 22 miles long, but it should be considered no more than a moderately strenuous one. It makes two long descents and ascents, but each are done along gradual grades over the course of several miles. There are ample opportunities to fish for trout or take long, leisurely dips and swims. Tent sites are usually easy to find, and water is plentiful.

The trailhead may be reached by taking exit 169 off I-64 at Lewisburg, driving US219 North for almost 32 miles, and turning left onto WV55/WV39 West. Make a right turn onto WV150/Highland Scenic Highway in an additional 6.5 miles (the Cranberry Mountain Nature Center is on the left), and continue for another 8.7 miles to the small parking spot for the North-South Trail {FS688} on the left.

Enter the woods and come to a four-way intersection at 0.4 mile. Turn left onto the North Fork Trail {FS272}, and begin a gradual descent along a grassy woods road lined by red spruce, bee balm, jewelweed, and Queen Anne's lace.

Queen Anne's lace was imported from Europe and is now found in all the lower 48 states and most Canadian provinces. Its quick diffusion can be attributed to its ability to take root in just about any open space—and to one of the clever ways it spreads its seeds. After the flowers die, the large seed-bearing umbel will often fall off and, being blown about by the wind, come to rest in some place far distant from the parent plant.

Stay to the right when you come to a Y-intersection at 2.2 miles, switchback to the right, and pass a small campsite just before crossing the Left Fork of the North Fork of the Cranberry River at 2.6 miles. The spruce trees are so thick that they form a tunnel over the trail at 3.3 miles, while the side road to the left at 3.4 miles leads about 200 feet to another small campsite.

Be alert at 4.3 miles. The trail leaves the old road on an indistinct pathway, descends to the right among the rough footing of many boulders and roots, and switchbacks to the left to return to the roadbed and ford the North Fork at 4.5 miles. Just a short distance later, it leaves the road again, this time ascending to the left and dropping back down in less than 700 feet.

The Fork By-Pass Trail {FS23} (some maps call this the Forks Spur Trail) comes in from the left at 6.2 miles. Stay right, leave the wilderness, and pass by the North Fork treatment station, which releases limestone in an effort to counteract the effects of acid rain and return the streams to their natural pH. Merge onto the treatment station road, turn right onto FSR102, and pass by the North Fork Shelter at 6.8 miles. This is the easy part of the hike, as the level roadway heads downstream along the South Fork of the Cranberry River. Bicycles and hand-pulled carts are allowed on the road. I have seen groups of more than ten people haul in gas grills, multiple coolers, huge tarps, large folding tables and chairs, and enough food to stay for a week. And that is why you should always carry a tent and not count on being able to spend the night in one of the shelters. Of course, you can't blame them. It's a great place for a low-cost family vacation. The kids can ride bikes up and down the road, older children can hike to secluded spots to do whatever it is teenagers do when no one else is around, and anglers in the family may cast a line for the stocked rainbow, brook, brown, and golden trout. On warm days, everybody

Third ford of the North Fork of the Williams River

can take a dip or sunbathe on the many flat rocks close to the riverbank.

Continue along FSR102, and the Tumbling Rock Trail {FS214} comes in from the right at 8.3 miles, just a few hundred feet before you pass the Tumbling Rock shelter.

Leave the forest road and the river behind by turning right onto the Birchlog Trail {FS250} at 8.9 miles. Swing left onto an ascending road at 9.0 miles, parallel Birchlog Run as it tumbles through thickets of rhododendron, and cross it in a forest of birch, hemlock, maple, and oak at 10.2 miles. The rate of ascent stiffens only slightly as the road fades to a pathway at 10.4 miles. Turn right onto the North-South Trail at 11.1 miles, follow the small ups and downs of a ridgeline, reenter the Cranberry Wilderness, and pass a small campsite to the right at 11.9 miles.

Make a left onto the Laurelly Branch Trail {FS267}—an old railroad grade—just 200 feet later, and pass another small campsite on the left at 12.1 miles. You are about to lose 1,000 feet in elevation in the next 3.0 miles, but for the most part it will be along a moderate grade. Cross the creek at 12.5 miles, and, at 13.1 miles, be watching for the twists and turns of a series of switchbacks.

The first ford of the Middle Fork of the Williams River at 15.0 miles is the most formidable stream crossing of the hike. It is a rock hop when the water is low, but during spring melt and times of heavy rain it can be dangerous. If you decide it is too risky (you're going to have to ford it twice more, too), retrace your steps back up the Laurelly Branch Trail, turn left onto the North-South Trail, and follow it back to your car.

Once across the river, turn right onto the Middle Fork Trail {FS271} (a large campsite is to the left) and ascend along a former Forest Service road that nature is reclaiming. If you feel like fording an extra time, there is a small campsite on the opposite bank, next to a waterfall in a side stream at 15.5 miles. The walk along this area is a pleasant one, as the Middle Fork is the quintessential Allegheny Mountain stream. Lined by hemlock trees and rhododendron thickets, it rushes through the narrow gorge it has carved out of the mountain, tumbling over rocks and creating eye-pleasing waterfalls like the one you can't help but admire at 15.8 miles.

Ford the river for the second time at 16.8 miles; the spectacularly deep and big swimming hole at 17.2 miles may be impossible to resist on hot days. Even though the river has narrowed, the third ford of the Middle Fork at 17.5 miles can still be a tricky crossing in high water, but you can usually make it across Slade Branch at 18.7 miles and North Branch at 19.0 miles fairly easily. The abundance of red spruce at 20.1 miles announces your return to the higher elevations of Black Mountain.

Turn right onto the wood sorrel-lined North Fork Trail at 21.1 miles, and, at 22.2 miles, arrive at the first intersection you encountered on the journey. Swing left onto the North-South Trail and return to your car at 22.7 miles.

In a speech commemorating the Wilderness Act of 1964, which set the stage for wilderness designation for the Cranberry Wilderness, West Virginia Senator Robert Byrd stated, "In no area has this Congress more decisively served the future well-being of the Nation than in passing legislation to conserve natural resources and to provide the means by which our people could enjoy them. One of the brightest stars in the constellation of conservation measures is the wilderness bill.

"In addition to land preservation, the act has encouraged the discovery of America's history, promoted recreation, provided for its diverse wildlife and ecosystems, and satisfied people's urge for solace and a return to wild places."

You have just experienced one of these wild places. If you enjoyed your time here, be sure to let your elected officials know that it and all such places across the country should continue to be protected and cherished.

20

Cranberry River/Lick Branch

Total distance (circuit): 8.7 miles

Hiking time: 5 hours, 15 minutes

Vertical rise: 1,460 feet

Maps: USGS 7½' Webster Springs, SW; U.S. Forest Service Recreation Guide for the Gauley District handout map

The Hike at a Glance

1.5   *Queer Branch Shelter*
1.9   *left onto Lick Branch Trail*
4.0   *left onto North-South Trail*
6.5   *crossing of Lower Twin Branch*
8.7   *end*

For those unable or unwilling to make the 22.7-mile circuit journey into the Cranberry Wilderness (see Hike 19), this 8.7-mile hike is a viable and rewarding alternative. Although your time in the woods will be less, you will still be exposed to the same beauty, plants, animals, and human history of the longer trek.

The area you will hike through used to be known as the 26,000-acre Cranberry Backcountry, but with the passage of the Omnibus Public Land Management Act in 2009, almost 12,000 acres of it was incorporated into the Cranberry Wilderness, adding an additional layer of protection for the land. The act was one of the largest pieces of environmental legislation to pass Congress in more than 25 years, designating more than 2 million acres of new wilderness and creating the National Landscape Conservation System. This mandates that the Bureau of Land Management make conservation a primary consideration on 26 million acres of land at more than 800 sites under its care.

Although the area is now closed to public motorized vehicles and bicycles, bicycles, equestrians, and hand carts are permitted on FSR76, which is on the edge of the wilderness. (See Hike 19 for more information.) These activities sometimes make the road appear to be quite busy, with people carrying more and moving about faster than just feet alone would permit. Camping is permitted throughout the hike; if you prefer, you could make base camp at the Cranberry Campground (picnic tables, water, and toilets). The outing can easily be accomplished as a day

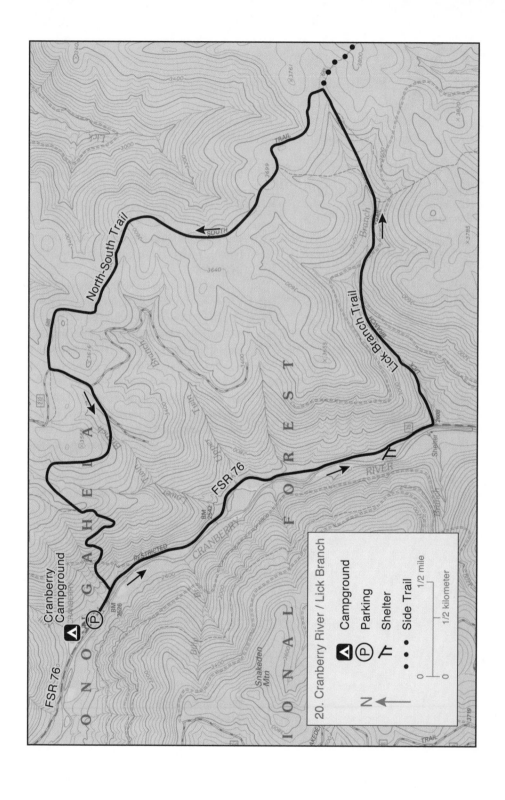

20. Cranberry River / Lick Branch

Campground
Parking
Shelter
Side Trail

N

0   1/2 kilometer
0   1/2 mile

trip, as there is only one short stretch of steep uphill. The rest of the hike is level, downhill, or on a gradually rising grade.

From the stoplight at the intersection of WV55/WV39 and Oakford Avenue in the center of Richwood, drive WV55/WV39 East for 1.0 mile, turn left onto Cranberry Road (WV6), and make another left onto FSR76 in an additional 2.4 miles. Passing by Big Rock Campground, FSR81, and FSR101, stay on FSR76 for 10.7 miles, and leave your car in the parking area at the far end of the Cranberry Campground. The trash cans encircled by a chain link fence should give some idea of how active the black bears are.

Begin the hike by walking around the gate and immediately passing by the ascending North-South Trail {FS688} on the left. Stay along the Forest Service road, enjoying the sight and sound of the Cranberry River. The river, with a few large hemlocks growing in the moist soil close to it, is stocked with trout, and you will most likely see a number of anglers trying their luck.

If you started the hike late in the day and are looking for a place to set up a tent, the side trails to the right around 0.4 mile will lead you to several possible campsites. Even if you're not going to spend the night, you should consider taking one of the trails to some great swimming holes a short distance upstream. The waters of Lower Twin Branch cascade down the hillside to your left at 0.75 mile, while the fragrance of milkweed fills the air of a well-used campsite at 1.1 miles.

Milkweed is such a common plant that it is easy to overlook the vital role it plays in the web of life. However, monarch butterflies, those resolute little creatures that weigh less than an ounce and yet migrate thousands of miles every year, don't overlook it—their survival depends upon it. Leaving their winter home among the evergreens of the high-altitude forests in central Mexico, they head northward in late winter. Flying through Texas, they spread out into the southern portions of the United States—and this is where the milkweed comes in. As monarch butterflies travel, they mate, but will lay eggs only on the various species of milkweed found in the United States and Canada. After laying eggs, that generation dies off and is replaced by the next one, which travels additional miles northward before it lays its eggs. Thus hopscotching from milkweed to milkweed, it will be the fourth or fifth generation that finally makes its way to southern Canada.

Triggered by cooler temperatures and decreasing daylight, the monarchs begin the return journey in late summer. Yet, they are genetically different from their ancestors. These southbound insects don't breed or lay eggs. Their lives consist of consuming nectar and expending the energy they get from it to fly to Mexico, where they spend the winter, and the process repeats itself.

The easy 1.6-mile walk from FSR76 and the Cranberry Campground to the Queer Branch Shelter (and pit toilet) makes the three-sided structure a popular destination that is often filled to capacity for days on end. However, you could also set up a tent nearby in one of several campsites located among the colorful jewelweed and viper's bugloss blossoms of late summer.

The small, double-layered waterfall at 1.9 miles signals you to turn left onto the Lick Branch Trail {FS212} and pass by a small campsite just a few feet later. The creek continues to tumble in small cascades, but the trail takes you away from the water to ascend steeply beside moss-covered rocks and below towering hemlock trees.

Swing left onto a grassy old logging road at 2.5 miles as the ascent becomes more gradual, but be alert at 3.1 miles. The trail makes a sudden left turn off the woods road,

Lick Branch

and if blazes happen to be absent, this turn would be easy to miss. Birch becomes more prevalent as you once again walk next to Lick Branch and cross one of its tributaries.

Be alert again at 3.7 miles. At a possible small campsite, the trail bears right away from the creek and rises to an intersection at 4.0 miles, where you want to turn left onto the North-South Trail. Interestingly (unless they have been replaced or removed by the time you hike here) you may have noticed that the sign at the Cranberry River said it was 3.0 miles to this point, but the sign here says it is only 2.0 miles back to the river. You now know the true length is 2.1 miles. No matter: You are here now, and this is a lovely spot, with the wind and bird songs being the only things to break the quiet. A few small spruce trees grow close to the intersection but are more or less absent anywhere else along the hike.

Rise to a small, lumpy campsite on the top of a low knob at 4.2 miles, noticing that the forest you are walking through on this easy terrain of minor ups and downs is completely deciduous. Keep watch, and you may see piles of scat, overturned logs, and scratched trunks that indicate that this is prime black bear habitat.

No one knows for sure exactly how many there were, but historians generally agree that black bears were numerous when settlers first entered what would become West Virginia. So many bears were killed for meat, fur, and sport that their numbers dwindled quickly. A demand in Europe for black bear fur for use in fancy military uniforms (the hats that Buckingham Palace guards wear are still made with it), and loss of habitat from unrestrained logging caused further declines in the population. By the mid-20th century, the state was home to fewer than 500 bears. Yet, the hiker of today has a good chance of seeing one. Bear hunting regulations, land purchases, reforestation projects, research programs, and the maturation of the previously logged forests have allowed black bears to thrive once again, and biologists now place the statewide population at more than 10,000.

Attain another knob at 6.0 miles, only to swing right and descend quickly along an old road. Bear right onto a grassy woods road at 6.2 miles and ascend, but be very alert less than 200 feet later. The trail makes a sudden left turn off the road and into the woods, but if the sign is absent it would be very easy to miss the turn. The pathway may be faint for the first few hundred feet but becomes more evident as you descend beside Lower Twin Branch and cross it at 6.5 miles.

Swing right onto an old road bed at 6.9 miles, but turn left off it less than 300 yards later, and descend via a series of switchbacks through a forest of poplar, maple, cherry, beech, birch, Indian cucumber root, mayapple, and rosy twisted-stalk. Because the leaves are similar, rosy twisted-stalk and Solomon's seal are sometimes mistaken for each other. The stem of the Solomon's seal is straight, while the other has a zigzagging stem. Get down on hands and knees to really understand how rosy twisted-stalk came by its common name. In one of those exuberant displays of fanciful artwork that nature seems to delight in, the stalks of the rose-colored, bell-shaped flowers emerge opposite the leaves and twist around the stem so that the blossoms end up drooping delicately beneath the leaves.

The hike comes to a close when you turn right onto FSR76 and return to your car at 8.7 miles. If you're staying in the campground, it is time to cook dinner, relax and—while listening to the hooting of a barred owl—read a good book by the glow of the setting sun. The Last Forest by G. D. McNeill would be a good choice, as its narrative begins just as railroads and loggers were moving into the Cranberry. After reading it, you will have a better understanding of what this land you walked through once was.

21

Falls of Hills Creek

Total distance (round-trip): 1.5 miles

Hiking time: 1 hour

Vertical rise: 260 feet

Maps: USGS 7½' Lobelia

The Hike at a Glance

0.3　Upper Falls
0.6　Middle Falls
0.75　Lower Falls
1.5　end

The Falls of Hills Creek is the showpiece pathway of the Gauley Ranger District. The Forest Service has lavished much attention onto the route, keeping it well maintained and building a number of staircases, observation decks, bridges, and boardwalks—both simple and complex—to enable you to hike with greater ease and enjoyment.

The attention is well deserved, for the 114-acre area is one of the prettiest waterfall settings in the state. Hemlock and rhododendron adorn the sides of the narrow gorge, creating shadows upon the dozens of wildflower species springing up from the forest floor, and letting in bits of sunlight to highlight the sparkling water of three separate falls. That's right. You can visit three waterfalls in just one short outing and get a geology lesson in the process.

It is not a hard walk, but you do descend hundreds of feet, and coming back up may be difficult for those not accustomed to climbing steps. Just take your time, and make as many rest stops as needed on the benches provided. Camping is not permitted, but the Forest Service's Summit Lake Campground is a short distance away. It might be a good idea to stop at the Cranberry Mountain Nature Center to check on the condition of the trail, for, time and again, landslides and fallen trees have caused the lower portions to be closed until the route can be reconstructed.

Take exit 169 off I-64 at Lewisburg, drive US219 North for almost 32 miles, and turn left onto WV55/WV39 West. Pass the nature center in another 6.5 miles, the road to

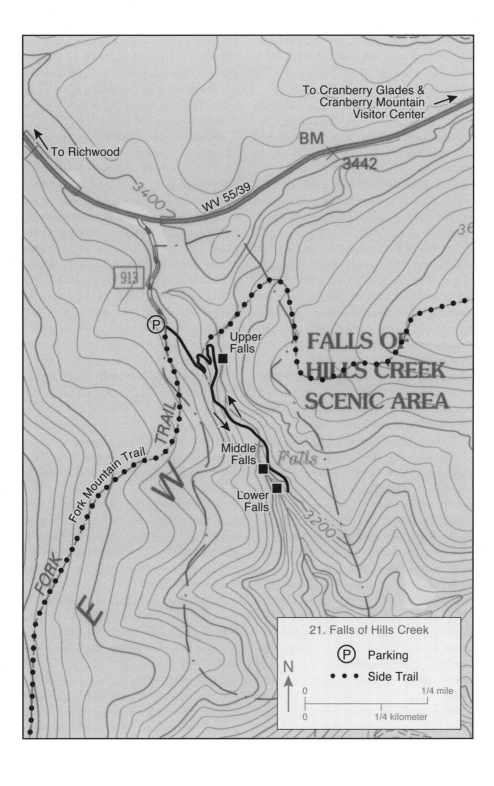

To Cranberry Glades &
Cranberry Mountain
Visitor Center

To Richwood

BM
3442

WV 55/39

3400

913

Upper
Falls

FALLS OF
HILLS CREEK
SCENIC AREA

Fork Mountain Trail

Falls

Middle
Falls

Lower
Falls

3200

21. Falls of Hills Creek

Ⓟ Parking

• • • Side Trail

N

0   1/4 mile

0   1/4 kilometer

the Cranberry Glades 0.5 mile later, and turn left onto the road marked for the falls in an additional 4.9 miles. The parking area is 0.3 mile down the road.

Begin by following the switchbacks of the paved, wheelchair-accessible pathway beside hemlock, rhododendron, mayapple, and striped maple. Bypass any side trails off this main route, and come to the overlook of the Upper Falls at 0.3 mile, where the pavement ends. This vantage point lets you watch the water clear the edge and drop into a pool 25 feet below.

The trail to the right at 0.4 mile returns to the parking lot; stay left and descend the steps. You came here to enjoy the falls, but the human handiwork can be just as visually pleasing. The lines of the stairs and short boardwalks lead downward, drawing your eyes to gaze onto distant objects as a well-framed photograph does. Although they grow naturally next to the stairs, the trilliums and foamflowers complement the surroundings so well that they appear to be part of an intentional landscaping scheme.

A short bridge takes you over Hills Creek in a setting that would ideally be soothingly quiet and serene, but you will be sharing it with a constant stream of other people if you are here on a nice weekend. The Forest Service estimates this pathway is the most heavily visited in the ranger district.

The platform to the right at 0.6 mile overlooks Middle Falls, but to get a much better perspective, descend several flights of metal steps that are attached to the hillside and hang out into space, and turn right onto a boardwalk to the superior view. Middle Falls drops 45 feet in this gorgeous grotto, towered over by rhododendron, hemlocks, and a mixture of hardwoods growing upon the rocks.

It's time to learn a bit about the geology of this area, where exposed layers of hard sandstone cover softer layers of red shale. The water of the creek cut into the underlying shale, which could no longer support the sandstone. As a result, blocks of the stone broke off, tumbled down the hillside, and created the falls you see today.

Continue descending on stairs and boardwalks into an increasingly narrower gorge, upon whose steep walls cling columbine, star chickweed, foamflower, white violets, and jewelweed. You are going to have to climb back up all those stairs, but the Lower Falls at 0.75 mile makes all of that effort worthwhile. The rock behind it has eroded into a crescent-shaped wall, allowing the water to rush over the brink and drop unimpeded for 63 feet to the base pool. Although it is no easy feat getting here, it is believed to be one of the most photographed waterfalls in the state, second only to easily reached Blackwater Falls (see Hike 12).

Take your time, and enjoy the chance to gaze once again upon the other two waterfalls as you retrace your steps and return to the parking lot at 1.5 miles. However, don't go home yet. Cranberry Glades is nearby, and like the hike you have just done, it is a not-to-be-missed place. A 0.6-mile, perfectly level boardwalk takes even the most out-of-shape visitors into four different bogs in the 750-acre glades. The plants and animals seen here are more commonly found in Canada and the northern parts of the United States, and several are at the southernmost point of their range.

To get there, drive back to WV55/WV39, turn right, go 4.9 miles, and turn left onto the road to Cranberry Glades (FSR102). Parking is on the right a little more than a mile later.

Walk onto the boardwalk and keep to the left, passing through rhododendron and hemlock to enter the openness of Round Glade, where fiddleheads, which had unfurled a

Just a few of the many stairs

month earlier at lower elevations, are still tightly wrapped in late May. At the edge of the bog grow speckled alder, wild raisin, and long-fruited serviceberry. Stop for a few moments to let your eyes sweep across this inspiring landscape, with the open glades ringed by spruce-crowned ridgelines.

The boardwalk swings into a bog forest of false hellebore, monkshood, tall meadow rue, and marsh marigold before crossing over Yew Creek. Insectivorous plants, such as sundew and horned bladderwort, grow next to the boardwalk. The pitcher plants you see here are not native but are the descendants of some that were planted as an experiment in the mid-20th century. A few additional feet of boardwalk over more glades and into the forest will return you to your car.

Aren't you glad you took the time to do these few extra minutes of walking?

22

Laurel Creek and Lockridge Mountain

Total distance (circuit): 8.8 miles	
Hiking time: 4 hours, 45 minutes	
Vertical rise: 900 feet	
Maps: USGS 7½' Minnehaha Springs	

The Hike at a Glance

0.2	cross FSR345
1.9	fourth footbridge
3.1	right at Y-intersection
5.2	shelter
6.8	large patches of rattlesnake weed
8.2	cross FSR345
8.8	end

Sometimes there is the urge to go on a weekend hiking trip without having to put in big miles. Without having to huff and puff up steep hills or use navigational skills to negotiate a route that is ill-defined or poorly marked. You just want a trip that will take you away from the bothers of everyday life, that will simply let you enjoy being in the woods and not present new difficulties to overcome.

If that's what you're feeling like, then the Laurel Creek Trail {FS466} is the place to be. Built by volunteers of the Older American Workers in 1975, the 8.8-mile hike makes for an easy weekend, with one short uphill and everything else level or having just minor ups and downs. The few stream fords are narrow and, except in times of extremely high water, easy to do. Tent sites are numerous about 2.0 miles after leaving the trailhead, while a shelter sits on a breezy hillside above the pathway a little more than halfway into the trip. A few mountain bikers have discovered the trail, but chances are good you will walk in solitude all weekend.

The beginning of the hike may be reached by taking exit 175 off I-64 at White Sulphur Springs, turning right onto US60 East, driving 4.8 miles, turning left onto WV92 North, and continuing for another 31.5 miles. Make another left onto WV92 North/WV39 West, and turn right into the Forest Service's Rimel Picnic Area just 0.2 mile later. (The picnic area may also be reached by driving WV39 East for 13 miles from the US219/WV39 intersection in Marlinton.)

Enter the woods, and turn right at the

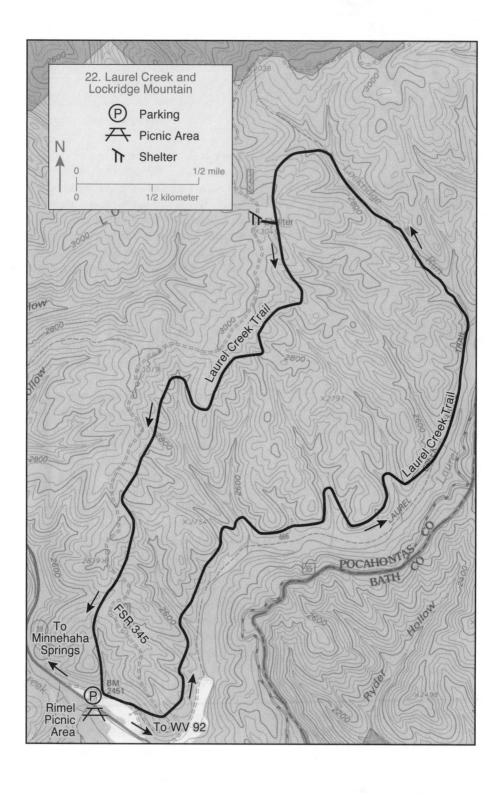

22. Laurel Creek and Lockridge Mountain

(P) Parking

Picnic Area

Shelter

N

0   1/2 mile

0   1/2 kilometer

Lockridge Mountain Trail

Shelter

Laurel Creek Trail

Laurel Creek Trail

Laurel Creek Trail

POCAHONTAS CO
BATH CO

Ryder Hollow

FSR 345

To Minnehaha Springs

Rimel Picnic Area

BM 2451

To WV 92

loop trail intersection on the blue-blazed Laurel Creek Trail. At 0.2 mile, cross FSR345 as you begin to gradually swing away from WV39, and walk upon a superbly built sidehill trail with almost no change in elevation. Constructed in the 1990s, this pathway enables you to stay high and dry, unlike the trail's former route on the valley floor, which was wet and muddy much of the time. Weave in and out of a number of draws, where footbridges take you across small water runs and hemlocks rise above a profusion of mushrooms and other fungi.

In days gone by, it was believed that fairies danced upon mushrooms and used the caps as umbrellas. We now know that mushrooms and other fungi play a much more important role in the forest. Possessing no chlorophyll—the matter that gives plants their green color—the fungi gain nourishment by feeding upon nutrients found in dead wood, leaves, and other forest litter. As this material breaks down, much of it returns to the air in a gaseous form, while the remainder, now mostly humus, returns to the soil and enriches it.

In addition, most plants have developed a relationship, known as mycorrhiza, with certain fungi in order to live. The fungi attach themselves to young plant roots and send hyphae, or fungal threads, into the soil, increasing the feeding capabilities of the root systems. Because the fungi are able to take in zinc and other important insoluble nutrients such as phosphorous, they allow the plants to survive in areas where these substances may be in short supply. In return, some of the carbohydrates the plant produces are transferred to the fungi—it's a win-win situation for everybody involved.

Soon after crossing the fourth footbridge at 1.9 miles, swing left onto an old roadbed, turn right to cross a final bridge, descend for a few hundred yards, and bear left onto an

Ascending to the ridgeline

old railroad grade to start walking upstream along Laurel Creek. Although none is established, there are numerous potential tent sites all along the route beside the creek. Pass through a small wildlife clearing at 2.5 miles. The activity of beavers around 3.0 miles may flood the trail in times of high water.

On the positive side, this added moisture enables jewelweed and cardinal flower to thrive. In their book, *Southern Wild Flowers and Trees*, published in 1901, Alice Lounsberry and Mrs. Ellis Brown were so taken by the cardinal flower that they wrote "Cardinal Flower is a wild flower about which the nation might feel a righteous pride, so intensely

Laurel Creek

coloured and velvety in texture . . . defying the artist's pigments to imitate them, and forming against their background of dark green and lustrous leaves a wild bit of colour almost without equal. Old men, urchins and little maids all seek it by the brook's side."

Bear right when you come to the Y-intersection at 3.1 miles. If there have been recent heavy rains, the trail may become part of the creek for the next several hundred feet. In addition, you may need to cross several runs that are just parts of Laurel Creek over-running its banks. Swing left at 3.6 miles to leave Laurel Creek, and begin the very grad-ual ascent along Lockridge Run. Cross the stream six times (this is the last sure water source before the shelter) as the trail passes through tunnels of rhododendron and hem-lock. At 4.6 miles, the ascent becomes pro-gressively steeper in the narrow draw along the more southern fork of Lockridge Run, which may be dry in late summer.

However, the climb does not last long, as the trail switchbacks out of the draw at 4.9 miles and onto a gradually ascending foot-path to soon gain the top of a spur ridge. Once again, the builders of this trail did an excellent job laying it out. Thanks to them, you get to cover the next several miles with almost no change in elevation.

At 5.2 miles, turn right to ascend 200 feet to the shelter sitting on top of the ridge and at the edge of a logged area, where tent sites abound on Lockridge Mountain's broad, flat crest. This is a pleasant place to be whether you are taking a break or are here for the night; ever-present gentle breezes carry bird songs through the air to serenade you.

Return to the main trail, and continue to stay just a few hundred feet below the top of the mountain, crossing one spur ridge after another, with little change in elevation. White snakeroot thrives in areas where sun-light reaches the forest floor, while mountain laurel and blueberry bushes make up the un-derstory in places where the forest canopy is more lush. You may also notice lots of acorns and squawroot. The acorns are here be-cause of the many oak trees, but so too is the squawroot. It is a parasitic plant with amaz-ingly small yellow flowers that grow on the roots of trees, especially oaks. The flower will probably not be what first catches your eye. It will be the stem. The plant produces no chlorophyll, so its entire stem is a sort of yel-lowish brown.

The cries of pileated woodpeckers are often heard in the forest around 6.8 miles, while rattlesnake weed grows in large patches for the first time on the hike. Rat-tlesnake weed and rattlesnake plantain are sometimes mistaken for each other because they both have similar-looking basal leaves. The telling difference is that the rattlesnake weed has reddish purple leaf veins instead of the rattlesnake plantain's white-veined leaves. In addition, the latter has stalks of tiny white flowers, while the rattlesnake weed's blossoms look like little yellow dandelions.

Cross FSR345 at 8.2 miles, and parallel it for several hundred yards before crossing a grassy woods road and descending quickly to your car at 8.8 miles.

23

Droop Mountain

Total distance (circuit): 2.5 miles

Hiking time: 1 hour, 15 minutes

Vertical rise: 280 feet

Maps: USGS 7½' Droop; park handout map

The Hike at a Glance

0.2   left onto the Minnie Ball Trail
0.6   lookout tower; begin following Musket Trail
1.1   left onto Cranberry Bogs Trail
1.7   begin following Horse Heaven Trail
2.0   begin following Overlook Trail
2.5   end

Following the Civil War Battle of Chicka-mauga in September 1863, Federal forces were being pushed farther westward by Confederate troops. In the hopes of severing the Virginia–Tennessee Railroad that was the supply line for the Confederates, Federal Brigadier General William W. Averell marched his troops eastward from Beverly, West Virginia, toward the rail line in Salem, Virginia. On November 5, 1863, a skirmish at Mill Point, about 8 miles south of Marlinton, slowed the movement somewhat, but Averell's superior numbers caused the men under the command of Confederate Colonel William "Mudwall" Jackson to retreat.

Throughout the night, Jackson's army placed artillery, built trenches, and otherwise fortified a site atop Droop Mountain, a high point with a commanding view of the Green-brier River Valley. Joined by troops under the command of Confederate Brigadier General John Echols, the smaller Southern army was able to withstand the first wave of attacks by Union forces. As the day of November 6 wore on, Federal troops in the 28th Ohio and 10th West Virginia regiments, under the command of Colonel Augustus Moor, at-tacked the Confederates' left flank. The Southerners were surprised but put up a tremendous resistance. As Moor said:

> Now rising and yelling like Indians,
> they poured a tremendous fire into
> the Twenty-eighth, advancing rapidly
> at the same time. This was the criti-
> cal moment of the day. I ordered the
> Twenty-Eighth Regiment to lie down

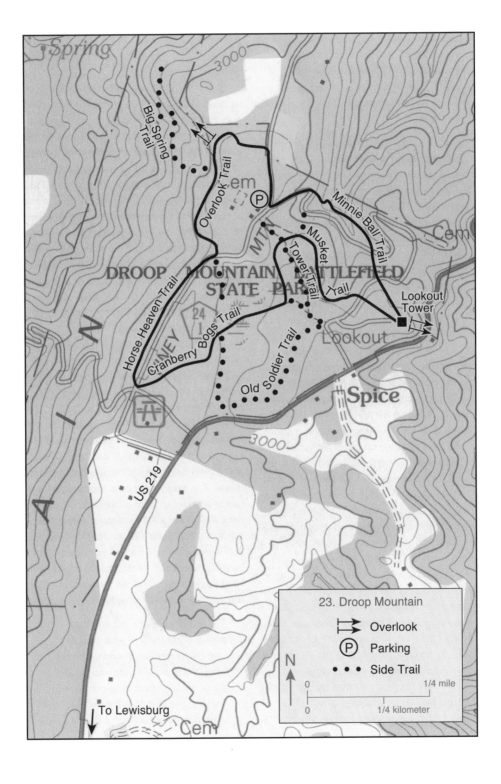

Big Spring Trail

Overlook Trail

Minnie Ball Trail

Cem

Cem

em

P

Musket Trail

Tower Trail

Lookout
Tower

DROOP MOUNTAIN BATTLEFIELD
STATE PARK

Horse Heaven Trail

Cranberry Bogs Trail

24
1

NEY

MTN

Lookout

Old Soldier Trail

Spice

US 219

3000

3000

To Lewisburg

Cem

23. Droop Mountain

Overlook

P   Parking

••• Side Trail

N

0   1/4 mile

0   1/4 kilometer

and fire by file. The sudden disappearance of the regiment and the increasing fire through the underbrush had an almost stunning effect upon the enemy. They hesitated.

On all sides, the Union army of about 4,500 continued assaulting the 2,500 men of the Confederate army, and by 4 PM, the Confederates were in retreat, ending the state's largest Civil War battle. Encumbered by prisoners and captured livestock, Averell decided to return to Beverly, waiting until December to lead a successful attack on the Virginia–Tennessee Railroad.

Decades later, John D. Sutton, a survivor of the battle and a member of the West Virginia House of Delegates, introduced legislation calling for a Droop Mountain memorial. On July 4, 1928, 125 acres of the old battlefield became West Virginia's first state-owned park when they were dedicated as the Droop Mountain Battlefield. From 1935 to 1937, men of the Civilian Conservation Corps built trails, roadways, cabins, picnic shelters, and other facilities. An additional 139 acres were acquired, and today the day-use state park has picnic shelters, play areas for children, and a small museum with items from, and displays about, the battle. A network of trails that winds through open meadows and into deep forests not only lets hikers enjoy the natural beauty of the area but also allows them to visit places that were important sites during the battle. Interpretive signs throughout the park provide additional details. As an added bonus, visitors can climb the six-sided log lookout tower built by the CCC for an Olympian view of the Greenbrier River Valley and surrounding ridgelines.

The park may be reached by taking exit 169 off I-64 at Lewisburg, driving US219 North for 25.0 miles and turning left into the park. Follow the main park road for 0.6 mile, and leave your car in the park office parking area.

Begin the foot exploration by walking out of the parking lot, turning left onto the paved park road, and following the route signed as leading to the lookout tower. However, be alert at 0.2 mile. Just after the road curves to the right, you want to bear left and enter the woods on the descending Minnie Ball Trail. As you walk along this ravine, think about the Union soldiers who had to climb this steep hillside, knowing the Confederates were waiting to fire at them from above. The vegetation may have been heavily trampled that day, but the pathway is so lightly used today that mayapple grows in the middle of it, and copious amounts of wood nettle crowd in from both sides.

Just after hearing water running underneath rocks you step over them at 0.3 mile, rise and cross a footbridge over a small water run lined by jack-in-the-pulpit. Step over another rivulet at 0.4 mile, and cross the paved park road twice as the ascent becomes steeper. The short climb ends at 0.6 mile, when you enter the level picnic area and swing left to climb the wooden lookout tower. You may have come only a short distance so far, but take a break to enjoy this magnificent vista. The words of John D. Sutton (from the book *Where People and Nature Meet*) ring true as you gaze upon Little Levels, the village of Hillsboro, the Greenbrier River Valley, and the mountains along the West Virginia–Virginia border:

The scene spread out before us was one of indescribable beauty and enchantment. Towering mountains, the smiling fertile plain and the famous historic Greenbrier River, flowing gently at the base of the mountain. Nowhere in all of our

Overlook of Hill Creek Valley with Jacox and Briery Knobs forming a backdrop

travels have we witnessed such scenic beauty or such a location for a great State Park.

From the tower, walk through the middle of the playground to begin following the Musket Trail. (Do not take the trail leading to the outhouses.) Cross a paved park road at 0.75 mile, and descend beside striped maple, huge oak trees, and the large stumps of chestnut trees. The size of the stumps is impressive, so imagine how large the chestnuts must have been at the time of the battle.

Turn uphill to the left at 1.0 mile, where flame azalea brightens the forest understory and a right turn would drop you to a park road. The four-way intersection at 1.1 miles presents you with an option. If you are tired or have run out of time, the park office and parking lot are a few hundred yards to the right. To continue the hike, stay to the left, now following the Cranberry Bogs Trail past skunk cabbage growing in moist areas beside the pathway. Mountain laurel and club mosses line the trail, while pine needles and mosses soften your footsteps.

The trail to the left at 1.2 miles goes back to the observation tower. Continue right along the Cranberry Bogs Trail, and pass under a utility line at 1.3 miles, with foamflower making up part of the understory. As you approach them from a distance, the flowers and their lacy stamens have a tendency to look like frothy foam balanced on the end of the long stem. This explains the common name, but several different sources give slightly varying accounts about how the plant received its genus name of *Tiarella*, which means "little tiara." Some say that the way the yellow pistils rise above the white petals resembles the points of a golden crown—referred to by the Greeks as a tiara. Others sources claim that the generic name is in reference to the headdress once worn by

Persians, as the shape of the pistils resemble a turban.

The small swamp to the right at 1.4 miles is at the heart of the cranberry bogs. It's definitely not as large as any of those at the Cranberry Glades (see Hike 21) but is certainly an environment not common to most of West Virginia. Black birch, hickory, red oak, and maple are part of the forest where you cross a woods road (the Old Soldier Trail) at 1.5 miles and gradually ascend. Be alert when you come to the unsigned Y-intersection at 1.6 miles. A left turn would take you to a picnic area. You want to keep right, cross the paved park road, and reenter the forest on a woods road, which is the Horse Heaven Trail, at 1.7 miles. It may not feel right for the first few hundred feet, but it soon becomes an obvious pathway lined by jack-in-the-pulpit and trillium and running along the top of low rock cliffs beside large rock formations.

Just as you come to the paved park road at 1.9 miles, a wooden bridge to the left crosses a small ravine to a bench, providing a peaceful spot to rest today, but this is the place where horses killed in the battle were disposed of. It's not something that is often touched upon by history books, but tens of thousands of horses were killed during Civil War battles. (At Gettysburg alone, 3,000 were killed.)

Turn left onto the paved road, but be alert 500 feet later. You need to swing left onto a dirt service road, and less than 100 feet after that make another left onto the Overlook Trail. The narrow passageways through large rock formations festooned with lichens, mosses, ferns, flame azalea, and painted trillium are reminiscent of the landscape in Beartown State Park (see Hike 24). At 2.2 miles is a cave that local lore claims was once a bear den. Also to the left is the Big Spring Trail, which descends steeply for

1,700 feet to end at its namesake water source.

You want to keep to the right, but make a left just a few feet later to enjoy an overlook of Hill Creek Valley, with Jacox and Briery Knobs forming a backdrop. Continue on the Overlook Trail, bypassing an unmarked trail to the right and staying left on the fainter pathway that passes by the remnants of trenches dug by Confederate soldiers. Turn right just before reaching WV22 at 2.4 miles, and return to your automobile at 2.5 miles.

The small museum, soldiers' graves, and several monuments are just a short walk away and will add to your knowledge of the battle. If you want to experience as much as possible what it was like to be at Droop Mountain on November 6, 1863, revisit the park on the second weekend of October on even-numbered years, when a reenactment takes place.

24

Beartown State Park

Total distance (circuit): 0.5 mile

Hiking time: 20 minutes

Vertical rise: 60 feet

Maps: USGS 7½' Droop

The Hike at a Glance

0.2   *interpretive signs explaining pits in the rock*

0.35 *interpretive signs explaining geology of the area*

0.5   *end*

This little outing is so short it can barely be considered a hike. Nevertheless, if you are in the area, you should not pass up the chance to walk through the fairy tale landscape of Beartown State Park. There are very few places in West Virginia where you can reap such a marvelous and rewarding payback for the small amount of energy you will expend and the few minutes of time you will invest here. It is such an easy walk that even those who are out of shape can handle it if they just take their time. This is also an excellent introduction for someone you are taking out on a hike for the first time. If you find the jaunt too short, you can always combine it with a walk on the trails of nearby Droop Mountain State Park (see Hike 23).

Beartown is a magical place. Atop the eastern summit of Droop Mountain, sandstone that formed during the Pennsylvanian Age, about 300 million years ago, has weathered and broken off into huge boulders, protruding cliffs, long rock walls, and nature-sculpted rock formations. Ice and snow often remain in the resulting deep crevasses until midsummer, while lichens, mosses, and ferns cling to life in bits of soil that become trapped in tiny cracks in the rock. A lush forest of hemlock and yellow birch towers over all of this, letting in small bits of sun that look like spotlights purposely pointing out certain spots to be accentuated and admired. If you approach with the right frame of mind, you can feel like a kid again, following the wooden boardwalk and staircases through a giant outdoor maze of rock labyrinths.

The state purchased the park's 107 acres

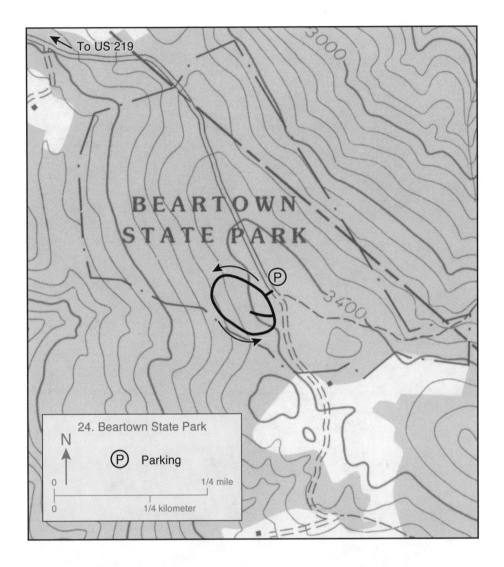

24. Beartown State Park

Ⓟ Parking

N

0 — 1/4 mile

0 — 1/4 kilometer

To US 219

BEARTOWN STATE PARK

in 1970 with funds from the Nature Conservancy and a donation from Mrs. Edwin G. Polan in memory of her son, Ronald Keith Neal, a former State Park Service student employee who lost his life in Vietnam in 1967. The name Beartown reflects local lore that the many caves and other openings in the rocks once made perfect winter dens for black bears. The park is open daily during daylight hours from April through October and may be visited at other times by advance arrangement with the superintendent of Droop Mountain Battlefield State Park. In order to preserve the natural features of the area, the West Virginia Division of Natural Resources has not developed the park, and the only facilities are a picnic table, outhouses, water pump, interpretive signs, and the boardwalk.

Beartown may be reached by taking exit

Boardwalk between rock walls in Beartown State Park

169 off I-64 at Lewisburg, driving US219 North for 22 miles, and turning right onto the road signed for Beartown State Park. The sign appears quickly after a sharp curve, so watching for it. Follow the road 1.5 miles to its end in the state park parking lot. (A 250-foot, wheelchair-accessible walkway permits an overview of the formations and access to one of the major crevasses. Parking for it is on the service road, 700 feet east of the main parking area.)

Start the walk by taking the pathway leading to the boardwalk, which soon begins to wind its way over and around huge boulder and rock formations and creeps into clefts, channels, and crevices in a forest of hemlocks, yellow birches, ferns, mosses, and lichens. Just a little more than 100 feet later, come to an intersection, turn right, and descend.

Adding to the feeling of being in a special place are the bits of quartz and mica, which sparkle on the sandstone like tiny mirrors. The overlook to the right at 0.1 mile has an interpretive sign explaining the large and small pits you see in the rocks. Some were created by noncementation of sand grains. (In other words, there was no bonding material to hold the bits of sand and rock together.) Other pits developed when cementing materials were leached away by water percolating along joints and planes in the porous sandstone.

Swing right and descend into a narrow passage whose rock walls almost have a neon glow to them from the large amount of mosses and other vegetation growing upon them. Some of the elephant ear lichen is more than 500 years old and was already well established decades before Columbus set out upon his voyages in the late 1400s.

The elephant ear lichen and its kin have played a large role in shaping the look of Beartown. Spreading across the surface of a rock, the lichens anchor themselves by way of minute, rootlike holdfasts, which pry loose small bits of the rock. In addition, a weak acid emitted by these plants chemically dissolves minerals in the rock, hastening additional wear. During cold weather, water that has seeped into these small cracks and openings will freeze and expand, splitting the rock apart in the same manner that the roots of trees and other plants do. Sometimes this process will take place over a large surface area, creating the long, rough rock facings you are walking by.

Take the next left at 0.25 mile and another left into a narrow defile at 0.35 mile to an overlook with interpretive signs discussing the geology of the area. Retrace the last few steps you took and go left. (A right turn would lead to a left turn onto a service road and a return to the parking lot in 700 feet.) Turn right when you find yourself back at the original boardwalk intersection at 0.4 mile, and return to your car at 0.5 mile.

For a chance to walk through natural formations of a different kind, drive back toward I-64 and Lewisburg, and follow road signs to Lost World Caverns. A guided tour will take you into giant underground chambers, through narrow hallways, and beside ever-growing stalactites and stalagmites.

25

Lake Sherwood

Total distance (circuit): 10.9 miles

Hiking time: 5 hours, 30 minutes

Vertical rise: 760 feet

Maps: USGS 7½' Lake Sherwood; USGS 7½' Rucker Gap, VA/WV; USGS 7½' Falling Spring, VA/WV; USGS 7½' Mountain Grove, VA/WV; Forest Service Lake Sherwood Hiking Guide handout map

The Hike at a Glance

0.9	right onto the Virginia Trail
1.5	left onto the Allegheny Mountain Trail
5.1	left onto the Connector Trail
5.6	left onto the Meadow Creek Trail
8.6	left onto the Lake Sherwood Trail
10.9	end

Lake Sherwood is one of Monongahela National Forest's largest recreation areas. Attractions include two swimming areas with hot showers and sandy beaches (one is on an island accessible by a footbridge), a concessionaire, boat and canoe rentals, three boat launches, and huge picnic areas with modern restrooms. Close to 100 tent and RV (no hook-ups) sites are available in three campgrounds with flush toilets, hot showers, and a sewage disposal station. The recreation area, which can easily accommodate more than 1,000 people, is open year-round, but services and facilities are limited from Labor Day to Memorial Day.

The 165-acre lake, named for the land's former owner, the Sherwood Land Mine and Mineral Company, was built in 1958 as a cooperative effort of the Forest Service, the U.S. Department of Agriculture, and the state Division of Natural Resources. It is reported to have good fishing for largemouth bass, bluegill, muskellunge, bullheads, and catfish. Meadow Creek, below the lake, is stocked with trout on an irregular basis.

With so much to offer and a location close to Lewisburg and White Sulphur Springs in West Virginia and Covington and Clifton Forge in Virginia, the recreation area is exceedingly popular and is usually busy almost every summer weekend. This 10.9-mile hike will help you escape the hustle and bustle of a noisy beach or crowded campground. If you wish to make it an overnight journey, backcountry camping is permitted anywhere except in the immediate vicinity of the lake.

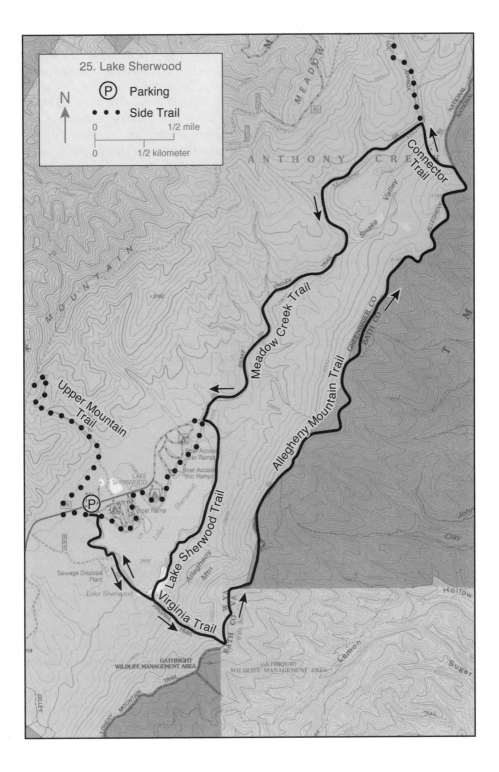

25. Lake Sherwood

P Parking
• • • Side Trail

0 _____ 1/2 mile
0 _____ 1/2 kilometer

N

Connector Trail

Meadow Creek Trail

Allegheny Mountain Trail

Upper Mountain Trail

Lake Sherwood Trail

Virginia Trail

LAKE SHERWOOD

Boat Access (No Ramp)

Boat Access (No Ramp)

Boat Ramp

Sewage Disposal Plant

GATHRIGHT WILDLIFE MANAGEMENT AREA

GATHRIGHT WILDLIFE MANAGEMENT AREA

Take exit 175 off I-64 at White Sulphur Springs, turn right onto US60 East, drive 4.8 miles, turn left onto WV92 North, and continue for another 15.6 miles. Turn right onto Lake Sherwood Road, and drive an additional 10.6 miles to bring you to the entrance station. Immediately afterward, turn right to the picnic areas, and make an immediate right to arrive at the trailhead parking.

Enter the woods behind the bulletin board, and come to an intersection. The Upper Meadow Trail {FS672} goes right. Bear left onto the blue- and yellow-blazed connector route. At 0.1 mile, swing right as another trail from the parking lot comes in from the left. Less than 300 feet later, make one more right, this time onto the main route of the blue- and yellow-blazed Lake Sherwood Trail {FS601}. Now walking beside the lake, you will see that it and the shoreline is a veritable dining table for the resident wildlife. The many square holes in the trunks of some of the trees were made by pileated woodpeckers in search of a meal of insects, while other trunks have been gnawed by beavers feeding upon the cambium, or inner layer of bark. Trolling about on long legs, great blue herons may be seen stabbing their long beaks into the shallow water in hopes of catching a fish for lunch or dinner.

Walk across the earthen dam at 0.6 mile, enjoying an unobstructed view of the lake. At the far end, curve right and cross an arched footbridge that is so attractive that it looks like it should be in a Japanese garden rather than spanning the dam's spillway. Rise to an intersection at 0.9 mile, where the Lake Sherwood Trail bears left. You want to stay to the right, now following the gradually ascending Virginia Trail {FS685}. The route is along an old roadbed that was used by early settlers, long before the Monongahela National Forest was established in the early 1900s.

The woods road fades at 1.25 miles, and the trail continues as a footpath at a steeper grade with a few rattlesnake plantain plants growing beside it. Attain the ridgeline at 1.5 miles, and turn left onto the Allegheny Mountain Trail {FS611}, another woods road. You now are walking on the West Virginia–Virginia border, with an occasional winter view into Bath County, Virginia, and onto Lake Moomaw, where there are also some good hiking opportunities. (Consult *50 Hikes in Northern Virginia*.) Although there is little evidence of anyone having camped anywhere along this undulating ridgeline, many possible tent sites can be found on the mountain's broad crest.

Be alert at 2.2 miles. The roadbed swings right, but you want to stay to the left and ascend a footpath that was originally constructed as a fire trail by the Civilian Conservation Corps during the Great Depression. Look upon the ground and you can learn a little bit about one of the many minienvironments this hike takes you into.

The abundance of acorns is evidence that oaks are some of the more dominant trees at this elevation. So, too, are the squawroot plants that are parasites upon the trees' roots. Acorns and squawroots are favorite foods of black bears, and, although you may not see a bear, the many piles of scat in this area are evidence that these large mammals have been enjoying the tasty treats. The yellow flowers of the false foxgloves are one more part of this circle of interrelationship. They also depend upon the nourishment they receive by being semiparasitic upon the oaks' roots.

By the time you have hiked 3.6 miles, the ridgeline is no longer broad, but narrow and rocky. The trail weaves around large boulders, sometimes descending a few feet to get around some rugged terrain, but always returning, often steeply, to the narrow spine

Lake Sherwood

of the mountain. There is a small, pleasant campsite at 4.4 miles, where the ridge becomes flatter and less rocky.

The Allegheny Mountain Trail comes to an end at 5.1 miles. Turn left and descend along the blue-blazed Connector Trail {FS604} beside mountain laurel and blueberry bushes. At 5.2 miles, swing right and pass through the middle of a wildlife clearing that in late summer is full of Queen Anne's lace and goldenrod. The latter is often blamed for causing the discomforts of hay fever.

However, this is unfair to goldenrod since its pollen is quite sticky—meaning it stays on the plants until picked up by visiting insects. The true culprit is ragweed, which blooms at about the same time as goldenrod and whose minute particles of pollen are blown about by the slightest of winds. At the far end of the clearing, begin to follow a woods road through the forest and ascend for a few hundred feet.

Another woods road comes in from the left at 5.5 miles; stay right and descend. However, be alert at 5.6 miles. The woods road continues to the right, but you want to make a sudden, hard left turn onto the much narrower blue-blazed Meadow Creek Trail {FS684}. Rhododendron and mountain laurel thrive in this moist area, where you hear the sound of flowing water for the first time since crossing the lake's spillway several miles back. The forest is so lush and full of vegetation compared to the open woods of the ridgeline from which you just descended that it almost feels like a jungle or rainforest. The ferns are thick, and it is interesting to note that most of the rhododendron is along the streambank, while the bulk of the mountain laurel is on the other side of the trail.

Rock-hop across Meadow Creek for the first time at 6.6 miles. The West Virginia Division of Natural Resources built this trail, formerly named the Snake Valley Trail, to provide easier access to the creek, which is a native trout stream. With vegetation often crowding in on the pathway, cross the creek eight more times.

Yet, be alert at 8.2 miles. You need to make a sudden left to cross Meadow Creek for the tenth, and last, time and to keep following the Meadow Creek Trail. (Continuing straight here would take you along a rough trail to the campground at the north end of Lake Sherwood.) The unmarked trail at 8.4 miles goes a few hundred feet into a swampy area created by the industrious work of beavers.

The Meadow Creek Trail comes to an end at 8.6 miles, where the Lake Sherwood Trail runs both left and right. You want to go to the left. (You could shorten the hike by about a mile by going right, but you would lose the quiet and solitude you have been experiencing, as that route goes by and through developed campgrounds, picnic areas, and swimming beaches.) The trail you have chosen to take is nearly level (with a few, short forays onto the hillside) as it wanders along the eastern shore of the lake.

The outing is almost done, so slow down and enjoy the time and scenery left to you. Lengthening shadows highlight the hundreds of stumps of young trees that have been gnawed down by the active beaver population. Clouds are reflected in the lake, dragonflies dart about just a few inches above the water, and water striders glide across the surface. Most of us learned in grade school that these lightweight creatures make use of surface tension to stay afloat. But how do they move about? A separate set of legs that extend beneath the water's surface are used like oars.

Return to the intersection with the Virginia Trail at 10.1 miles. Turn right, cross the footbridge over the spillway, and retrace your steps to return to your waiting automobile at 10.9 miles.

Before leaving here, you might want to consider doing another circuit hike of almost equal length by following the Upper Meadow Trail {FS672}, Meadow Mountain Trail {FS610}, Connector Trail, Meadow Creek Trail, and Lake Sherwood Trail on the western side of the lake. A handout map, available at the entrance station, shows this network of pathways and provides brief descriptions of them.

26

Anthony Creek

Total distance (circuit): 5.4 miles

Hiking time: 3 hours

Vertical rise: 1,040 feet

Maps: USGS 7½' Anthony

The Hike at a Glance

1.7   intersection with the Anthony
        Creek Trail
3.1   shelter
4.3   first viewpoint
5.4   end

An amiable saunter into a stream valley, a climb of a bit more than a mile to provide a cardiovascular workout, an easy ridgeline walk, and a quick, but rather gentle descent with a succession of good views. What more could you ask for in a day hike?

Well, in addition to the above, there are an abundance of level tent sites and a trailside shelter, which you could use to turn this hike into an overnighter, the route is lined with more than its fair share of spring and summer wildflowers, and you have the option of making the journey a combination hiking/fly-fishing outing by casting a line into the trout-stocked waters of Anthony Creek. To top it all off, there is a small beach on which you can soak up some sun after cooling off in a large pool at a wide bend in the creek.

A final option is to use the Forest Service's Blue Bend Recreation Area as a base from which to explore this hike and/or many of the other outdoor opportunities in the area. Set among the shade of hemlock trees and rhododendron thickets are a picnic area and campground with flush toilets, hand pumps, and water fountains.

The recreation area may be reached by taking exit 175 off I-64 at White Sulphur Springs, turning right onto US60 East, driving 4.8 miles, and turning left onto WV92 North. Make a left on WV16/2 in an additional 9.4 miles, and turn left into the recreation area in another 3.9 miles.

Begin the hike by following a pathway through the picnic area, crossing Anthony Creek on a well-constructed swinging

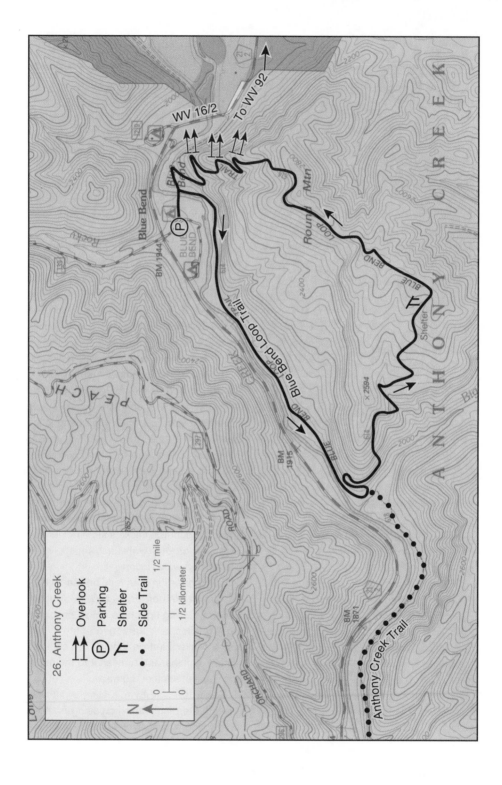

26. Anthony Creek

Overlook
P Parking
Shelter
Side Trail

N

0   1/2 kilometer
0   1/2 mile

WV 16/2
To WV 92

Blue Bend
Blue Bend
BM 1944
BLUE BEND
Rocky

Round Mtn
BLUE BEND LOOP
Shelter

PEACH

CREEK

Blue Bend Loop Trail

BLUE BEND

x 2594

BM 1915

ROAD

ORCHARD

BM 1857

BM 1871

Anthony Creek Trail

ANTHONY CREEK

bridge, and coming to an intersection of several trails. Turn right and follow the Blue Bend Loop Trail {FS614} downstream, walking by white and birdsfoot violet, mayapple, rhododendron, geranium, and chickweed. On bright, sunny days, the creek almost looks green as it reflects the leaves and needles of ash, poplar, sycamore, maple, beech, hemlock, and pine.

In early summer, you can identify another member of the forest, basswood, by noticing the many bees flying about its hanging clusters of small, yellow-tinged white flowers. Later in the year, you may find basswood honey for sale in some of the nearby country stores, as its strong flavor has been considered a treat by many generations of Appalachians.

More wildflowers, such as trillium, columbine, and jack-in-the-pulpit grow under the moss- and tripe-covered rock outcrop at 0.4 mile. You usually don't expect to find beavers living beside such a swiftly moving stream, yet the unmistakable mark of their gnawing is on a number of trees close to the often-dry water run you step over at 0.6 mile. Beavers are rodents, which make up more than half of all animal species in the world. In West Virginia, rodents range from tiny half-ounce mice to beavers that may weigh more than 60 pounds.

There is a T-intersection at 1.7 miles. The Anthony Creek Trail {FS618} goes to the right, crosses Big Draft, and continues for 3.8 miles to its end at the Greenbrier River on Anthony Station Road. You want to bear left and begin a switchbacked ascent, continuing to follow the Blue Bend Loop Trail. The pathway is now obviously less used, as pads of moss in the middle of the pathway soften your steps, and the trailside ground vegetation changes to wintergreen and plantain. Crushing a wintergreen leaf will delight your olfactory nerves, while chewing on a leaf will freshen your mouth and give your taste buds a treat as you continue to climb.

The switchback to the right at 2.5 miles is done in a forest where oaks (and the squawroot that parasitizes the trees' underground root systems) become more common as you continue to gain elevation. For another refreshing aroma, crush a leaf of the flowers of hoary mountain mint, which are a part of the ground cover where you cross a water run at 2.8 miles. Hopefully, the rivulet will be running when you pass by here, as this may be the last chance for water if you are planning on spending the night in the shelter at 3.1 miles. The spring about 300 feet down the ravine, behind the shelter, should be counted on for water only in wet weather.

The trail continues beyond the shelter by following a woods road along the undulating ridge to the summit of Round Mountain at an elevation of 2,960 feet. Be alert at 3.5 miles. Soon after you begin a quick descent, the Blue Bend Loop Trail takes its leave of the woods road, turns left onto a pathway, and drops into a woodlands of striped maple, rhododendron, hemlock, wintergreen, and trailing arbutus. You may have to get down on hands and knees, brush away some forest litter, and lift up the evergreen leaves of the trailing arbutus in order to finally see its blossom. This Lilliputian flower's delightful scent almost led to its demise. In the early part of the 20th century it was so highly prized for floral bouquets that commercial diggers nearly wiped out the country's entire native population. To this day it remains protected by law in many states in the hope that it will reestablish itself.

It is time to take a break when the trail makes a switchback to the left and you come to the first of the views at 4.3 miles. The mountainside drops precipitously in front of you, revealing a rural landscape of green

Third scenic view

meadows and country homes spread across the valleys created by Anthony and Little Creeks. The setting is so serene that it can call to mind Ambrogio Lorenzetti's fresco *The Effects of Good Government in the Countryside*. The second viewpoint at 4.5 miles takes in the same scene from a little more diminished elevation, while the third one at 4.8 miles is from an even lower perspective.

Upon reaching Anthony Creek at 5.1 miles, switchback to the left (the trail to the right is a fishermen's pathway), and cross the swinging bridge over the creek again. Before returning to your car at 5.4 miles, you should take the short walk to the right to the beach and the swim that was promised to you in the introduction of this hike. Having walked through the peace of a typical Allegheny Mountain forest, and now having your cares washed away by the cold water of the creek, you may come to truly appreciate the words of Ralph Waldo Emerson (from the poem "Musketaquid"): "A woodland walk, a quest for river grapes, a mocking thrush, a wild rose, or a rock-living columbine, salve my worst wounds."

Southern West Virginia

27

Kate's Mountain

Total distance (circuit): 8.9 miles

Hiking time: 5 hours, 15 minutes

Vertical rise: 1,480 feet

Maps: USGS 7½' Glace; USGS 7½' White Sulphur Springs; park handout map

The Hike at a Glance

1.7	right onto WV60/32
1.9	left onto Holsapple Trail
4.5	left onto WV60/32
5.0	vista
5.3	right onto Rocky Ridge Trail
7.6	right onto WV60/14
8.4	intersection with Mabel Doway Trail
8.9	end

It was in the warming temperatures of spring 1892 that botanist John Kunkel Small, while exploring the environs of Kate's Mountain, came upon an unknown plant growing in a shale barren. With cloverlike leaves and white, round flower heads, the plant came to be known as Kate's Mountain clover, not only because it was discovered here but also because for many years this remained the only place it was found.

The clover was not the only plant first discovered on the shale barrens of Kate's Mountain. About 15 years prior to Small's explorations, Gustav Guttenberg recorded finding a nodding flower that lacked petals, but had thick, purple sepals, and was later named white-haired clematis. In 1903, Kenneth M. Mackenzie found the mountain pimpernel, an upright plant with several terminal clusters of tiny yellow flowers.

For many years after their discovery, each of these plants was believed to exist only on Kate's Mountain and nowhere else in the world. It is now known that they are found in, and are endemic to, shale barrens in several Mid-Atlantic and southern states. Yet, they grow in such small numbers that they are certainly not common plants, and, in fact, Kate's Mountain clover is listed as rare, threatened, or endangered in every state in which it is found.

Much of Kate's Mountain is within the boundaries of 5,130-acre Greenbrier State Forest. Unlike the state forests in many other states that are managed primarily for timber and have few amenities, a large percentage of West Virginia's state forests offer a variety

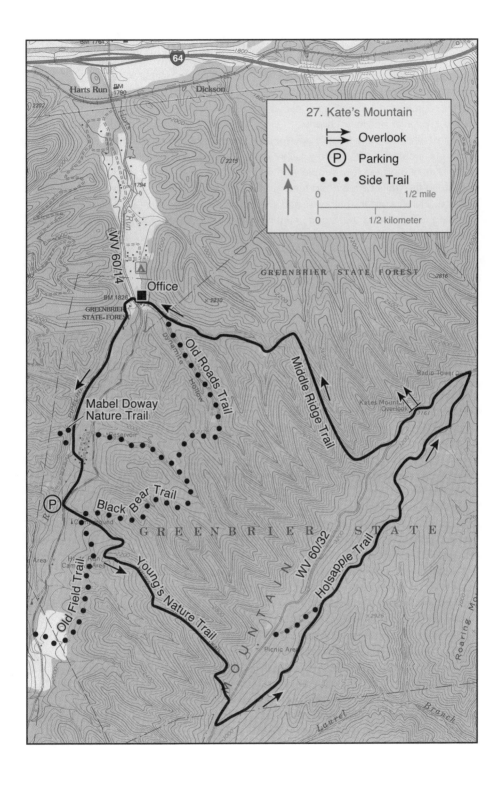

27. Kate's Mountain

→ Overlook
Ⓟ Parking
••• Side Trail

N

0 _____ 1/2 mile
0 _____ 1/2 kilometer

64

Harts Run
BM 1790
Dickson

WV 60/14

Office
BM 1826
GREENBRIER
STATE·FOREST

GREENBRIER STATE FOREST

Old Roads Trail

Dynamite Hollow

Mabel Doway
Nature Trail

Reservoir

Middle Ridge Trail

Radio Tower

Kates Mountain
Overlook

Black Bear Trail

Ⓟ

Campground

Picnic Area

GREENBRIER STATE

Old Field Trail

Young's Nature Trail

WV 60/32

Holsapple Trail

MOUNTAIN

Picnic Area

Roaring Mo

Laurel Branch

of outdoor opportunities and visitor attractions. Greenbrier State Forest has a campground (hook-ups and hot showers), rental cabins, game courts, picnic areas, a seasonal nature program, and a swimming pool that is extremely popular with local children.

Almost all of the state forest's developed areas are located in the narrow valley of Harts Run, leaving the few people who do hike along the trails with a good feeling of isolation. (Hunters use the pathways and surrounding forest during the various hunting seasons, so take proper precautions.) All the trails are well marked and signed at intersections, but this is not a hike for those who are out of shape. The trip starts in the valley and climbs steeply for more than 1,000 feet to the ridgeline. The descent is even steeper.

Yet, there are compelling reasons to put yourself through all of this. Botanists list 15 species of plants that are confined to shale barrens, and 14 of them grow upon the slopes and ridgelines of Kate's Mountain. Deer, opossums, raccoons, chipmunks, black bear, squirrels, woodpeckers, turkeys, grouses, quail, and close to 250 other species of birds have been seen here. In addition, there is a spectacular view that more than makes up for the huffing and puffing.

The park and trailhead may be reached by taking exit 171 off I-64 at White Sulphur Springs, driving south on WV60/14, and entering the forest in 1.2 miles. Trailhead parking is on the right (do not block the gate), 1.4 miles later.

Begin the hike by diagonally crossing the paved park road and ascending into the woods along the orange-blazed Young's Nature Trail. Pass by the group campsite at 0.2 mile, and 500 feet later stay to the left, where the yellow-blazed Old Field Trail comes in from the right. Yellow star grass and pink and flame azalea are part of the forest at 0.4 mile, where the green-blazed Black Bear Trail

comes in from the left. Stay to the right to continue along Young's Nature Trail, possibly stepping on a puffball or two.

Almost all of us enjoyed popping puffballs when we were kids (and some us still do as adults) to see the little clouds of dust they produce. Puffballs are the fruiting organs of fungi that grow from mycelia, threadlike roots that permeate the ground or other matter from which the fungus gains nourishment. The dust is the plant's minute spores, and by having stepped on the puffball you have released them to the wind to be carried off somewhere to start new puffballs.

Studying another one of nature's methods of reproduction, the winged seed pods of the striped maple, may help take your mind off how steep the ascent becomes at about 0.9 mile. Also, be on the lookout for one of the mountain's other rare plants. Swordleaf phlox has been found in only a few places in West Virginia and several bordering Virginia counties. Its bright purple-to-pink flowers bloom from May through early July.

It may slow you down, but the steep climb lasts only a short time, as you attain the ridgeline at 1.7 miles and turn right onto unpaved WV60/32. Don't let the easy walking lull you into missing the important left turn at 1.9 miles onto the red-blazed Holsapple Trail. This former logging road continues with very slight ups and downs, providing pleasant and easy walking beside star moss, dogwood, and geranium.

The route to the left at 2.9 miles leads to WV60/32 and a state forest picnic area. Stay right, but keep to the left when a different logging road comes in from the right at 3.9 miles. Begin a gentle rise, and, at 4.5 miles, turn left onto unpaved WV60/32, soon passing a radio tower.

You have been walking for a long time, so take a rest break when you come to the

Westward view from Kate's Mountain

dramatic view of the mountains and ridge-lines to the west and north at 5.0 miles. Most impressive is the deep gap that I-64 enters between White Rock and Greenbrier Mountains. You are having such a slow-paced day here in the mountains that it almost makes you wonder why all of those people on the highway are in such a hurry and moving at such high rates of speed.

Continue on your way, but be alert at 5.3 miles, as you need to bear right and ascend through mayapple on the yellow-blazed Rocky Ridge Trail, attaining the 3,200-foot summit of Kate's Mountain at 5.4 miles. Local lore states the mountain is named for one of the area's early settlers, Kate Carpenter. She and her infant daughter hid in the hollow of a rotting log to escape the wrath of a Native American raiding party that had scalped and killed her husband, Nathan.

From the summit, the trail begins what is one of the longest and most unrelentingly steep descents in the state; use caution. Just about the time your knees scream, "Stop! We can't handle any more," the trail switchbacks to the left at 6.4 miles and onto a gently descending sidehill trail. However, be alert at 6.6 miles. The pathway makes a sudden switchback to the left onto a somewhat faint route. (If you continue straight, you will go down a steep embankment.)

Turn right onto a former logging road at 6.7 miles, but be alert only 400 feet later, where you turn left and descend the pathway to cross a small creek. The route will be much easier to follow once you merge onto a woods road at 6.9 miles and descend through hemlocks and other evergreens. One of Kate's Mountain's most interesting plants is the box huckleberry, which grows in large colonies, often below rhododendron and pine thickets. Although the plants appear to be individuals, they are actually connected by a continuous underground root system, making them all part of one single plant. Past generations of mountaineers found the berries to be a delicious treat and used them in jams, jellies, and pies.

Cross the creek a couple of more times, and stay to the right when the red-blazed Old Roads Trail comes in from the left. Pass by the route to the archery and muzzleloading rifle ranges, emerge from the woods, pass by the state forest office, and turn right onto paved WV60/14 at 7.6 miles.

Almost immediately make a left onto the forest superintendent's residence driveway. (A sign says DO NOT ENTER, but you are permitted here if you are hiking—just respect the privacy of the family living here.) Although it is just a gravel service road you continue to follow, you are compensated by the beauty of the large hemlocks that line the burbling waters of Harts Run. The blue-blazed Mabel Doway Nature Trail goes off to the right at 8.4 miles. Stay on the service road, cross the run on a footbridge, and walk by several rental cabins. Turn into the driveway for Cabin #12 at 8.6 miles, and make a right onto the trail marked as leading to the picnic area. The hike comes to an end when you bear left onto the service road and return to your car at 8.9 miles.

If you enjoyed the outing, but feel as though you missed or had trouble identifying the various species of plants for which Kate's Mountain is known, consider coming back here in the spring, when volunteers and park personnel conduct the annual Show-Me Wildflower Hike.

28

The Appalachian Trail

Total distance (one way): 14.9 miles

Hiking time: 8 hours, 45 minutes

Vertical rise: 2,800 feet

Maps: USGS 7½' Narrows, VA/WV; USGS 7½' Peterstown, WV/VA; USGS 7½' Lindside, WV/VA

The Hike at a Glance

1.8   cross VA641
4.0   spring
6.4   Rice Field
8.3   side trail to unreliable spring
11.8   Symms Gap
12.8   left onto the Groundhog Trail
14.9   end

The Appalachian Trail (AT) follows the crest of the Appalachian Mountains for more than 2,100 miles from Springer Mountain, Georgia, to Mount Katahdin, Maine. Although other people had put forth similar ideas, a 1921 magazine article by Benton MacKaye is generally regarded as having provided the impetus for the AT. MacKaye saw a post–World War I America that was becoming urbanized, machine-driven, and removed from the positive aspects of the natural world.

In October 1923, the first miles to be built for the AT were opened in Harriman–Bear Mountain State Park, New York. On August 14, 1937, the final section was constructed in central Maine. A remarkable aspect of the trail is that nearly every bit of effort expended on its behalf has been done by volunteers. The Appalachian Trail Conservancy (ATC), the organization overseeing volunteer efforts, estimates that somewhere between two and three million people enjoy some portion of the pathway annually.

The trail comes in contact with southeastern West Virginia a few miles east of Peterstown. Traversing Peters Mountain along the West Virginia–Virginia border, it zigzags across the state line for close to 13 miles. At one moment on this hike you will be in West Virginia, another time in Virginia, and sometimes one foot will be in one state while the opposite foot is in the other. Highlights are the commanding views onto waves of Allegheny Mountain summits and rural farmlands from Rice Field and Symms Gap Meadow. Water is scarce, so start out with plenty.

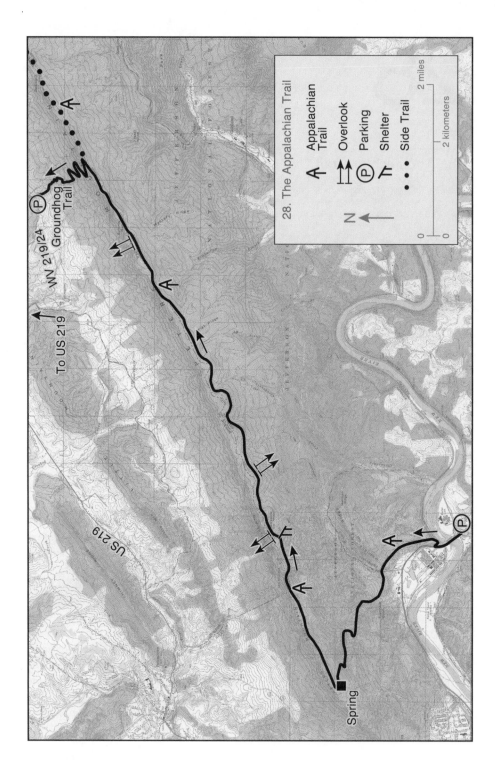

28. The Appalachian Trail

Appalachian Trail
Overlook
Parking
Shelter
Side Trail

N

2 miles

2 kilometers

0
0

WV 219/24
Groundhog Trail

To US 219

US 219

Spring

You will need to do a car shuttle in order to complete this one-way hike. Drive US219 North for 6.1 miles from its junction with WV12 in Peterstown. Turn right onto WV219/21 (Painter Run Road), go 1.3 more miles, turn left onto WV219/24 (it may be unsigned), and continue for another 0.5 mile to the trailhead parking on the right.

To park your other car, return to Peterstown and continue on US219 South to Rich Creek, Virginia. Follow US460 East for less than 10 miles, and cross the New River. Parking is available at the far end of the bridge in the small shopping center on the left. Ask permission at the business before you leave your car.

Please note: A major relocation is planned for the first few miles of this hike. It will still start from the same point, but keep an eye out for the AT's white blazes and signs; if the route differs from the description in this book, follow the blazes. The overall distance may increase slightly, but you will still be able to easily accomplish this as an overnight hike.

Start the trip by following the white blazes back across the Senator Shumate Bridge over US460. Here, you see the Hoechst Celanese chemical plant. You may not enjoy the its ugly behemoth of industrial architecture, the roar its machinery produces, or the clouds of pollutant-laden smoke it pours into the atmosphere, but realize that almost all of us are responsible for its existence. Those of us who purchase garments and equipment made of synthetic fibers help keep the company profitable.

Turn right at the far end of the bridge, enter the woods on a narrow pathway, and negotiate several small ups and downs (do not drink or treat any water in this area—it is very tainted) before crossing VA641 (Stillhouse Branch Road) at 1.8 miles. Reenter the forest on a rising woods road, but leave it at 3.0 miles to ease the rate of ascent, since the road becomes a steep, rocky pathway with just a few switchbacks.

To save a long trip to get water when you are at the shelter at about 6.3 miles into the hike, you might want to fill your bottles at the small spring close to the trail at 4.0 miles. Once you attain the ridgeline at 4.1 miles, warm-weather flowers—such as black-eyed Susans and Queen Anne's lace—line the pathway. The openness of two pipeline crossings (at 5.5 miles and 5.7 miles) and a utility line right-of-way at 5.9 miles hint of better views to come and contrast nicely with the cool shade provided by lush vegetation.

Breaking out of the woods and into Rice Field, you may be moved to burst out in a song from *The Wizard of Oz*—"You're out of the woods/you're out of the dark/ . . . step into the light!"—because now you know why so many people take such delight in doing this trip. Peters Mountain may be just as magical, and as varied, as that mythical Land of Oz. In the 6.4 miles you have been hiking, you have already enjoyed a cool drink from a mountain spring, watched the antics of chattering chipmunks, walked by the tall trunks of chestnut oak and red maple trees, looked down onto the New River Valley, maybe had a small flock of turkeys scatter upon your approach, and listened to the soft buzzing of bumblebees maneuvering from mint to clover.

Now you are graced with the chance to take in the spacious western view. Cattle graze directly below, and rectangular fields of nearby farms alternate with strips of woodland, turning the landscape into a patchwork quilt of greens, browns, and golds. Receding into the horizon is a vast jumble of West Virginia mountaintops. This is a great place to watch the sunset.

Situated in the woods, 20 feet or so from the meadow, is the Rice Field Shelter, its machine-cut logs unstained and shining

Rice Field

brightly amid leafy surroundings. The water source for the shelter may be found by following the blue-blazed trail steeply down the mountainside for 0.5 mile.

(At this point I feel obligated to become a bit of a gossip and let you in on some behind-the-scenes trail politics: After the shelter was built in 1995, members of the Kanawha Trail Club put up a plaque dubbing it the Star Haven Shelter. This certainly appears to be an innocent enough name—and an appropriate one, since you can sit on the edge of the field and gaze upon the heavens. However, it just so happened that the club's trail supervisor at the time was Jo Ann Starr. The Forest Service, which has always held to the practice that shelters are not named for living persons, felt the plaque honored Ms. Starr and refused to recognize the Star Haven name. This is why you will find that the structure is simply called the Rice Field Shelter in all government and Appalachian Trail Conservancy publications.)

Reading the shelter register, you may find numerous entries exclaiming the beauty of the sunsets and the great abundance of stars visible from the field. Other hikers write about being serenaded by whip-poor-wills as they drift off to sleep. If nothing else, your lullaby for the night will be the lonesome, but somehow comforting sound of train whistles echoing off the hillsides above the New River Valley.

Resuming the hike, reenter the woods at 6.9 miles and follow the small ups and downs of the narrow ridgeline, soon walking through the wide cut of a power line right-of-way that lets you gaze upon Pearis Mountain to the south. The trail to the right at 8.3 miles leads 150 feet to an unreliable spring.

True to their name, spring beauties are some of the first to emerge as the weather gets just a bit warmer. With flowers of pinkish white, they can line this section of the AT in such great quantities that they may appear to be patches of slowly melting snow. The flowers, which usually last only about three days, are bisexual, but the female and male parts mature at different times, preventing self-pollination. Deer browse on the tiny flowers and leaves, while chipmunks, mice, Native Americans, the early settlers, and even some people today have found the root of the plant to be quite delectable and nutritious. Tasting like radishes when raw, the roots have been likened to potatoes, with a sweet, chestnutlike flavor when baked or boiled in soups or stews.

Merge onto a woods road at 11.4 miles and enter Symms Gap Meadow, whose lack of trees lets you once again enjoy views into West Virginia. The trip is almost over, and you have time to linger, so take a break, lie down, and watch the clouds drift by. If you are here in the fall, you may be treated to more than just clouds, as hundreds, maybe even thousands, of raptors zip by on their way south for the winter.

Sometimes as early as mid-August, ospreys, American kestrels, and a few bald eagles may start the procession. However, the migration begins in earnest in the middle of September, when the broad-winged hawks take to the skies. Peak daily sightings of several thousand are not uncommon, and on record days more than ten thousand have

been reported. In the early weeks of October, peregrine falcons join the movement, as do the smallest hawks, the sharp-shinned, and the larger, but fewer-in-number Cooper's hawks. Red-tailed hawks fly by the leafless trees of November, not as large flocks, but usually as solitary birds. Making their way to a warmer climate at about the same time are red-shouldered hawks and northern harriers. Soaring over a Peters Mountain that could be covered by December snows, northern goshawks and golden eagles bring the migratory season to a close.

Descend into Symms Gap at 11.8 miles, turn off the old road, and ascend on a rough and rocky trail. It is time to take your leave of the AT at 12.8 miles and turn left onto the Groundhog Trail. It was built by volunteers of the ATC, West Virginia Scenic Trails Association, and Kanawha Trail Club in the 1980s to provide access to the AT from West Virginia. Although it is not maintained as well as the AT, it is an easy, switchbacked route that brings you down the western slope of Peters Mountain and returns you to your car at 14.9 miles.

You have now walked more than 12 miles of the Appalachian Trail. You only have approximately 2,160 miles left to complete its entire length.

29

Pipestem State Park

Total distance (circuit): 7.3 miles

Hiking time: 4 hours

Vertical rise: 1,120 feet

Maps: USGS 7½' Pipestem; USGS 7½' Flat Top; park handout map

The Hike at a Glance

1.3   right on Canyon Rim Trail
1.6   Heritage Point Overlook
2.2   right onto River Trail
2.8   left onto County Line Trail
3.5   Indian Branch Falls
4.7   left onto the horse trail
5.1   right onto Lake View Trail
5.7   right onto Lake Shore Trail
6.7   right onto Law Hollow Trail; few feet later, left onto Den Tree Trail
7.3   end

Early in the 20th century, many people, including West Virginia Attorney General Howard B. Lee and Hinton newspaper publisher John Faulconer, had stated that the beauty of the Bluestone River Canyon and the land around it was worthy of being preserved as a park. The reality would have to wait until the 1960s, when the federal government provided funds for economic development in West Virginia's pockets of low employment and income.

Dedicated on Memorial Day 1970, Pipestem Resort State Park, with rolling lands upon the Allegheny Plateau, steep canyon walls, and a narrow strip of bottomland beside the Bluestone River, has become a premier destination in southern West Virginia. There is something here for just about everyone: two golf courses, a driving range, and a pro shop; miniature golf; tennis and basketball courts; swimming pools; the Mountain Artisans Shop featuring West Virginia–made arts and crafts; two gift shops; and several restaurants and snack bars. The year-round campground has full hook-ups, heated bathhouses, laundry facilities, and a playground. Fully equipped rental cottages provide electric heat and fireplaces. Seven-story McKeever Lodge (open year-round) sits on the lip of the canyon (make sure to ask for a room with a canyon view when making reservations), and Mountain Creek Lodge, open seasonally and accessible by the aerial tramway, is located on the canyon floor.

The park's amphitheater, which can accommodate 2,000 people, hosts concerts,

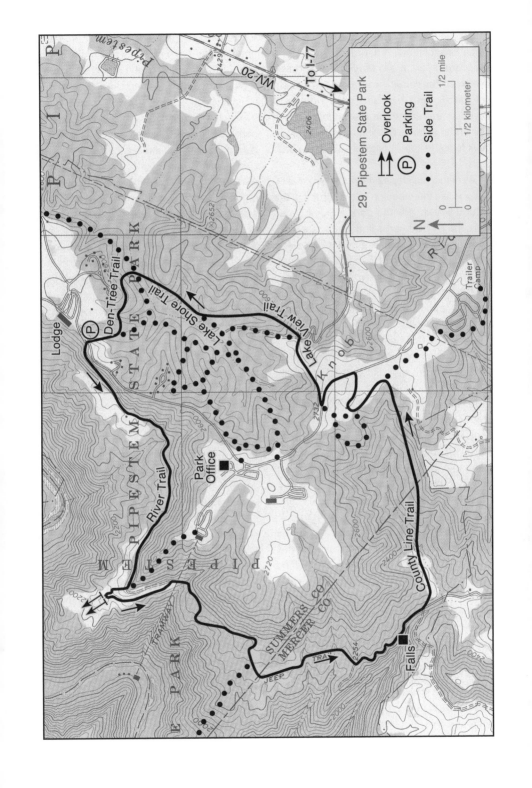

29. Pipestem State Park

nature events, evening programs, and theatrical productions. A nature center is open year-round (with a varying schedule), overnight horseback camping is available seasonally, and trail and pony rides and hayrides are offered on a scheduled basis. The artificial Long Branch Lake tempts anglers to try their luck for trout and largemouth bass.

All of this development and activity makes it sound like there couldn't be much left of the natural world. Yet, the park encompasses more than 4,000 acres and numerous pathways wind into its more remote places. The more-than-1,000-foot difference in elevation—with deep, moist, hollows and dry, rocky sandstone outcrops—provides many different environments for a diverse assemblage of plants and animals.

Almost 100 species of trees and shrubs grow above so many wildflowers that it takes an eight-page pamphlet just to list them. More than 160 kinds of birds have been recorded here, with wild turkeys, chickadees, titmice, and nuthatches living year-round, and warblers, vireos, and flycatchers flying south for the colder months. Among the many animals are salamanders, toads, frogs, turtles, snakes, bats, beavers, red foxes, coyotes, weasels, otters, deer, bobcats, and black bear.

This 7.2-mile hike takes in a view of the canyon, a small waterfall, the nature center, and the lake. The trailhead may be reached by taking exit 14 off I-77 (located a few miles north of Princeton), following WV7 eastward for 2.6 miles, and turning left onto WV20 (Athens Road). Continue for another 9.2 miles, and turn left into the park. (Soon after this is a parking area on the right for a short trail leading to the Bolar Lookout Tower. The few minutes it takes to walk to the tower is amply rewarded with one of the best views in southern West Virginia.) Just over 2.0 miles

from the park entrance is a road to the left that goes by the park office and to the aerial tram. Stay right, and pull into the parking area on the right for Long Branch Lake just 0.9 mile later.

Begin the hike by diagonally crossing the park road and descending along the orange-blazed River Trail (a dirt service road) lined by oak, maple, striped maple, and hemlock. The road to the right at 0.4 mile leads to a clearing. Stay left and continue to descend beside the large leaves of buckeye trees.

Turn right at 1.3 miles, and descend along the blue-blazed Canyon Rim Trail, soon coming to an old homesite clearing. Swing to the right and continue to descend. Many families lived on small farms near the canyon rim when land for the park was purchased in the 1960s, and reminders—such as this crumbling chimney and house foundation—may still be found in various locations.

Turn right at 1.6 miles, and descend steeply to Heritage Point Overlook, a sandstone outcrop. There are no constructed barriers to keep you from falling into the abyss, so use caution as you wander around, peering into the canyon and onto the Bluestone River. Perched high on the other side of the gorge is a cabin, which was once the home of the local Farley family. While you might sight golden eagles in winter and a bald eagle year round, the large birds you may happen to spot riding the thermals are most likely vultures.

Although black vultures (with white patches on the wing tips) are seen in the Allegheny Mountains, turkey vultures are much more common. In flight, their 6-foot wingspan creates a distinctive and easily identifiable V pattern. Historically, turkey vultures had been thought to depend upon their sense of smell to locate carrion, but recent studies have shown that, like the black vultures, their keen eyesight plays a much more important role.

Reconstructed log home

When ready to leave, walk back to the last intersection, and to return to the River Trail by a different route, keep to the right. Having made your way back to the homesite clearing, make a sharp right to, once again, continue on a different route than the one you came in on. You might hear a high-pitched *squeenk* or a low, twangy *c'tung* from the green frogs you surprise as you pass a small pond at 2.1 miles. Also listen for the short, raspy quacks of wood frogs—the park naturalist once counted more than 250 of them around the pond on one of his walks in late February.

The park is home to at least nine species of frogs and toads, and their calls can add a melodious presence to your excursion. Listen for the high-pitched *peep* of spring peepers, the low croak of pickerel frogs, the raspy *wreenk* of mountain chorus frogs, the loud discordant *w-a-a-h* of Fowler's toads, the trill of American toads that can last for close to a half minute, and the quick trill of gray tree frogs.

Turn right onto the River Trail at 2.2 miles, and pass under the tramway, whose cleared swath provides a nice view onto the river and Mountain Creek Lodge. Reenter an open forest of oak, ash, maple, walnut, poplar, and hemlock, and cross a small stream tumbling down the mountainside. The vegetation of club moss, wild ginger, and walking fern is more lush than it has been so far on the hike.

The walking fern is such an interesting plant that it warrants stopping for a few moments to admire it. The fronds, which can grow to be more than a foot long, rise from black rootstocks and spread out in a circular fashion. They arch over until they touch the ground, where they take root and, without the aid of spores that most ferns use to reproduce, form new plants. These repeat the process and soon there may be an entire colony of ferns *walking* across rock facings, boulders, fallen trees, and other spaces upon the forest floor.

The River Trail turns right at 2.8 miles and descends the canyon wall to the Bluestone River. However, you want to bear left, now following the red-blazed County Line Trail. Stay left again when an old road comes in from the right at 3.2 miles. Indian Branch Falls at 3.5 miles is the classic mountain waterfall, dropping on its crescent-shaped bowl to its basin pool about 35 feet below.

Be alert at 3.6 miles. The County Line Trail, which you want to continue to follow, makes a turn to the left in a forest that in the early morning is alive with the songs of vireos and warblers. Pay attention again at 4.4 miles as the County Line Trail swings left and ascends a rough and rocky treadway that soon becomes steeper.

At 4.7 miles, turn left onto a wide dirt road, whose churned dirt marks it as part of the park's horse trail. Bear right at 4.8 miles, and rise a few feet to walk by a reconstructed log home and other structures that were moved from various sites within the park. (One of the buildings had originally been in the vicinity of Heritage Point Overlook.) A few more feet up the hill is the nature center, where restrooms and water are available when it is open.

Continue by following the sign directing you into the woods along the Dogwood Trail, walk about 0.2 mile, turn right to walk on the main park road, and watch for the left turn onto the old roadbed that is signed as the white-blazed Lake View Trail.

A dirt road comes in from the right at 5.3 miles; stay left, but keep right at the next intersection in 500 feet. Less than 300 feet beyond this is another intersection with a faint road coming in from the right. Swing left, still following the Lake View Trail. There is another intersection just a few hundred feet beyond this. The Horse Trail comes in from the left. Keep right, descend, and turn right onto the blue-blazed Lake Shore Trail at 5.7 miles. If you are walking here in early evening, you might get to hear the deep *jug-o-rum* call of bullfrogs coming from Long Branch Lake, which is visible through the vegetation.

Alder grows in the wet area at 6.7 miles, where you pass below the lake dam and come to an intersection. Make a right turn onto the white-blazed Law Hollow Trail, but be very alert. Just a few hundred feet later you want to make a left onto the narrow, lightly used, and red-blazed Den Tree Trail. After a short rise, level out, and join an old woods road at 6.9 miles.

At 7.1 miles, drop down a few feet, turn right onto the paved handicapped-accessible road to the lake, and soon turn right to ascend the wood and gravel steps to return to your car at 7.3 miles. It is hoped that you made arrangements to spend the night in one of the lodges or cottages, or set up a tent in the campground, because tomorrow morning you could set out upon a new exploration of a different part of the park (see Hike 30).

30

Bluestone River

Total distance (circuit): 3.6 miles

Hiking time: 2 hours, 10 minutes

Vertical rise: 720 feet

Maps: USGS 7½' Pipestem; USGS 7½' Flat Top; park handout map

The Hike at a Glance

1.0   *left onto the Farley Loop Trail*
2.1   *old fence line*
2.9   *left at T-intersection*
3.6   *end*

This outing has a bit of a twist to it: You will take the aerial tramway in Pipestem State Park (see Hike 29) to the Bluestone River and the beginning of the hike. The ride, which is certainly an attraction unto itself, will be free if you are staying at the park's Mountain Creek Lodge. If not, the round-trip ride costs only a few dollars.

After the collision of continental plates raised the Allegheny Plateau millions of years ago, water began the process of erosion. Rising on East River Mountain in Virginia, and flowing more than 70 miles to the New River near Hinton, West Virginia, the Bluestone River has carved out a gorge that is more than 1,000 feet deep. Like most of West Virginia in the 1800s and early 1900s, the gorge and the land around it were heavily timbered and mined for coal, and the river ran black with coal dust and raw sewage discharged from numerous mining camps.

Thanks to the efforts of those who fought hard for strict environmental controls, the canyon walls are now covered in a second-growth forest punctuated by large rock outcrops, and the river is populated with smallmouth bass, catfish, and bluegill.

Although this is a rather short trip along the river and onto the heights of the canyon wall, it is a rugged hike that should be done by only those who are fit and sure-footed. The climb will test calf muscles and lung capacity, while the descent is on a very steep and rocky pathway that, in some places, is almost nonexistent and is almost always just barely wide enough to put your feet side by side. If your fear of heights increases while

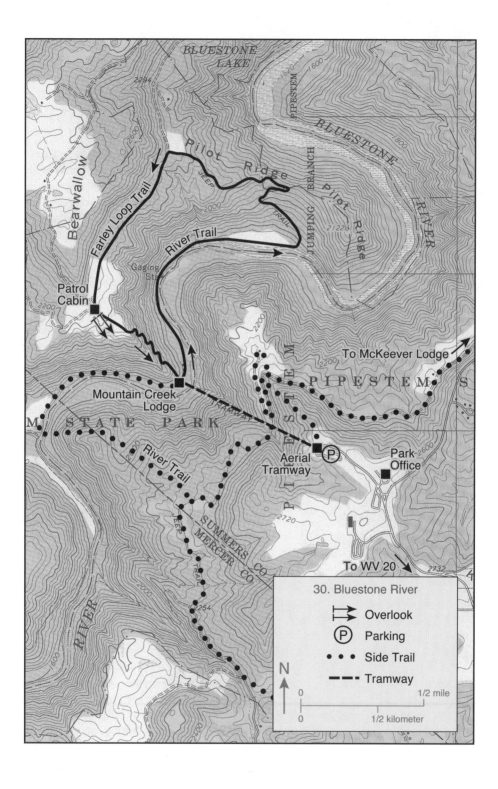

BLUESTONE LAKE

Bearwallow

Farley Loop Trail

Pilot Ridge

JEEP TRAIL

River Trail

BLUESTONE

Pilot Ridge

JUMPING BRANCH

BLUESTONE RIVER

Gaging Sta.

Patrol Cabin

To McKeever Lodge

PIPESTEM S

Mountain Creek Lodge

TRAMWAY

M STATE PARK

River Trail

SUMMERS CO.
MERCER CO.

PIPESTEM

Aerial Tramway

P

Park Office

To WV 20

30. Bluestone River

⇥ Overlook

Ⓟ Parking

• • • Side Trail

– – – Tramway

N

0   1/2 mile
0   1/2 kilometer

going down such routes, you might want to consider doing the trip in the opposite direction.

Pipestem State Park and the aerial tramway may be reached by taking exit 14 from I-77 (located a few miles north of Princeton), following WV7 eastward for 2.6 miles, and turning left onto WV20 (Athens Road). Continue for another 9.2 miles and turn left into the park. Turn left 2.1 miles later, go past the park office, and continue to the parking lot for the Canyon Rim Center and tramway.

(The tram usually operates daily from mid-May through the last weekend in October. If you want to do this hike at any other time of the year, or find that the tram happens to be closed, you will have to add about 8 miles to the journey by walking the Canyon Rim Trail from the Canyon Rim Center to the River Trail, fording the Bluestone River, and following a gravel road to the Mountain Creek Lodge.)

As you ride the tram down, look across to the small cabin perched on the hillside on the other side of the gorge—you will be standing there in about 3 miles.

Begin the hike by walking to the front of the Mountain Creek Lodge and following the orange-blazed River Trail downstream along an old road with slight ups and downs. The logs, brush, and other debris swept downstream and deposited far from the river show just how high the water can get after heavy rains. However, the walking is easy, so you have the luxury of watching for snapping turtles, kingfishers, great blue herons, bullfrogs, and northern water snakes along the banks. Be on the lookout for copperhead snakes throughout the hike.

Cancer root, a parasitic plant that resembles Indian pipe and is also known as naked broomrape, grows on the hillside, while lyre-leaved sage, a member of the mint family, flourishes in the sandy soil beside the trail. Its lower lip makes a landing site for insects, whose weight causes the plant's stamens to dip down and deposit pollen on an insect.

The trail can get very muddy, especially around 0.9 mile. Expect to get wet and mucky feet. Be alert at 1.0 mile. The River Trail comes to an end, and the old road continues through Bluestone National Scenic River for 8.5 miles to Bluestone State Park. Known as the Bluestone Turnpike, it was used by soldiers during the Civil War and by local people as late as the 1940s.

You, however, want to turn left onto the Farley Loop Trail, which may be overgrown for the first few hundred feet. Once past the open area, populated by the yellow blossoms of coreopsis, you will begin to rise quickly. Even though the route ascends by way of a number of switchbacks along an old, washed-out woods road bordered by yellow star grass, the climb is quite steep in a number of places.

The old fence line and large crowns on some of the trees at 2.1 miles are evidence that this land was once used for agricultural purposes. A faint road comes in from the right, but you want to swing left, going past large piles of stones that farmers removed from the soil so that they could grow their crops. A short trail leads to one of the two small family cemeteries near the route of the hike.

The walking is easier now as you continue on the Farley Loop Trail, traversing a nearly level shelf on the mountain's hillside. The forest is open and pretty, and many ferns grow along the old road bank. Bobcats live in the park, but it is unlikely that you will see any on this hike, since they are elusive and primarily nocturnal. Yet, just knowing that they are there is an exciting thought, and there is always the possibility that you may see one of their paw prints in the soft soil of the old

View from the porch of the Pleasant Farley cabin

road. The tracks are about 2 inches in diameter (front and hind) and are almost rounded. No claw marks are made, but all four toes and the heel pad from each paw are usually visible. Heel pads are concave in front—giving them a scalloped look—and lobed in the rear; this distinguishes this track from that of canines, which are lobed only in the rear and have no scalloping in the front.

Turn left when you come to the T-intersection at 2.9 miles, soon coming to the cabin you saw while riding on the tram. It was once the home of the local Pleasant Farley family and is now used as a park patrol cabin and facility for guided horseback camping trips. As you sit on the porch, enjoying the impressive view of the main Pipestem lodge perched upon the very lip of the gorge, you may begin to wonder how the park came by its name. The most widely accepted story is that it comes from the *Spirea alba* bush, locally called pipestem because its long, hollow, woody stems were incorporated into the clay and corncob pipes used by Native Americans and early settlers.

When you are ready to leave, continue beyond the cabin on a descent that soon becomes extremely steep along a very narrow pathway. While holding onto tree trunks to keep your balance and looking down to know where to place your feet, your eyes may catch glimpses of squawroot growing below oak trees and stonecrop clinging to small cracks in the rock.

At 3.4 miles, a 50-foot pathway leads to the Raven Rock Overlook for a view southward into the gorge. The main trail begins a switchbacked, but still steep descent that returns you to the tram and Mountain Creek Lodge at 3.6 miles.

The trip may have been short, but hikes always work up a good appetite, so head over to the restaurant for dinner before taking the tram ride back out of the gorge. Many people claim that the quality and type of food served here is the best to be found in any West Virginia state park.

31

Bluestone Lake

Total distance (circuit): 5.0 miles

Hiking time: 3 hours

Vertical rise: 1,080 feet

Maps: USGS 7½' Pipestem; park hand-out map

The Hike at a Glance

0.6   left at Campsite #14
1.5   right onto Big Pine Trail, left onto Boundary Trail 250 feet later
2.6   Gib Lilly Hollow
3.6   walk past Cabin #17
3.9   left onto Rhododendron Trail
5.0   end

After 2,000-acre Bluestone Lake and its dam were completed under the direction of the U.S. Army Corps of Engineers in the 1940s, Bluestone State Park was established in the 1950s as a recreational site to draw tourism dollars into an economically depressed area. Located along the western arm of the lake, the 2,000-acre park became remarkably popular and, in order to keep up with growing numbers of visitors, amenities and attractions were added through the years.

Today, it offers two campgrounds with a dump station and warm showers, a primitive campsite accessible only by boat, and modern cabins with heat that may be rented year-round. A variety of paddle and motorized boats are available for rent, or you may use park facilities to launch your own craft. Picnic areas, children's playground, game courts, an activities building, and seasonal nature and recreation programs bring many families to the park for day, weekend, or weeklong visits. Other folks come to go warm-water fishing for muskellunge, channel catfish, crappie, and largemouth, smallmouth, and striped bass.

A hike in the park will not deliver you to any roaring waterfalls nor open up any grand vistas of the surrounding countryside. What it will do is provide you with the opportunity to escape the activity in the developed part of the park and meander through quiet woodlands, surveying the different small parts of the forest that come together to make up the whole. Redbud, cardinal flower, comfrey, and rattlesnake weed grow under the deciduous forest canopy of buckeye,

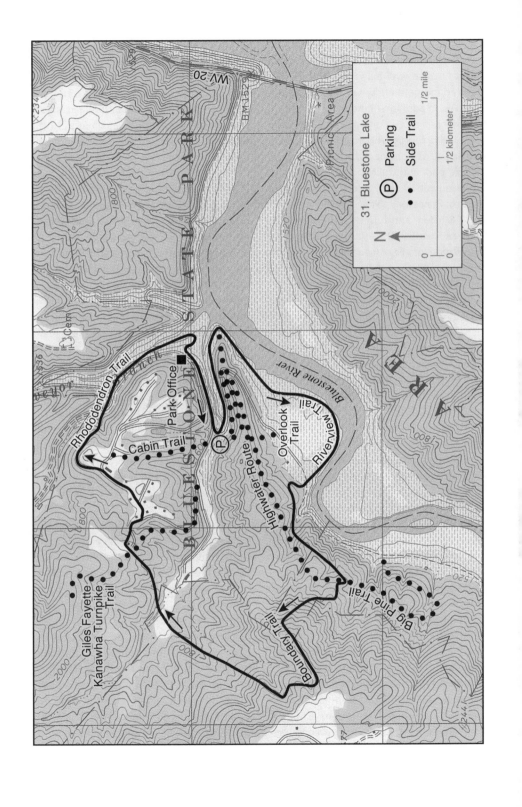

locust, maple, poplar, and ash. Beside the small streams are sycamore and cardinal flower, while you may see cattails and hooded mergansers when walking beside the lake. In addition, there is the possibility of coming in close contact with a box turtle, deer, wild turkey, red fox, bobcat, mink, skunk, squirrel, chipmunk, or black bear.

The park and trailhead can be reached by taking exit 14 off I-77 (located a few miles north of Princeton), following WV7 eastward for 2.6 miles, and turning left onto WV20 (Athens Road). In 9.2 miles, you will pass by Pipestem State Park (see Hikes 29 and 30). Drive an additional 8.3 miles and turn left onto WV20/2, which is the entrance road for Bluestone State Park. Continue to the intersection of several routes next to the park office. Take the one signed as leading to the campgrounds and continue for another 0.25 mile to the sign for the Riverview Trail on the left. Park in a small area to the right of the road, making sure not to block the service road.

Begin the hike by descending along the blue-blazed River View Trail in a moist forest of sycamore, redbud, willow, joe-pye weed, and cardinal flower. Cross the creek and come to a picturesque 5-foot waterfall at 0.25 mile, where in times of high water there will be a small, but inviting pool in which to wade. At 0.3 mile, another small falls goes down a series of rock steps and slides across some smooth rocks in a fluid motion— and marks the point where the trail makes a sudden turn to the right and ascends.

The trail leading to the right at the top of the rise is the high-water route that should be used in case the lower pathway is flooded. Keep left, walking by the large leaves of yellow buckeye trees and looking at the lake through the vegetation. Turn left onto the paved campground road at 0.6 mile, but 100 feet later turn left again, through campsite

#14, and continue following the River View Trail along the shore of Bluestone Lake.

Be on the lookout for hooded mergansers floating in the narrow stretch of water between you and the small, cattail-lined island. The hooded may be the smallest of North America's mergansers, but they have one of the species' most distinctive characteristics. On the back of the male's head is a fan-shaped crest of black-tipped white feathers that may be raised and lowered. The female's crest is made up of light brown feathers that are not as densely packed as the male's. All mergansers are diving ducks that have tooth-like notches on their beaks, which are used to catch fish, frogs, and insects.

Avoid all trails rising to the right as you also try to avoid the stinging nettles closing in on the pathway. Pass by the swimming pool at 1.0 mile, and begin to rise, soon crossing the paved park road and ascending on switchbacks lined by lyre-leaved sage and some wonderfully large trees. Turn right onto the green-blazed Big Pine Trail at 1.5 miles, only to make a left onto the white-blazed Boundary Trail 250 feet later. Walk under towering oaks, steeply ascend toward the top of a knob, and level out at 1.9 miles, where the pathway follows a sidehill trail below the summit.

At 2.0 miles, begin a gradual descent into a pretty forest of many ferns and an occasional beech tree. This is the most isolated you will feel on the hike as the route continues to descend into a hollow devoid of human sounds, but alive with bird songs early in the morning.

Oftentimes we hikers get caught up in the movement of the trek and fail to appreciate the beauty of the forests we pass through. Stop, sit down, and open your eyes and ears to the wonders of the natural world. The trees towering dozens of feet above you began as small seeds and nuts less than an

Bluestone Lake

inch in diameter, while the ferns started out as spores not much larger than a speck of dust. The warblers and vireos that fill the woods with song were once nothing more than a liquid mass inside tiny eggshells. Laboring unseen, worms, ants, and insects work the soil that makes all life possible. Although seemingly commonplace, such things are tiny miracles that should not be overlooked or forgotten.

Resuming the hike, pass through Gib Lilly Hollow at 2.6 miles, where lush vegetation may overtake the trail. Cross a small stream rolling over boulders in miniature cascades, and begin to ascend, waking by an occasional comfrey plant, squawroot, or rattlesnake weed. Continue with a series of small ups and downs, passing by old fence lines in a woodland of locust, maple, poplar, and ash. At 3.4 miles, stay on the Boundary Trail when it comes in contact with the orange-blazed dirt bed of the Giles, Fayette, Kanawha Turnpike. Long abandoned, the road's construction was authorized by the Virginia Assembly in 1838, and it was used by nine-year-old Booker T. Washington (1856–1915) on his journey of freedom from close to Roanoke, Virginia, to Malden, West Virginia.

Walk past cabin #17 at 3.6 miles, following the paved road and soon keeping left at intersections where roads to the right lead to cabins #19–21 and #22–24, and #26. Just after passing the activities building (water and restrooms available when open) at 3.9 miles, turn left, and descend along the red-blazed Rhododendron Trail. Despite the steepness of the hillside, the pathway descends at a somewhat gradual rate. Cross the paved park road at 4.1 miles, and rock-hop Surveyors Creek, where box turtles are often seen and lush mosses completely cover boulders lining the waterway. Poison ivy also grows lushly.

Pass a small picnic area at 4.5 miles, turn right to rise along the paved boat launch road, and come to an intersection of roads at 4.75 miles. Take the one signed as leading to the campgrounds, and return to your car at 5.0 miles.

There is another excellent walk you should do before leaving this area. Drive back to WV20, turn left, follow it for several miles, and just before you would cross the river into Hinton, bear left onto WV26. Pass by the Brooks Falls area (with an approximately 2-mile trail that is also worth hiking) in another 4.0 miles, and pull into the Sandstone Falls parking area in an additional 4.0 miles. Spanning the New River, the falls are 1,500 feet wide and, divided by a number of islands, drop 10 to 25 feet.

A 1.0-mile circuit trail takes you across bridges and observation decks for a close-up view of the falls and an ambulation of the interesting Flatrock community environment around them. Plants include arrowhead, water willow, fringe tree, lizard's tail, and more than 50 different composite plants. Among the animals are great blue herons, kingfishers, mussels, hellgrammites, crayfish, mallards, bullfrogs, eastern river cooters, and other turtles.

32

New River Gorge

Total distance (circuit): 5.6 miles

Hiking time: 3 hours, 20 minutes

Vertical rise: 1,120 feet

Maps: USGS 7½' Fayetteville; Park Service handout map

The Hike at a Glance

0.6 cross Kaymoor Trail
0.8 end of Kaymoor Miner's Trail; retrace steps
1.0 left onto Kaymoor Trail
2.0 Craig Branch waterfall
3.1 right onto Craig Branch Trail
5.6 end

In the not-too-distant past, West Virginia's New River Gorge was known for two things: the spectacular view from Hawk's Nest State Park and the interminably twisting two-lane US60 that had to be negotiated to reach it. Woe unto you if you got behind a coal truck crawling uphill. Terror unto you if one came barreling downhill, inches from your back bumper.

The views and the trucks are still around, but the construction of four-lane US19 and the establishment of the New River Gorge National River changed the area's image. The gorge is now known for great rock climbing, BASE jumping from the country's longest single arch bridge (on the third Saturday in October), and arguably the country's best whitewater rafting down the New and Gauley Rivers. (This reminds me of a bad joke from my childhood: Do you know how the New and Gauley Rivers got their names? Well, many years ago some Native Americans were paddling up the Kanawha River when they came to a confluence and one of them shouted out: "Golly, a new river!")

What are often overlooked are the 80-plus miles of trails coursing the national river's 70,000 acres, and this is where I, your beneficent hiking guide, come in. I explored most of the routes and am going to direct you to two of the best (Hikes 32 and 33).

You should begin your first visit to the national river at the Canyon Rim Visitor Center (north of Fayetteville off US19) to obtain maps, brochures, and other information. Close by, the 2.5-mile Endless Wall Trail

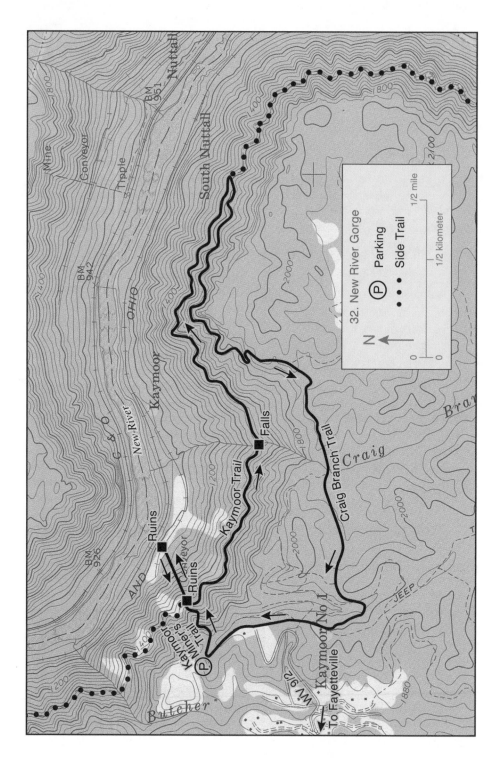

goes to spectacular views downward, and two short pathways lead to overlooks of the bridge spanning the 876-foot (at this point) deep gorge.

For a walk into the gorge, where coal mining was king in the late 1800s and early 1900s and thousands of people lived, drive to Fayetteville on US19. Follow WV16 through downtown Fayetteville, and turn left onto WV9 (Gatewood Road) in 0.6 mile. Continue for another 2.0 miles, make a left onto Kaymoor No. 1 Road (WV 9/2), and follow it to its end at the Park Service parking area in an additional 1.0 mile.

Be aware that this hike involves descending and ascending hundreds of stairs, which can be strenuous and taxing for those not used to such an activity.

Walk back up the road you drove in on for a few hundred feet, turn left, and descend along the Kaymoor Miner's Trail. The upper town of Kaymoor, of which there is little evidence, had more than 100 single-family dwellings and a population of more than 500. It was established in 1899, and in the 1950s people moved out. The trail follows the route of the Kaymoor Haulage, a 250-foot cable car that carried 15 people at a time down to the mine opening near the gorge floor.

At 0.4 mile, a 35-foot waterfall goes down a rock facing whose small steps churn the stream into whitewater. The hemlock trees and rhododendron growing beside it ensure the setting will have a greenish tint to it at any time of year. Old shacks and other reminders of an industry no longer here are scattered along the Kaymoor Trail that you cross at 0.6 mile.

Continue the descent, now on hundreds of steps. In some places you can see the tracks of the cable car directly underneath the staircase. Come to the end of the steps at 0.8 mile and walk into what may feel like a Tarzan "Lost City" setting. Cement blocks, tipple, valves, old equipment, and buildings have trees and vines growing over, and sometimes through, them.

Even though you are wandering around an old mining site, its present condition makes it hard to imagine just how much activity went on in the gorge. Just a few miles upstream is the town of Thurmond, located within a few feet of the river. During the coal boom days, it boasted opera houses, hotels, saloons, and more than 400 residents. More than a dozen passenger trains a day came through town, with the depot serving as many as 95,000 customers a year. Today, Thurmond has a population of fewer than 10, and the restored depot is a Park Service visitors center. (The movie *Matewan* was filmed here. Check out the video—it's an excellent portrayal of miners' struggles in the early 1900s.)

Walk back up steps and, at 1.0 mile, turn left onto the Kaymoor Trail, lined by jewelweed and mayapple. Look onto the ground after a rain and you may see efts wandering about. These little creatures are actually immature newts that, soon after being born in water, lose their gills, develop lungs, and forsake water for land. Spending the next several years as terrestrial beings, they forage for snails, worms, spiders, caterpillars, and other invertebrates. Upon reaching maturity, they become newts and return to water to live out their adult lives.

The waterfall to the right of the trail at 2.0 miles is Craig Branch dropping down the gorge to the river, visible hundreds of feet below through the vegetation. Enjoy the lush greenery of the hemlock trees—if they are still alive by the time you hike here. Having no resistance to the hemlock woolly adelgids, insects which suck the sap from the base of the trees' needles, eastern hemlocks have been dying at an alarming rate. Almost all the

New River Gorge

hemlocks in Virginia's Shenandoah National Park are dead, and some botanists predict a virtual elimination of the species in the not-too-distant future.

Be alert at 3.1 miles. You want to make a sudden switchback to the right to ascend the Craig Branch Trail, an intersecting roadway. (If you are here in wet weather, you may want to go straight for a couple of hundred feet to enjoy another waterfall before making this turn.) Tulip poplar blossoms cover the ground in mid-May as you make two switchbacks in quick succession with rock walls towering overhead.

A faint road comes in from the left at 4.1 miles. Stay on the main route, lined by blood-root in late March and early April. Because the plant must endure the cold temperatures of early spring, the bloodroot's leaves stay curled around the stems to conserve warmth, and do not fully expand until pollination occurs. Since insects so vital to the pollination process are scarce at this time of year, the flower—which usually only lasts two to four days—has developed the ability to produce copious amounts of pollen. This helps insure self-pollination if no insects happen by. To protect its reproductive parts, the flower closes up at night until pollination does occur.

Pass through a gate, walk by the trail-head, and return to your car at 5.6 miles.

33

Grandview

Total distance (round-trip): 3.6 miles
Hiking time: 2 hours
Vertical rise: 160 feet
Maps: USGS 7½' Prince; Park Service handout map

The Hike at a Glance

Grandview. Bona Vista. Buena Vista. With today's contractors usurping such romantic-sounding names, it is a good probability that there is a "Grandview" housing development somewhere close to where you live. This hike, however, is the real deal. Overlooks in the Grandview section of the New River Gorge National River treat visitors to some of the gorge's most spectacular vistas, and this outing, only moderate in difficulty, delivers you to each one.

Take exit 129 from I-64 (east of Beckley), drive on Grandview Road (WV9) for 4.7 miles, enter the national river area, and follow the road to the main overlook and visitors center in another 0.5 mile.

Leave your car in the upper parking lot, and walk onto the pathway signed as leading to the Main Overlook. After just a few seconds of walking, you are rewarded with a view from the national river's highest point. Standing at 2,500 feet above sea level, your eyes can take in 7 miles of the gorge, with the river flowing close to 1,100 feet below you. This vista is, by far, one of the most photographed scenes of the New River.

After enjoying the view, retrace your steps for about 100 feet and turn right onto the Castle Rock Trail, a winding footpath through a woodlands of rhododendron tunnels, green ferns, and mossy rocks. The Park Service does not recommend this trail for young children because of uneven footing and steep drop-offs. At 0.3 mile, walk below the very lip of the gorge, which is composed of rock walls that display layers of alum, sandstone, and coal. After only 0.5 mile of

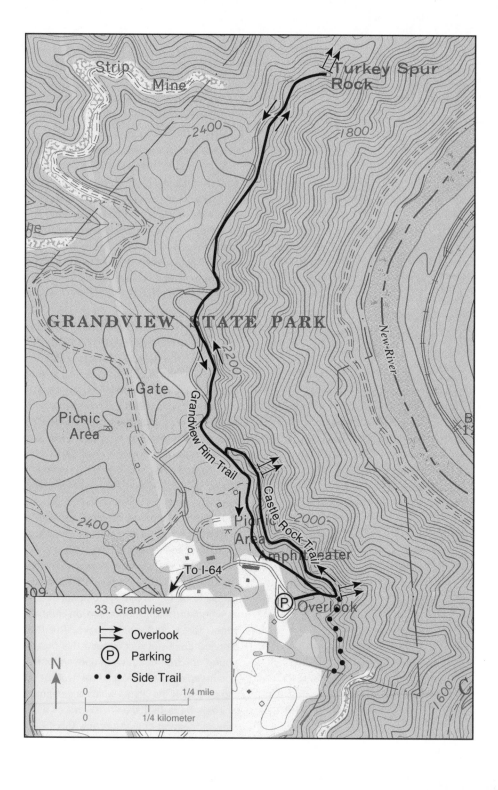

Strip Mine

2400

1800

GRANDVIEW STATE PARK

2200

New River

Gate

Picnic Area

Grandview Rim Trail

Castle Rock Trail

2000

2400

Picnic Area

Amphitheater

To I-64

P Overlook

B 1

109

Turkey Spur Rock

1600

C

33. Grandview

⇥→ Overlook

Ⓟ Parking

•••• Side Trail

N

0 _____ 1/4 mile
0 _____ 1/4 kilometer

hiking, you are treated to another view of the river, this one looking onto the waterway as it flows westward.

Rise and turn right onto the Grandview Rim Trail (formerly called Canyon Rim Trail) at 0.7 mile to begin paralleling the Turkey Spur Road and enjoying additional glimpses into the gorge. Pass through a rhododendron tunnel at 0.9 mile, and walk next to squawroot and hemlock trees. Be looking for fire pinks after descending steps and slabbing along the right side of a knoll at 1.5 miles. The unmistakable, richly scarlet, 1- to 2-inch flowers have five petals that are notched—sometimes deeply. Several may grow on thin stalks from the axils of the upper leaves. Because the plant has tiny hairs covered in a sticky substance along the length of its stem that capture ants and other insects and prevent them from reaching the flower's nectar, fire pink is sometimes commonly referred to as catch fly. Yet, the brilliant red of the flower is a natural attractant to hummingbirds, which are often seen flitting from plant to plant and enjoying drinks of the sweet juices by dipping their long beaks into the flowers' narrow tubes.

Continue across the parking lot at 1.7 miles, and ascend 150 steps, delivering you to three different observation platforms with nearly 360-degree views. From these you can look out upon the Stretcher's Neck Bend of the gorge and the towns of Quinnimont and Prince. Beside the steps is what the Park Service refers to as "nature's air conditioner," a cleft in the rock from which cool air rises.

Return to the parking lot, and retrace your steps along the Grandview Rim Trail to the intersection with the Castle Rock Trail at 2.9 miles. To walk a different route than the one you came in on, keep to the right on the Grandview Rim Trail, and ascend gradually. The forest is especially rich and diverse here,

with birch, oak, maple, fringe tree, flame azalea, teaberry, and Indian cucumber root being some of the most prominent plants.

Indian cucumber root is an intriguing-looking plant that rises on a single stem to a whorl of leaves about halfway up its length and continues on to a second whorl on top. The uppermost leaves can hide the small, dangling, yellow flower. However, it is such a comely little flower that you should stop for a few moments to give it a thorough examination. Lifting it onto your fingers, you will notice that the three long stigmas curve gracefully back over the entire flower and are tinged in a brownish red. The tiny stamens, which are close to the same color, stick straight out. Later in the year, the leaves add dashes of color to the forest understory by turning red and offsetting the dark purple hues of the plant's small berries.

Turn left onto the short trail at 3.1 miles to the North Overlook for a final grand view of the New River's horseshoe bend. Return to the main trail and continue on your way, bypassing the trail on the right that leads to picnic shelter #1 and returning to your car at 3.6 miles.

Do not drive away immediately if you are here in mid-May or early June. Just a short walk over to the far parking lot will take you to an occurrence that visitors to the Mount Rogers National Recreation Area in southern Virginia are willing to hike several miles of the Appalachian Trail to experience. Making one of the most colorful displays found anywhere in this area, the parking lot's middle island will be ablaze with thousands upon thousands of Catawba rhododendron blossoms. The light-pink-to-dark-pink-to-rich-purple flowers are about 2 inches across, are open bell-shaped, have five lobes, and grow in large and ornate clusters.

If you are here in winter, you can use the plant's leaves to determine the temperature.

New River Gorge from the Castle Rock Trail

In order to protect their soft undersides from the desiccating effects of cool breezes, the leaves begin to droop and curl under. The tighter the curl, the colder it is. When the leaves are wrapped around themselves to about the size of a choice cigar, the temperature is hovering around freezing; the diameter of a cheap cigar means that it is getting into the twenties and the teens. If you are out here when the leaves have become no larger than a cigarette, you better be wearing lots of layers–the temperature is mighty close to zero.

There is still one more reason to visit Grandview. For decades, Theatre West Virginia has been presenting two excellent outdoor musical dramas in the amphitheater during the summer months. *Honey in the Rock* is a dramatization of West Virginia's birth during the Civil War, and *Hatfields and McCoys* is an account of the state's most famous feud.

34

Twin Falls Resort State Park

Total distance (round-trip): 8.0 miles

Hiking time: 4 hours, 15 minutes

Vertical rise: 960 feet

Maps: USGS 7½' Mullens; park hand-out map

Of the resort state parks in West Virginia, Twin Falls is one of the least developed—and that is a good thing. The golf courses in the other parks occupy so much land that they can be intrusive, and their lodges and banquet facilities are so large that you may feel as if you are attending a convention with hundreds of other people instead of visiting a quiet place in the outdoors. The lodge at Twin Falls, perched upon a knoll with pleasant views, has only 20 rooms, so crowds are not a problem, and the 18-hole golf course is confined to the narrow Black Fork Valley.

However, the 3,776-acre park does not lack amenities. There is a full-service restaurant, a small café open seasonally, a gift shop, a swimming pool, game courts, and picnic areas. The campground has electric hook-ups, laundry facilities, and hot showers, while fully equipped cottages have fireplaces and electric heat to make them available for rent every month of the year. The staff at the nature center conducts educational activities and special programs year-round, and a small museum and the Pioneer Farm provide insight into the area's past. Also, located at 2,400 feet above sea level on the Allegheny Plateau, the park receives a significant amount of snow and is a favorite place for local cross-country skiers.

Hiking trails wind onto hillsides and into narrow hollows, and this outing takes you on two round-trip pathways leading to a couple of nice viewpoints and next to the two waterfalls for which the park is named. Compared to some of the high, crashing, roaring waterfalls found in other parts of the state,

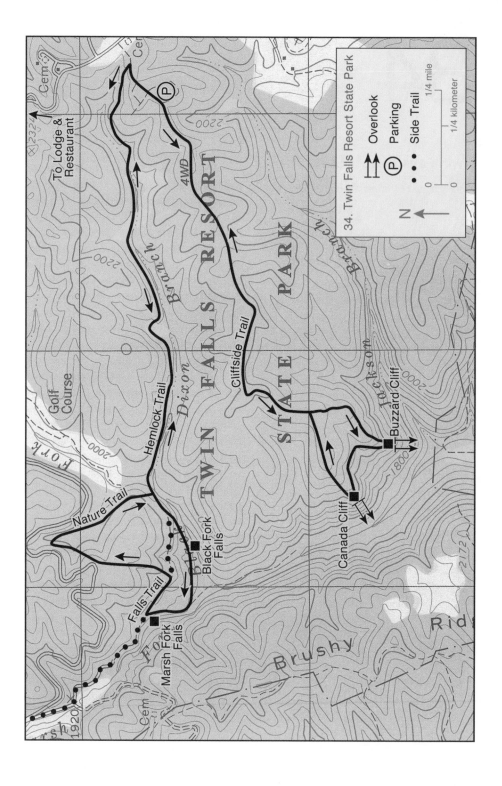

the twin falls are rather meek and mild, but their settings are just as attractive and fit in well with the understated atmosphere and beauty of the park. Also, remember: "It is the journey and not the destination that matters."

You will park your car in the middle of these two round-trip routes, so you could decide to do each on separate occasions if you don't have the time or inclination to do the entire outing all at once. All of the park's trails are well signed and marked.

Twin Falls Resort State Park may be reached by taking exit 42 from I-64/I-77 at Beckley and following WV16 South/WV97 West for 3.8 miles. Turn right onto WV54 South/WV97 West, go another 13.9 miles, turn right onto WV97 West, continue an additional 5.4 miles, turn left onto Bear Hole Road (marked with a Twin Falls sign), and enter the park several miles later. To reach the trailhead, follow signs to the campground, turn right onto the campground entrance road, and continue just past site #23 to a small parking lot on the right.

Walk around the gate and onto the red-blazed Cliffside Trail, a woods road through hemlock, beech, maple, hickory, and oak. Oaks make up close to 60 percent of all the trees growing in West Virginia and are found in nearly every environment except the highest elevations. All of the state's oaks are deciduous. The red oaks, with bristle-tipped leaf lobes and acorns that stay on the tree for two years before maturity, include the northern red, scarlet, pin, and black oaks. Among the white oaks, with rounded leaf lobes and acorns that mature in a year, are the chestnut, post, white, and chinkapin oaks.

Many birds are active only during the early morning and evening hours, but hikers walking past the dogwood trees lining the route at 0.3 mile are likely to hear the call of pileated woodpeckers during any daylight hour. The faint trail to the left at 0.5 mile is the abandoned Bear Wallow Trail, named for a water-filled, shallow depression in the forest floor that bears have used to cool off during the hot temperatures of summer.

With a wildlife clearing to the right at 0.9 mile, swing left and come to a Y-intersection at 1.1 miles. Bear left, descend, and pass through a rhododendron and mountain laurel tunnel with wintergreen berries forming little red dots on the ground.

Stay left again when you come to the next intersection at 1.4 miles, and descend less than 200 feet to Buzzard Cliff. The rocky promontory overlooks the narrow valleys of Jackson and Halsey Branches and out across a succession of ridgelines. If you are here near sunset, you may not only be treated to the pinkish glow spreading across the landscape but also to the yipping of a pack of coyotes emanating from the valley floor and echoing off the hillsides.

All of that barking, howling, and yipping serves a purpose. It is used as a vocal way to mark territory, keep family members in touch with each other, and communicate while on the hunt. Some observers say that, at times, coyotes appear to howl just for the fun of it or, like humans joining together in song, do it as a purely social activity.

Walk back to the previous intersection, and turn left onto a rough and rocky trail on a sloping hillside populated by galax, a plant not found as often on the Allegheny Plateau as it is in the Blue Ridge Mountains of Virginia. A left turn at the intersection at 1.6 miles takes you on a descent of less than 300 feet to Canada Cliff. It has somewhat the same view as Buzzard Cliff but is a bit more concentrated on Brushy Ridge across the narrow Cabin Creek Valley. If the streams are running high, and the wind blowing just right, you might hear the sound of the two falls you will be visiting later in the hike.

Return to the intersection, stay left, and

ascend steeply for several hundred feet. Having returned to the Y-intersection at 2.0 miles, bear left and retrace your steps, possibly catching sight of several deer or noticing the club moss you missed on the way out. Return to your automobile at 3.2 miles. If this is all the time you have, drive away with plans to do the rest of this outing another day. If not, take a short break and enjoy the snacks and drinks you had left stashed in the car.

When ready to resume, walk the paved road back out to the campground entrance, but be alert a few hundred feet later. Just behind the registration building, turn left onto the blue-blazed Hemlock Trail, a woods road descending by hemlocks, mayflowers, ferns, and club mosses. You may not even notice when you cross the headwaters of Dixon Branch because the small water run at 3.7 miles is often dry. The gas line right-of-way at 3.8 miles is the same one you stepped over earlier on the Cliffside Trail.

The narrow valley you are walking into has such a feeling of isolation that you may forget that the lodge and golf course are a short distance away. The wild turkeys often seen here add to this sense of being removed from the modern world. These birds came by their name in a roundabout way. It was originally used for African guinea fowl that had been imported into Europe from Turkey. When large birds started being shipped from America to Europe in the 1500s, they were often confused with the guinea fowl, so both came to be called turkeys—and the name has stuck ever since. Continue along the road with towering hemlocks providing shade and rhododendron plants making this a walk through greenery at any time of year.

Come to an intersection at 4.6 miles. Turn left and, although it may not seem like the trail, walk through a dry, rocky streambed before crossing the creek and coming to the intersection with the Falls Trail at 4.7 miles.

Bear left and follow that pathway's yellow blazes downstream, enjoying the small drops and riffles of the rhododendron-lined water. If you don't mind its steepness, take the trail to the left at 4.8 miles to the base of 15-foot Black Fork Falls.

If you don't take the trail to the left, continue on the main route, now following the course of an old railroad grade. When the grade widens into a road at 5.1 miles, notice that you are now following a different creek upstream. Just a few feet before you would walk onto a paved pathway, take the trail to the left to descend to Marsh Fork Falls (also known as Foley Falls for Marion Foley, who operated a mill nearby). The 12- to 15-foot falls are appealing enough, but what a grand swimming hole its basin pool is! Its deep water (in times of wet weather) beckons you to wade in, and a few flat rocks will allow you to relax and soak up the little bit of sun that makes it through the hemlocks and rhododendron.

Rise back to the main route, and make a hard right onto the pavement, which ends in just a few feet. Continue to follow the yellow blazes, but at 5.5 miles, turn onto the white-blazed Nature Trail and rise into a cool, hemlock-dominated forest. At 5.8 miles, swing right beside a parking lot, go a few feet, and reenter the woods, still following white blazes and descending into a more deciduous forest. The route you are following is another old railroad grade, evidenced by the indentations from the cross ties that are still visible.

Cross a small water run at 6.0 miles, swing right, and follow the rivulet downstream, soon walking on the paved golf cart track for a few feet before leaving it and staying to the right on the Nature Trail. The intersection with the Falls Trail at 6.4 miles should look familiar. Bear left, cross the creek, and renegotiate the rocky streambed of the Hem-

Buzzard Cliff Overlook

lock Trail. Come to another familiar intersection at 6.5 miles, turn right, and ascend, retracing your steps back to your car at 8.0 miles.

Other trails in the park include the 0.75-mile Buck Run Trail, the paved 0.25-mile Twin Oaks Trail, and the 1.3-mile Huckleberry Trail, which passes through Pioneer Farm. The 3.5-mile Poke Hollow Trail goes by the Tolliver Cemetery and into a number of forest types. The Still Run Ridge, Horsepen Knob, and Pathfinder Trails could be combined for a full afternoon's worth of hiking along steep terrain and old farmland.

35

Panther Wildlife Management Area

Total distance (circuit): 5.6 miles

Hiking time: 3 hours, 30 minutes

Vertical rise: 1,320 feet

Maps: USGS 7½' Panther; USGS 7½' Iaeger; state forest handout map

The Hike at a Glance

0.8	swimming hole
1.6	left onto ascending roadway
2.0	left at intersection
2.9	straight at four-way intersection
3.7	lookout tower
4.6	diagonally cross woods road
5.6	end

Unless you live in the area, Panther Wildlife Management Area is one of those you-really-have-to-want-to-get-there types of places. Located close to the very southernmost point of the state, it is far removed from any four-lane highways and takes a considerable investment in driving time to reach.

In fact, the entire region in which the wildlife management area is situated is a world apart. Isolated from the rest of West Virginia, things are still a little rough around the edges—and that is its allure. Malls and supersized discount stores are few and far between, large luxury resorts occupying thousands of acres are nonexistent, home-style cooking is what you will find in the restaurants, and mom-and-pop enterprises are the norm. The mountains are more rugged than those to the east, rising more in jumbles than in long ridgelines. This is West Virginia's coalfield, and while driving on the narrow roadways, you may often look into the rearview mirror to see the grill of an overloaded coal truck barreling down the mountain just inches from your back bumper.

Much of this may change. Four-lane highways have been proposed, and there are always ever-evolving plans for "economic development." The time to visit is now, before this place loses its rough edges, before roadsides are littered with fast-food restaurants instead of being bordered by modest homesteads. Visit now, before other folks learn of the charms of this place, and while you can still explore pathways in relative peace and quiet, rarely encountering another foot traveler.

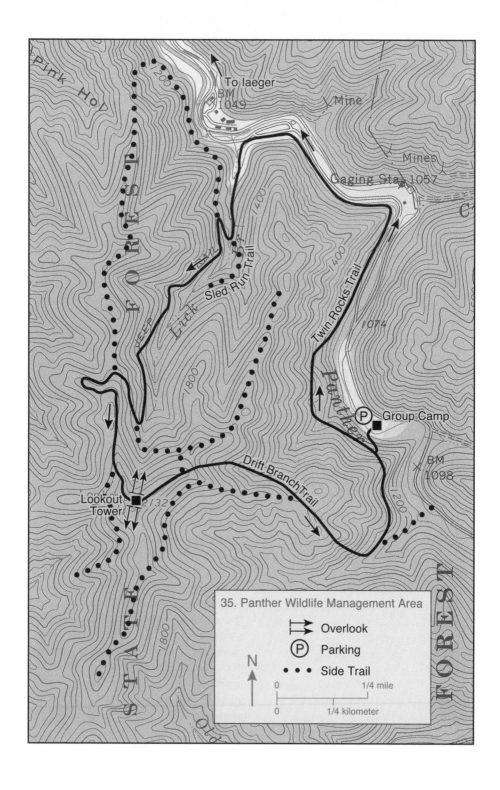

35. Panther Wildlife Management Area

⊢→ Overlook

Ⓟ Parking

••• Side Trail

N

0   1/4 mile

0   1/4 kilometer

Panther Wildlife Management Area's charms lie in the fact that it, too, is a little rough around the edges. This is not a place where you will be mollycoddled with a luxury lodge to stay in or have warm showers in a campground's heated bathhouse. There is no lodge, and the small campground and picnic area have only pit toilets.

Looking at it another way, this lack of overblown, unnatural attractions and facilities keeps away the large numbers of people who need such things in order to have a good time and ensures that the wildlife management area remains a relatively quiet place for those who enjoy the outdoors for its simple pleasures. (There is a swimming pool that is a favorite of local children on hot summer days.)

This circuit hike will take you to a lookout tower at the wildlife management area's highest point (2,065 feet) for a grandstand view into three states. Wildlife management areas are administered under the multiple-use philosophy, which means that the extraction of timber and other natural resources, such as gas, is permitted. Much of the hike follows the unsigned roads that were built for these activities, so you will have to pay attention to the directions given below to make sure which way to turn at each intersection. The hiking trails are signed but are not blazed.

Take exit 1 off I-64 at Bluefield and follow US52 West (watch for many twists and turns in town) for approximately 50 miles. A little more than 1.0 mile north of Iaeger, turn left onto Panther Road, go 6.7 miles, bear left at the Y-intersection, bear left again at the next intersection, and follow this road to the wildlife management area boundary. Another 2.8 miles will lead you to the second parking lot for the Group Camp.

Walk across the footbridge over Panther Creek, and turn left upstream through hem-

The view from the tower takes in three states.

locks and rhododendron and into a garden of wildflowers. Trillium, foamflower, showy orchis, jack-in-the-pulpit, black cohosh, wild geranium, and bloodroot will be with you on different parts of the hike. The showy orchis grows best in moist soils, so it will be one of the first flowers you see along the creek. Blooming from April through June, the ornate blossom is fertilized by bumblebees, which visit the flower to feast upon the abundant nectar found inside its tube. In addition, the spur of the lower lip contains a sweet syrup high in sugar content.

Within a couple of hundred feet of beginning the hike, swing right on the Twin Rocks Trail, rise onto the hillside, and, at 0.3 mile,

---

Panther Creek

bear right at an intersection (you will return via the pathway to the left). Walk under utility lines at 0.5 mile, and reenter the woods.

If you are the first person of the day to be walking here, you may become what Appalachian Trail thru-hikers have dubbed an *arachnidiot*—one who flails arms wildly at the hundreds of spider webs stretched across the trail. Wolf spiders are the largest and most common spiders in West Virginia. After the young emerge from the egg sac, they climb onto their mother's abdomen and are carried by her for quite some time. If the mother is killed, the young will scurry away, which gave rise to an old myth that a dead spider immediately produces hundreds of little spiders to take its place.

Descend along a woods road to return to the banks of Panther Creek at 0.7 mile. If you don't mind wading into the water in sight of the paved park road at 0.8 mile, there is a nice swimming hole at the bridge over the creek. Continue to follow the woods road, which is now a gravel service road. Pass by residences on both sides of the creek at 1.1 miles, and maintenance buildings and the forest office at 1.5 miles.

Be alert when you come to the Y-intersection at 1.6 miles. You want to turn left onto the less-used roadway that ascends past what was evidently a garbage dump. The guttural calls of ravens often accompany hikers as they gradually rise beside small Lick Branch. Look up and you may get to witness one of nature's most beautiful and acrobatic displays of flight. Ravens soar and glide like hawks, but they also fold their wings and dive for long distances like peregrine falcons. In addition, they execute barrel rolls and tumbles and drop objects to catch them in flight.

Do not take the Sled Run Trail that ascends to the left at 1.8 miles. (I came upon an eerie scene when I decided to take this pathway on one of my other visits here. It was early morning and the fog was still settled on the hillside when I came around the corner to the small family cemetery at the trail's end. I had been told the cemetery had not been used for decades, but there, barely discernible through the mist, was a large, plain pine casket sitting beside the gaping hole of an open grave.)

Continue to follow the road as it swings to the right. Coltsfoot is one of the first flowers to line the road in late winter and early spring; at 2.0 miles reach an intersection and bear left. Do not go left or right when you come to the four-way intersection at 2.9 miles. Continue straight, curve to the left 500 feet later, and continue to ascend. Cardinals, the state bird of West Virginia, are often seen flying from tree to tree along the road's edge. With their bright red plumage, they were named after the robes worn by the cardinals of the Catholic Church. Female cardinals are brown, with just a hint of red on their wings, tail, and head.

Avoid the road to the left at 3.0 miles, but stay to the left at the Y-intersection at 3.3 miles. You can go in either direction when you come to the loop road around the lookout tower at 3.7 miles. The steps of the tower are extremely steep and can be intimidating to those afraid of heights. However, you can still enjoy a 180-degree view to the east from the third landing, while the fourth opens up a partial view to the west. If you go all the way to the top, the vista includes the landscape in three states: West Virginia, Virginia, and Kentucky.

To continue the hike, take the route that descends behind the fire warden's cabin. However, be very alert at 3.9 miles (just about 600 feet from the tower), as the left turn onto the Drift Branch Trail can be easily missed. Soon begin a steep descent beside a utility line. Cross a dirt road at 4.1 miles,

The mist of a humid day is highlighted by the sun.

and continue to descend, with level stretches mixed in with steep ones and fire pink and tall meadow rue adding color to the forest.

Cross a woods road diagonally to the left at 4.6 miles, and soon enter a cool, deep, shaded draw, with stinging nettle closing in on the pathway. The pile of rocks in the small clearing to the right is all that remains of a log cabin that once stood next to Drift Branch. The antics of squirrels jumping from limb to ground and back again may entertain you in this woodlands of black gum, chestnut oak, and sourwood.

Turn left onto the Twin Rocks Trail (which may or may not be signed) and walk on the side of the hill; the route to the right descends to the park road. After having hiked 5.3 miles, you will have returned to the first intersection you encountered on the journey. Turn right and retrace your steps back to the Group Camp at 5.6 miles.

Be sure to make a stop at Pinnacle Rock State Park on the drive back to I-64. A parking lot on US52 gives you access to the 0.1-mile trail that leads to the towering rock structure and scenic views.

36

Carnifex Ferry Battlefield State Park

Total distance (circuit): 2.0 miles

Hiking time: 1 hour

Vertical rise: 220 feet

Maps: USGS 7½' Summersville Dam; park handout map

The Hike at a Glance

0.2	intersection with Pierson Hollow Trail
0.6	Pillow Rapids Overlook
1.0	picnic area
1.6	cross WV23
2.0	end

It became obvious during the early days of the Civil War that the western part of Virginia wanted to break away from the state and remain a part of the Union. In order to occupy territory and prevent this from happening, Confederate troops were sent into the area. The clash with Federal soldiers on July 3, 1861, at Phillipi is considered by many to be the first land battle of the war. Various other conflicts that occurred during the following months, in which the Confederates were kept out of the northern part of present-day West Virginia, set the stage for what would happen at Carnifex Ferry.

Land was traded back and forth between the two forces in the southern part of the region, with a former Virginia governor, Confederate Brigadier General John B. Floyd, establishing a camp on the Patterson farm overlooking Carnifex Ferry on the Gauley River. On September 10, 1861, soldiers under the command of Union Brigadier General William S. Rosencrans attacked the encamped southern troops. Although Confederate casualties were far fewer than those inflicted upon the opposing forces, Floyd decided to give in to superior numbers and retreated across the ferry during the night.

Western Virginia continued to experience skirmishes throughout the next few years, but the Union retained virtual control during the remainder of the war, ensuring the safety of delegates meeting in Wheeling and enabling the statehood movement to proceed without any serious threats.

Carnifex Ferry Battlefield State Park preserves 156 acres of land on which the battle

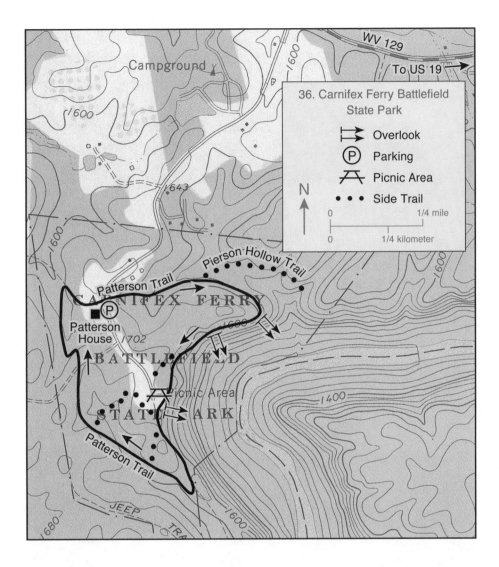

took place. A monument, gravesite, replica cannon, wooden fences, and a museum in the refurbished Patterson farmhouse help visitors recall earlier days. Established in the 1930s, the park is a day-use area with picnic shelters and facilities (open seasonally), game courts, softball field, and playground. There is no campground or backcountry camping permitted, but on the drive to the park, you will pass by a couple of Sum-

mersville Lake/U.S. Army Corps of Engineers and Gauley River National Recreation Area/National Park Service campgrounds.

The 2.0-mile Patterson Trail weaves in and out of forest and meadow and by several important battle sites. It traverses a moderate terrain, with just a few very short, steep sections, making it an ideal hike for children. There is enough variety to keep them interested—lots of deer, squirrels, and

Copperhead Overlook

rabbits; several impressive views of the Gauley River; and a small water run in which they can search for small aquatic creatures. The playground is located in the middle of the hike, so if the little ones lose interest, one adult can stay with them while they swing and slide and the rest of your group continues with the hike. If the kids get so tired that the entire trip has to be called off, your car will be parked just a few hundred feet from the playground.

Carnifex Ferry Battlefield State Park may be reached from the intersection of US19 and WV129, a few miles south of Summersville. Drive WV129 West, coming to an overlook of Summersville Lake in 1.2 miles, crossing Summersville Dam in another 1.3 miles, and turning left onto Carnifex Ferry Road (WV23) in an additional 2.7 miles. Enter the park 0.7 mile later, and continue to the Henry Patterson House parking lot on the right in another 0.2 mile.

Cross the paved park road, and descend into the woods on the Patterson Trail. If you are here in the spring, look for the holly tree's tiny white blossoms that develop into the rich red berries we are all familiar with around Christmas. The hollow you are walking into was the site of the mistaken killing of several Union soldiers by their own comrades as they came back from a mission at night.

The Pierson Hollow Trail that descends to the left into a cove forest at 0.2 mile comes to a dead end in a short distance. Once it is turned into a loop trail, which park plans call for, it will be more enticing to follow. For now, you want to keep right on the Patterson Trail to ascend through hemlock, poplar, maple, dogwood, and an abundance of ferns.

Do take the short trail to the left at 0.5 mile to the Copperhead Overlook for a grand view of the Gauley River twisting its way through the gorge hundreds of feet below.

Return to the main trail, and continue on your way, ascending on a pathway lined by mountain laurel and rhododendron. The Pillow Rapids Overlook provides another glance onto the river at 0.6 mile. Even from this far away, it is easy to see why it is considered one of the premier whitewater paddling rivers in the eastern United States.

The pathway to the right at 0.7 mile leads to the ball field. Stay left on the Patterson Trail, and come to another overlook of the river at 0.9 mile, where you begin circling around the picnic area. Walk along the left side of a picnic shelter at 1.0 mile, and descend along the road marked with a sign for Carnifex Ferry and Patterson Trail. This is the road that Floyd's men retreated upon after the battle. It goes just a bit more than a mile to the ferry site on the river, but you need to be alert at 1.1 miles.

Take your leave of the road and turn right onto a pathway to continue along the Patterson Trail into a forest of rhododendron, hemlock, and holly. The blossoms of the mountain laurel make their appearance at just about the time flame azalea flowers are withering away in mid-spring. Some observers have remarked that the latter's golden petals remind them of the glow that spreads across an Allegheny Mountain sky at sunset.

An unmarked trail at 1.2 miles (that some old park maps identify as the Nature Trail) leads right to the picnic area. Keep left, descend, parallel, and then cross a small water run. The trail to the right at 1.4 miles is another part of the old Nature Trail that leads to the picnic area. Stay to the left, and gradually ascend through groves of hemlocks that provide year-round shade. Walking through this peaceful scenery, it may be hard to imagine a deadly battle having taken place here, but the words of Confederate Captain

Robert Winn Snead paint a vivid picture of what it was like:

> Boom went the cannon of our enemy, the large balls whistling over our heads. Our men fell flat on the ground . . . then came a terrible shot of a shell, it burst and fell all around us. The bullets fell like rain whistling and whizzing over our heads and into the logs we lay behind.

Cross WV23 at 1.6 miles, and descend on a pathway lined by running cedar. The flame azalea puts on a great display in early May at a small footbridge that goes over a wet area at 1.7 miles. Ascend, switchback to the right, and return to the Patterson farmhouse at 2.0 miles.

Close by is the grave of Confederate soldier Granville Blevins. He did not die from a wound received during the battle but passed away from fever four days before the conflict took place. He was not alone in his fate. Nearly two-thirds of the soldiers who died during the Civil War did so from some kind of disease and not from battle.

A reenactment of the Carnifex Ferry Battle usually takes place in the park in September of odd-numbered years. Check with the park office to verify specific dates.

37

Cedar Creek State Park

Total distance (circuit): 2.2 miles
Hiking time: 1 hour, 15 minutes
Vertical rise: 580 feet
Maps: USGS 7½' Glenville; park hand-out map

The Hike at a Glance

0.6	attain the first knob
0.9	descend
1.4	cross WV17
1.8	walk by ponds
2.2	end

Cedar Creek State Park is situated in the western foothills of the Allegheny Mountains at what is, geographically, almost the center of the state. The highest point is only 1,448 feet, but that does not mean the hiking will be easy. The terrain is a jumbled mass of narrow valleys and twisting ridgelines that may only be reached by ascending steep hillsides dominated by oak and poplar trees. The lack of far-reaching views is more than compensated by the opportunity to walk pathways that appear to be rarely trod. On a gorgeous summer weekend when the campground was filled to capacity and every table in the picnic area occupied, I did not see one other hiker as I explored every trail in the park.

On the other hand, wildlife is abundant on the 2,483 acres. In the lower elevations and edges between field and forest, watch for rabbits, chipmunks, grouse, quail, and groundhogs. Raccoons, deer, opossum, squirrels, wild turkeys, and an occasional black bear are likely to be seen anywhere in the park. There is also a variety of butterflies, amphibians, and reptiles, and among the many birds that have been spotted are black and white warblers, American redstarts, Canada geese, northern parulas, yellow warblers, water thrushes, ovenbirds, prothonotary warblers, red-eyed vireos, and orchard orioles.

Recreational facilities within the park include picnic sites and shelters, game courts, miniature golf, a swimming pool, three trout-stocked fishing ponds, and paddleboat rentals. The campground (which is extremely popular) has electric hook-ups, hot showers,

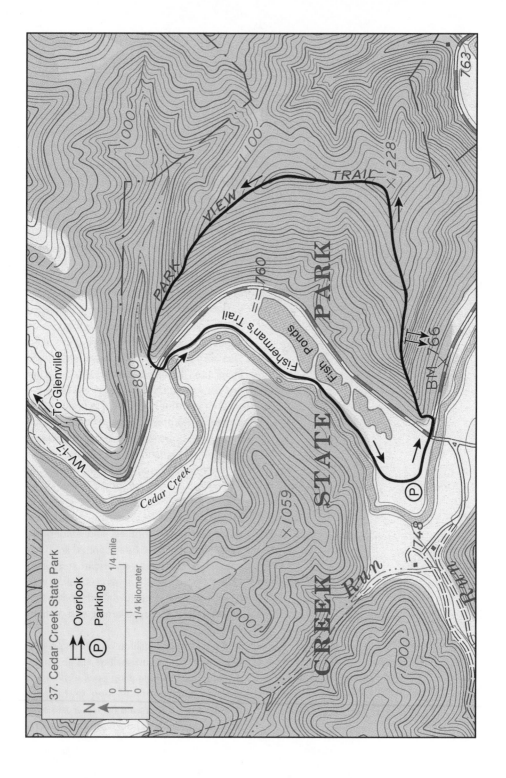

37. Cedar Creek State Park

▲ Overlook
Ⓟ Parking

0 1/4 mile
0 1/4 kilometer

N

WV-17

To Glenville

Cedar Creek

PARK VIEW TRAIL

Fisherman's Trail

Fish ponds

CEDAR CREEK STATE PARK

763

×·1228

760

800

× 1059

BM 766

748

Run

Run

1000

1100

1000

1000

laundry facilities, and a camp store, and nature and recreational programs are offered from Memorial Day to Labor Day.

A large percentage of the development in the park was done by workers employed by a number of federal and state social work programs. Sadly, most of these, including the Aid to the Dependent Children of the Unemployed, State Temporary Economic Program, and Emergency Employment Program, are no longer funded. Not only did the workers make many improvements in state and national parks and forests, but they also received needed paychecks and job skills. The entire country would be well served if programs such as this were revived.

The hike described here takes you onto a ridgeline and beside Cedar Creek so that you may experience most of the environments the park has to offer. Its variety and fairly short distance also make it a good choice for an outing with children. Just be sure the kids (and maybe even you) are up to tackling the first portion of the trip. It only lasts for a little more than 0.5 mile, but is it ever steep!

From the intersection of WV5 and US33/US119 in Glenville, drive southward on US33/US119 for 4.6 miles, turn left onto WV17 (Cedar Creek Road), and continue for another 4.2 miles, where you will turn right into the paved lot next to the park's fishing ponds.

Walk back to WV17, go past the park entrance, and onto the blue-blazed Park View Trail. Because this path immediately ascends at such a steep grade, very few people hike on it, making the foot tread barely discernible in places. A rock outcrop at 0.4 mile will provide a view onto Cedar Creek valley—if the vegetation has recently been cut back.

Attain a knob at 0.6 mile, swing left, descend, and climb to another high point at 0.8 mile, walking amid some wonderful, old, burled, and gnarly oak trees. A chance to watch the squirrels go about their daily lives is a good excuse to sit down and recover from gaining this elevation so quickly.

A squirrel's long, luxuriously furred tail, which makes up half its body length, serves a plethora of purposes. On hot days, the tail is curled over the back and head as a sunshade and is used as an umbrella on rainy days. It wraps around the body like a warm blanket when temperatures drop. The tail helps balance the squirrel when the animal is climbing trees, running along branches, and jumping from limb to limb. It also acts as a rudder to enable quick changes in direction. These tree-dwelling creatures, especially red squirrels, are territorial, and males will fluff out their tails when two of them are vying for dominion over the same area or a female. What may be most outstanding is that the tail can be used as a parachute. Many observers have seen squirrels fall from great heights but land unharmed because their fanned-out tails greatly reduced the rate of descent.

Descend steeply at 0.9 mile, watching for the blue blazes, as the trail may be hard to locate among downed limbs and fallen trees. Come to WV17 at 1.4 miles, where you may see a groundhog feasting on roadside vegetation or a variety of birds searching for insects or berries to nibble upon.

Like the squirrels' tails, birds' feathers are remarkable things. The fluffy down feathers are the ones closest to the body and trap air to form an insulating layer. Body feathers not only add warmth but have also evolved into bright colors and shapes used during courtship rituals. Tail feathers are used for balance while on the ground or for steering while in flight. Interestingly, a bird's wings are covered with the fewest feathers. The long, outer wing feathers are usually narrower on their leading edges, a design that produces

Cedar Creek State Park fishing pond

lift as the feather slices through the air. Inner wing feathers point away from the wind, not across it, and help smooth the flow of air.

Cross the road, walk to Cedar Creek, and turn left upstream onto the Fisherman's Trail. This is a decidedly different environment than what you had been walking through on the ridgeline. Opulent patches of poison ivy make up a large part of the heavy undergrowth, and sycamore trees grow in the moist soil beside the creek. Even in a densely packed, mixed forest you can easily spot the sycamores by the gleaming white bark on their upper portions. If conditions are right, a sycamore can live for centuries and can have the largest trunk diameter of any hardwood tree in the eastern part of the country. In earlier days, its hollow trunks provided homes for the now-extinct Carolina paroquet, the only member of the parrot family native to the United States.

You will probably no longer be alone when the pathway takes you by the park's three fishing ponds at 1.8 miles. Anglers will be casting for trout, white bass, and catfish, and families will be laughing and joking as they move about on paddleboats.

The ponds were constructed in the 1960s on land that had been used for agricultural purposes, but they wouldn't hold water because of the loamy soil. In order to keep the water from seeping into the ground, a large plastic sheet covered with clay was placed at the bottom of each pond. What engineers had not anticipated was that the natural decomposition of gases under the plastic sheet resulted in it rising to the surface and falling back down again as the gas bubble escaped. It was such an interesting—and entertaining—sight that crowds of visitors came out on weekends just to watch it happen.

Turn left when you come to the ball field, walk by the park office, and return to your car at 2.2 miles.

On a historical note, it is believed that the log cabin that currently serves as the campground check-in office was originally built in nearby Troy around the turn of the 20th century. What is known for sure is that it was moved to Glenville in 1928, and served as a gas station for 54 years, before being moved once more in 1982, to be rebuilt in the park. Also on park grounds is a reconstructed one-room schoolhouse authentically furnished with a potbellied stove, student desks, and inkwells. Guided tours are offered on Saturdays during the summer season.

An additional hiking opportunity in the park is the network of trails that emanates from the campground. The Two Run, North Boundary, and Stone Trough Trails can be combined for several more hours of woods walking.

38

Stonewall Resort State Park

Total distance (round-trip): 1.9 miles

Hiking time: 1 hour

Vertical rise: 140 feet

Maps: USGS 7½' Roanoke; park hand-out map

The Hike at a Glance

0.3 left at intersection
0.8 right at loop trail intersection
1.0 right at loop trail intersection
1.9 end

If any state park ever deserved having the word *resort* in its official name, this is it. Within its 2,000-plus acres are a sprawling, huge, 198-room lodge; lakeside cottages; three restaurants; a golf course designed by Arnold Palmer; indoor and outdoor pools; a fitness center; bicycle rentals; and spa complete with massage therapy, facial treatments, body therapies, and sundeck. There is also a marina with close to 400 slips and a bait shop, with fishing boat, pontoon boat, houseboat, and kayak rentals. The campground has full hook-ups, hot showers, and a playground.

Named for the famous Civil War Confederate general who was born nearby, Stonewall Jackson Lake was completed in the mid-1980s, when the West Fork River was dammed for the purposes of flood protection, water quality control and supply, and recreation. The park was created soon afterward, and there are a number of aspects that are still under development. There is an entrance fee, which is a rare thing in the West Virginia state park system and hopefully not a harbinger of fees being imposed at other places. As is to be expected for a place on the edge of a 2,650-acre lake, the emphasis is on water activities, but a few trails have been built to let you explore the land.

An excellent way to spend a day here would be to rise early enough to take the described hike out to its farthest point to watch the sun rise over the lake, go to the lodge for a leisurely lunch, spend the afternoon watching for ospreys as you kayak along the edge of the lake, and spend the evening swimming in the pool, or–better yet–having a full massage. The hike is so short and on such easy terrain that small children should have little trouble doing it.

The park is conveniently located a short distance from I-79. Take exit 91 (a few miles south of Weston), drive US19 South for 2.7 miles, and turn left into the park. To reach the beginning of this hike, follow the main route (bypassing all turnoffs to the marina, golf course, and lodge) for 1.7 miles, and leave your car in the small turnout on the left, just before the road curves right toward the lakeside cottages.

Start by rising onto the Autumn Laurel Brooke Trail for just a few feet and following a sidehill trail beside maple and buckeye trees. Although the large, shiny, brown nuts of the buckeye are attractive, and for some reason satisfying to hold in the hand, they should never be eaten. They contain a toxin, esculin (some sources spell it aesculin), that destroys red blood cells. Effects of poisoning include vomiting, stupor, twitching, paralysis, and in some cases–most often involving children–death. Yet, while on a visit in 1784 to Colonel Morgan Morgan in what is now West Virginia's Northern Panhandle, George Washington was so impressed with a variety of the tree that produces red-to-purple flowers that he gathered a number of its seeds and planted them at Mount Vernon.

In a younger forest with smaller trees, come to an intersection at 0.3 mile, and swing to the left. The trail to the right leads to the lakeside cottages. At 0.4 mile, rise steeply for less than 50 feet. Views of the lake soon appear through the vegetation, while deer tracks may make indentations in the soft dirt of the trail, and box turtles are often seen meandering into the undergrowth. There is no mistaking this reptile because, of all the turtles in the United States, this is

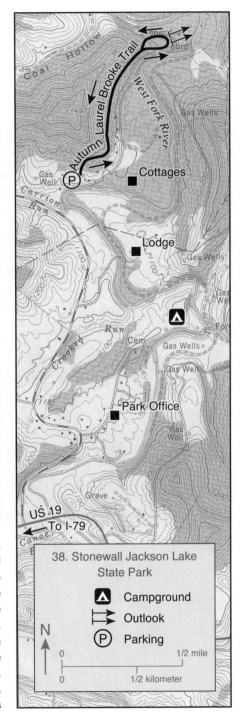

Stonewall Jackson Lake

the only one able to "box" itself in completely by closing its shell. Of the more than three dozen species of reptile that exist in West Virginia, at least 14 are turtles, 5 are lizards and skinks, and 22 are snakes. Reptiles and amphibians are often mentioned together because both are cold-blooded vertebrates. The reptiles can be distinguished from the amphibians by their body scales and claws, which are absent on the amphibians (except for some tropical and subtropical species).

Come to a loop trail intersection at 0.8 mile. Stay right and follow the pathway around a finger of land jutting into the lake. This is the best point on the hike to look out upon the water, so take a break, sit down, and think about this huge lake you are walking next to. Located at 1,073 feet above sea level, it is 26 miles long, has 82 miles of shoreline, and is 68 feet deep. Remember, where you are standing now was once a ridgeline overlooking the West Fork River's narrow valley.

Evidence of beavers having once inhabited this land can still be seen from the old chew marks on the ironwood and other trees. Ironwood has also been commonly called musclewood tree, a reference to the sinewy, muscled look of its trunk and bark. Except for dogwood, it is the hardest wood in the forest, much harder than hickory, locust, oak, or ash. It escapes the lumbermen's purview because it rarely grows more than 30 feet high and its trunk almost never becomes more than a foot thick. Being an understory species, it provides shade to wildflowers and mosses, and its nuts are a favorite food of pheasants, rabbits, deer, and other woodland creatures. In his book *A Natural History of Trees of Eastern and Central North America* Donald Culross Peattie states "Everything about this little tree is at once serviceable and self-effacing. Such members of any society are easily overlooked, but well worth knowing."

Return to the loop trail intersection at 1.0 mile. Stay right and retrace your steps back to your automobile at 1.9 miles. It's time to grab some lunch, after which you can rent a kayak and head out onto the water, knowing that a full-body massage in the evening will take away any aches and pains that may result from the day's activity—and you could spend tomorrow walking the park's other trails. The 0.5-mile (one way) Overlook Trail wanders through an old-growth field to a view of the lake and marina, while the 3.5-mile (one way) Hevener's Orchard Trail passes through mature timber, open fields, and an early succession forest.

39

Lewis Wetzel Wildlife Management Area

Total distance (circuit): 3.5 miles

Hiking time: 2 hours, 15 minutes

Vertical rise: 800 feet

Maps: USGS 7½' Center Point; USGS 7½' Folsom; WMA handout map

The Hike at a Glance

0.9	*left onto High Knob Trail*
2.0	*left onto Lesin Run Trail*
3.3	*left onto road*
3.5	*end*

With 51 of them spread throughout the state, state wildlife management areas (WMAs) are probably West Virginia's most often overlooked parcels of public back-country lands. (An additional federal 30 WMAs are located on national forest land in the state.) Except during hunting season (usually late October through early January and again in early spring), when it might be best to avoid them, many of the areas can go for weeks on end without anyone visiting their inner reaches.

While state parks were primarily established to provide outdoor recreation and state forests founded for silviculture, wildlife management areas were created with the emphasis on protecting and harvesting game animals. Habitats for waterfowl, white-tailed deer, ruffed grouse, fish, rabbits, squirrels, and others are often artificially created and maintained.

Within the last few decades, many people have come to view these areas as also places of conservation for nongame species and areas of recreation for the general public. In many ways, WMAs can't be beat if you are looking for a primitive experience and few crowds. Amenities such as picnic areas, restrooms, and the like are usually nonexistent, and trails are sometimes nothing more than informal, unmarked pathways created by the footsteps of occasional hunters.

In an area of the state where large tracts of public land available for outdoor recreation are somewhat slight, 12,448-acre Lewis Wetzel Wildlife Management Area provides the opportunity to enjoy the beauty

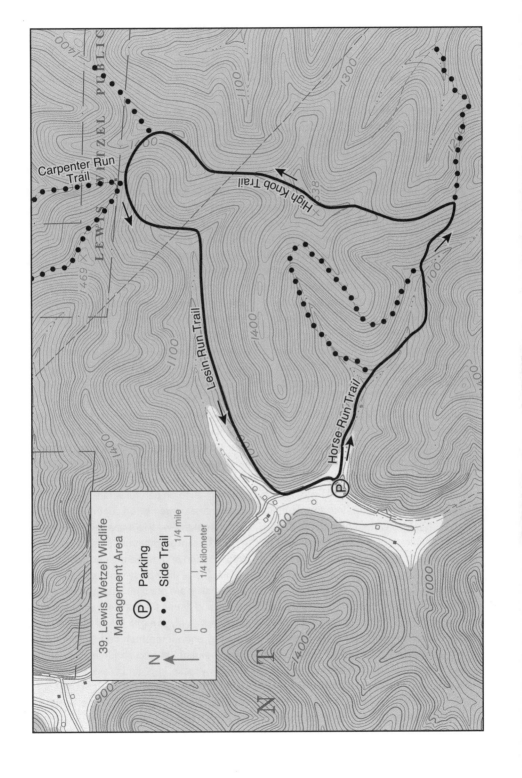

Carpenter Run
Trail

High Knob Trail

Lesin Run Trail

Horse Run Trail

LEWIS WETZEL PUBLIC

1400

1300

1100

1100

1200

1400

1400

1100

1200

1400

1100

900

1000

1000

1400

900

N
T

N

39. Lewis Wetzel Wildlife
Management Area

P Parking
•••• Side Trail

0   1/4 mile
0   1/4 kilometer

of foothills located on the western edge of the Allegheny Plateau and along the eastern reaches of the Ohio Valley. The rugged terrain ranges in elevation from 736 feet to 1,560 feet. Wildlife includes squirrels, ruffed grouse, deer, turkeys, raccoons, mink, muskrats, foxes, groundhogs, coyotes, black bear, skunks, opossums, and rabbits. Local people maintain that rattlesnakes are especially numerous.

As with most of the state's WMAs, the forest road-and-trail system is rarely maintained, routes are not blazed, and intersections may not be signed. It is suggested that you save this outing until you have a fair amount of outdoor experience and are comfortable with the feeling of not knowing exactly where you may be at any given moment. With this in mind, the wildlife management area can provide one of the most primitive hiking experiences you will find. Backcountry camping is not permitted; a small campground with pit toilets is located near the beginning of the hike.

Take exit 125 off I-79 (a few miles north of Clarksburg), and follow signs to WV131 North, which you will turn left onto in 0.4 mile. Make another left onto US19 in an additional 6.5 miles, turn right onto WV20 in less than 1.0 mile more, and follow that route for nearly 29 miles to turn left onto Buffalo Run (WV82). Soon after entering the WMA, come to an intersection, where you want to turn left toward the campground. The small trailhead parking turnout is 1.1 miles later, just before you would enter the campground.

The wildlife management area is named for one of West Virginia's earliest citizens, whose skill as a hunter and marksman have drawn comparisons to Daniel Boone and Simon Kenton. Lewis Wetzel's fame was such that numerous songs and stories were written to tell of his exploits. After one of his brothers was killed by Native Americans in 1777, he gained another reputation. Depending on which source you read, he became "a defender of the feeble settlers" or a ruthless "killer of Indians with only vengeance on his mind."

Start the hike by following the Horse Run Trail around the gate and onto the woods road across the paved road from the pullout area. (Make sure you take the road that is gated and not the one that parallels Meathouse Run along the edge of the campground.) The open meadows fade away as you ascend into a mixed hardwood forest and come to a Y-intersection at 0.3 mile. A fainter road rises steeply to the left; stay right, soon climbing steeply and overlooking a pretty stream hollow. Be alert at 0.6 mile. Just after dropping to a low point, you will come to another Y-intersection. Stay to the right, and resume the steep climb, which becomes even more so after you pass a gas well at 0.7 mile.

Attain the ridgeline at 0.9 mile, and turn left onto the unsigned High Knob Trail. (To avoid descending the other side of the mountain, do not continue straight.) Maple and oak are dominant on this undulating ridgeline, where you are likely to see numerous deer and turkey tracks in the mud of the pathway. Also be careful where you step, for rattlesnakes are often seen here and throughout the wildlife management area.

Snakes are ectothermic, meaning they are cold blooded and derive their body heat from the air. Since their body temperature fluctuates, snakes are dormant through most of the winter, and during the hot weather of summer often move only at night. It is at this time that you may encounter them during the day, as they seek shelter and shade and might be hidden by rocks, logs, and thick undergrowth.

At 1.2 miles, reach the top of the knob, which provides a good view of the surrounding jumble of mountains when the leaves are

Along the Horse Run Trail

off the trees. During the warmer months, a flash of brilliant color may go zipping by you. Wintering in the tropics during the cold weather months, scarlet tanagers return to breed in the eastern United States in spring. There is almost no mistaking the male for some other bird at this time of year. Its body is covered by rich scarlet feathers, while the tail and wings are a deep black. In late summer and early fall, the red feathers are replaced with dull green ones, which remain all winter. The female is green throughout the year, with just a hint of black on her wings.

Come to a faint intersection at 1.3 miles, where you want keep to the left and descend steeply past black cohosh, which will be blooming if you are hiking during the summer. Also commonly called fairy candles, the plant has tall spikes of tiny white flowers whose small petals fall off soon after opening, leaving behind fluffy masses of tiny pistil and stamens. Another common name is bugbane, given for its unpleasant odor said to be repellent to insects.

Be sure to pass by any faint trails or roadways so that you will ascend to the top of a second knob on the main ridgeline at 1.8 miles, but be very alert at 2.0 miles! You need to turn left and descend onto the unsigned Lesin Run Trail. Depending on recent foot (and unauthorized ATV) traffic, this route may appear to be heavily traveled or only faintly discernible. Either way, it will become an obvious woods road within a few hundred feet.

Be very alert again at 2.2 miles. Just as you come into a gap, there is a trail to the right that drops along Carpenter Run. You want to take what might be the less obvious route descending to the left. The rate of descent soon moderates when you begin walking beside Lesin Run. Cross the creek and one of its tributaries at 2.5 miles, continuing downstream and bypassing any intersecting routes.

The trail and the creek become one at several points, and just about the time you might think you have taken the wrong route, you emerge from the woods and turn left onto the campground road at 3.3 miles. If you arrive here around dusk, you might get to watch bats make amazing aerial acrobatic moves as they snare insect after insect.

Of the 13 species of bats that have been confirmed in West Virginia, the little brown myotis, eastern pipistrelle, and red bat have been seen in the wildlife management area. With close to 1,000 species worldwide, bats make up one out of every four species of mammals. Ranging in size from the Kitti's hog-nosed bat, weighing less than an ounce, to the flying fox bat, with a wingspan of more than 6 feet, bats feed on fruit, pollen, nectar, frogs, fish, mammals, and even blood, but the diet of all of the state's bats is exclusively insects. In fact, you might want to shout a word of thanks to them: It is estimated that a single little brown myotis will consume more than 500 mosquitoes per hour, or more than 2,000 during the course of one night's feeding.

The hike is over when you return to your car at 3.5 miles.

40

Cooper's Rock State Forest

Total distance (circuit): 8.9 miles

Hiking time: 5 hours

Vertical rise: 980 feet

Maps: USGS 7½' Lake Lynn; state forest handout map

The view into the Cheat River Canyon is so spectacular and breathtaking that it consistently draws hundreds of people into Cooper's Rock State Forest every week throughout the year. Locals bring visiting friends to see it, travelers routinely pull off I-68 to stretch legs and gaze into the geological wonder, and the outing has almost become a rite of passage for freshmen students from nearby West Virginia University. After having come here once and discovering all that the state forest has to offer, a large percentage of people return here time and again to walk, hike, mountain bike, birdwatch, rock-climb, cross-country ski, fish, and hunt. The campground (electric hookups and hot showers) and picnic areas have playgrounds for the kids, making the facilities popular with families—so this state forest fills up quickly on nice weekends.

Iron ore played a large role in the early history of this area. An abundance of limestone and low-grade iron ore was discovered in the late 1700s, and for the next 100 years, furnaces dotted the countryside. Vast amounts of timber were cut and turned into charcoal to feed the furnaces' voracious appetites. As coal began to replace charcoal for fuel, and large deposits of ore were discovered in the Great Lakes region, the industry faded away and was replaced by logging for the next half century. Reminders of these days, when natural-resource extraction was the primary use of the land, can still be found, and many of the old road and railroad grades are now part of the state forest's trail system.

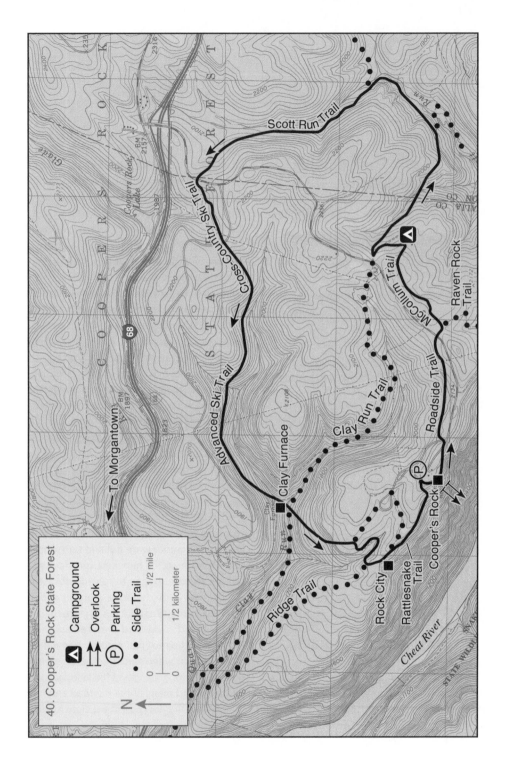

Scott Run Trail

Cross-Country Ski Trail

Advanced Ski Trail

McCollum Trail

Raven Rock Trail

Roadside Trail

Clay Furnace

Clay Run Trail

To Morgantown

68

Clay Furnace

Ridge Trail

Rock City

Rattlesnake Trail

Cooper's Rock

Cheat River

40. Cooper's Rock State Forest

Campground
Overlook
Parking
Side Trail

1/2 mile
1/2 kilometer

0
0

N

The initial plot of land for the state forest was acquired in 1936, with workers from the Civilian Conservation Corps building many facilities and structures while camped here from 1936 to 1942. Now the largest state forest in West Virginia, Cooper's Rock State Forest's 12,713 acres are bisected by I-68, with the area north of the interstate being used, in cooperation with the West Virginia University Division of Forestry, as a place for timber management, forestry research, teaching, and demonstration. Although there are hiking trails wandering throughout this area, most of the recreational opportunities are concentrated on the land south of the interstate.

From the intersection of I-79 and I-68 at Morgantown, follow I-68 East for 15 miles, take exit 15, turn southward on WV73/16, enter the state forest, and follow the road for 3.0 miles to its end.

Leave the car in the parking area, walk toward the concession stand, and turn left onto the Overlook Trail. The temperature will drop a few degrees as you enter the deeply shaded hemlock and great rhododendron forest. West Virginia's official state flower, the great rhododendron has white petals and usually blooms in June, about a month later than the pink-to-purple blossoms of the Catawba rhododendron.

At 0.1 mile, turn right onto the wooden bridge taking you over the cleft and onto Cooper's Rock for soaring views into the canyon and of the Cheat River flowing hundreds of feet below. Portions of Morgantown may be seen to the west. The view of the New River from Hawks Nest State Park in the southern part of West Virginia may get better press coverage, but this vista is equally awe-inspiring. A local legend says the state forest and rock you are standing upon were named for a convict who hid out in the rugged area around the overlook. Although

a fugitive from the law, he was a cooper by trade and continued to make barrels, which he sold in the communities nearby.

Return to the trail, turn right, and take the paved route for a few feet past rhododendron and mountain laurel. When the pavement ends at a picnic shelter, stay to the right on the footpath, and come into another parking lot, where you need to turn right along the main forest road you drove in on.

At 0.4 mile, turn left onto the first paved road you come to, but be alert less than 300 feet later, as you want to turn right onto the (possibly) unsigned Roadside Trail, and reenter the woods. (This route can be identified by the post of an underground phone cable next to it.) A road pullout is just to the right of the trail at 0.75 mile. Stay on the pathway as striped maple becomes part of the forest understory, pass under utility lines at 0.9 mile, and walk along the edge of a wildlife clearing bordered by some wonderfully large spruce trees at 1.0 mile.

The male catkins of these evergreens emanate from the leaf axils and grow in stamens that are arranged spirally. The shorter female flowers grow from the ends of the twigs. The cones, which always hang down, have thin, leathery, wooden scales with thinner, papery scales between them.

Cross the paved forest road at 1.1 miles, walk around a gate, and follow the Raven Rock Trail. Less than 300 feet later, that pathway goes off to the right. You want to stay left along the dirt road. However, be alert at 1.3 miles, as you need to turn left onto the McCollum Trail signed as leading to the campground (it may or may not be orange-blazed). Although it rarely encroaches on the trail, greenbrier is abundant and grows up and over much of the surrounding vegetation. The plant is easy to identify, as it is the only woody vine in the eastern United

Cooper's Rock Overlook

States with both thorns and tendrils—those thin, twisted things growing from the base of each leaf that look like roots and which the plant uses to attach itself to whatever it grows upon.

At 1.5 miles, swing to the right of a knob, whose summit is accentuated by huge boulders and luxuriant patches of hay-scented ferns. You will be next to the campground registration building (soda machines and rest rooms) when you break out of the woods at 1.9 miles. Turn left onto the paved campground road, but just before arriving at the main forest road, turn right at 2.2 miles and reenter the woods on the yellow-blazed Scott Run Trail, an old logging road.

A footbridge takes the route across a stream at 2.6 miles, and as the terrain rises, abundant laurel blossoms make this a very pretty walk during late May and into June. Be alert at 3.0 miles. The Scott Run Trail, which you want to follow, makes a sudden left turn off the woods road you have been walking along. (The white-blazed road continues across Scott Run.) Cross a tributary at 3.2 miles, and walk next to Scott Run, which at this point is a small stream. Yet, it is still deep enough to provide some nice pools in which to cool your feet while listening to the Woody Woodpecker—like calls of pileated woodpeckers and looking at the tiny partridgeberry flowers, in bloom from late June through early July.

Walk over three more footbridges. By the time you cross the final one at 4.4 miles, Scott Run is not much more than a trickle. Soon swing to the left and, if you have a sharp eye, you might see blue-eyed grass growing next to the trail. Members of the iris family, about a dozen species of blue-eyed grass grow in eastern North America. About the only thing separating one from the other are leaf length and branching patterns, but all have delicately small flowers with golden stamens. Most have blue petals, but some blossoms are yellow, making identification even more complicated.

Cross the main forest road diagonally to the right at 4.8 miles, walk to the far end of the day-use parking area (pit toilets), and reenter the woods at 5.0 miles on the Cross-Country Ski Trail. Gradually rise, taking care to not let your legs brush against the stinging nettle that hangs across the trail. The route swings right at 5.1 miles and slabs the hillside on the former route of a rail line. Slowly healing pits and depressions in the earth are evidence of old charcoal hearths and iron ore mines that furnished materials for the nearby Clay Furnace while it operated during the mid-1800s.

Pass under utility lines at 5.3 miles, cross a paved forest road, and reenter the woods on the Intermediate Ski Trail. At 5.4 miles, stay right on the Advanced Ski Trail signed as leading to the Henry Clay Furnace, and gradually descend, looking into the Right Fork of Clay Run Valley. Avoid the trail descending to the left at 5.75 miles; stay to the right along the hillside and cross a footbridge over a small water run at 6.3 miles. This may be the quietest part of the hike, as the interstate traffic noise has faded away and few people come this way.

Standing above it on the trail at 7.0 miles, the Clay Furnace looks like a Mayan ruin in the jungles of Mexico. Ferns grow out of its sides, while bushes and small trees top its crown. (This may not be the case when you get here if plans to clean and stabilize the furnace are carried out.) Built in the 1830s, this was a cold blast furnace that produced pig iron, which was transported by rail to the Cheat River. In its heyday, the furnace employed about 200 people and was the focal point of the town built up around it—although you would be hard pressed to find any evidence of the town's existence today.

After studying the furnace, cross the footbridges over Clay and Right Fork of Clay Runs, and come to an intersection. The route bearing off to the left, the blue-blazed Clay Run Trail, goes about 2.0 miles to the campground. You want to keep to the right, but in a few feet avoid another trail going off to the right, and stay left on the route signed as leading to Rock City. Ascend more steeply than you have so far.

The intersection at 7.6 miles may not be signed, but you want to bear right, follow a couple of switchbacks uphill, turn left onto a woods road, and come to another intersection at 7.9 miles. The white-blazed Ridge Trail goes to the right; keep left to go toward Rock City, staying on the main route when passing well-worn trails that branch off it. Swing to the right around a huge picnic shelter at 8.1 miles, and come to the sign pointing to Rock City. Go in here and play. I have not included any mileage along this route, as you could wander around for a long time among these large rock formations that are somewhat reminiscent of the slot canyons in America's Southwest. If you let yourself go and be a kid again, this can be the highlight of the hike. I have seen entire families spend hours in here, traversing narrow corridors and climbing in and out of small caves that lead to other passageways.

When done with this fun activity, return to the picnic shelter. Turn right onto the blue-blazed Rattlesnake Trail, which has its own version of Rock City, as you wander below tall cliffs, into narrow clefts, and over huge boulders—all the while walking along the lip of the canyon. Watch for the blue blazes, as the route can become confusing at times. Be alert at 8.7 miles. You need to make a hard left onto a trail that may not be identified by blazes, ascend, make a right, and come to the final intersection of the journey at 8.8 miles. Take the route that will lead you to the concession stand and your car, finishing the trip at 8.9 miles. It's time to study the state forest map again; there are at least 30 more miles of trails to be explored here.

41

Oglebay Park

Total distance (round-trip): 3.9 miles

Hiking time: 2 hours, 15 minutes

Vertical rise: 420 feet

Maps: USGS 7½' Wheeling

The Hike at a Glance

0.5	Schenk Lake
0.9	begin following Habitat Discovery Loop Trail
1.05	left onto the Falls Vista Trail
1.25	Oglebay Falls
1.5	left onto Hardwood Ridge Trail
2.3	loop trail intersection and Hardwood Falls Overlook; retrace steps to Schenk Lake
3.4	Schenk Lake
3.9	end

In the 1920s, Earl W. Oglebay willed his 700-acre summer estate of "splendid drives, magnificent shade trees, beautiful gardens, lawns, and rolling meadows" to the citizens of Wheeling for "as long as the people shall operate it for purposes of public education and recreation." Since then, Oglebay Park has become one of the top tourist attractions in West Virginia, with more than 3.5 million visitors annually and, according to the City of Wheeling, is the only major self-sustaining public park system in America.

One of the things that makes Oglebay Park so much more than the usual municipal parks—which often bring to mind a small area with a few sports fields, several picnic tables, possibly an exercise trail, and a couple of pit toilets—is its size. New York's Central Park has only 843 acres, and the City Park of New Orleans encompasses 1,500 acres, while additions to Mr. Oglebay's gift have brought Oglebay Park, now at 1,650 acres, the distinction of being one of the largest municipal parks in the country.

Yet, size alone is not enough to draw people to a place. Perched atop the low knolls and rolling terrain of West Virginia's Northern Panhandle, Oglebay is attractive to visitors because its many facilities appeal to a wide range of people. History and art lovers can wander through the Carriage House Glass Museum—with more than 3,000 pieces of Wheeling glass—or take in the period-decorated Mansion Museum. Those who have trouble pulling themselves away from malls have seven distinct shops to browse in. Golf addicts can tee off on a choice of

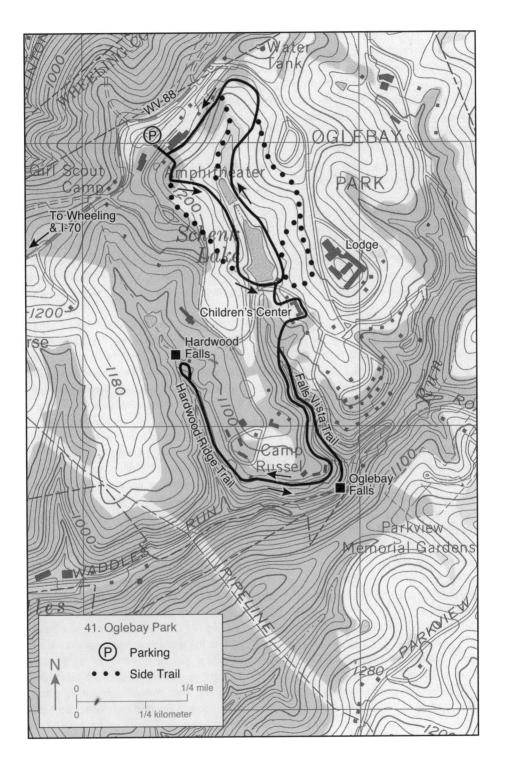

41. Oglebay Park

Ⓟ Parking

•••• Side Trail

N

0   1/4 mile

0   1/4 kilometer

courses, equestrians may participate in guided trail rides, and gourmands have given the Ihlenfeld Dining Room, with a panoramic view of the manicured grounds, a number of awards for its presentations of regional specialties. Birdwatchers have open spaces and forested lands in which to pursue their hobby, and wildflower lovers can seek out the more than 180 species of blossoms that have been identified in the park.

With the ambience of a mountain inn, Wilson Lodge has more than 200 guest rooms, with indoor pool, fitness center, and massage therapy. For those wanting a place of their own, close to 50 fully equipped cottages can accommodate 12 to 15 people. (There are no camping facilities, but a commercial campground is located next to I-70, about 10 miles east of Wheeling.) Other attractions include miniature golf, fishing, pedal boat rentals, playgrounds, picnic areas, tennis courts, and a heated outdoor pool. Of the many special events, the Winter Festival of Lights, which covers more than 300 acres, is the country's largest light show and attracts more than one million visitors.

Oglebay's forte is how well it can introduce small children to the natural world. Playgrounds and picnic areas are located next to many different environments, so the kids will see and experience a variety of plants and animals; the 30-acre Good Zoo features exotic species that don't live in West Virginia; and the Benedum Planetarium opens young eyes to the wonders of the night sky. The $2 million Schrader Environmental Education Center has a number of excellent displays, a hands-on children's area, and a staff eager to pass on its knowledge. Seasonal day camps provide a fun and educational time in the outdoors.

The best way to experience all the park has to offer is to walk its network of pathways. To allow you to take in as much as possible, this hike follows both the paved trails that wind through the developed areas of the park and the dirt routes that explore the park's undisturbed forest and dead-end at small, but pretty waterfalls. If your idea of hiking does not include pavement, you could bypass the first part of this outing by parking, and starting and ending the hike, at the environmental education center. Doing so would shorten the trip by about 1.5 miles.

Oglebay Park may be reached from exit 2A off I-70 in Wheeling. Drive US40 East for 0.5 mile, turn left onto WV88 North, and continue for another 2.6 miles. Turn right into the park at the first sign, make an immediate left, go an additional 0.2 mile, and leave your car at the fountain to the right of the visitors center.

Begin the hike by going by the fountain with its hanging flower baskets, descending the steps, and turning right on the red brick pathway for a view of the surrounding hillsides and the park's small fishing pond. The 16-acre Bissonnette Gardens you are walking through are a re-creation of those that existed on the Oglebay estate near the turn of the 20th century. In spring there will be daffodils, hyacinths, tulips, and pansies. Fuschias, begonias, impatiens, petunias, and geraniums will delight the eyes in the warmer months, and fall brings forth thousands of chrysanthemum blossoms.

Turn left to descend the concrete and grass steps beside a small flower and vegetable garden, turn right at the first paved pathway, walk by the amphitheater, and follow the route as it bends to the left and descends. At 0.2 mile, take the first paved path to the left, and almost immediately turn right and walk beside the fishing pond. (If you get confused by all these twists and turns, just head downhill and you will end up at the pond.) Beyond the pond, come to a Y-intersection at 0.5 mile, go left, walk beside

Arbor and fountain near the visitor center

Schenk Lake, and come to the boat-rental house, where you want to walk through the small tunnel and into a playground of swings and slides.

After having passed those delights of childhood and the miniature golf course at 0.75 mile, turn left and ascend (do not go down the steps to the right) to the environmental education center (where restrooms and water are available). Go behind the building, at 0.9 mile enter the woods on the Habitat Discovery Loop Trail, soon passing a small amphitheater, and come to an intersection at 1.0 mile. Cross the footbridge, ascend steps, and come to an intersection in less than 300 feet. Swing left onto the Falls Vista Trail, and descend beside the foot-high waterfalls of the small Schenk Run. The little gorge you are in becomes deeper as the pathway continues, with hemlocks adding shade to the already sunlight-challenged terrain.

However, thousands of jewelweed plants thrive in the small places where there are breaks in the forest canopy. Folk medicine has long held that the juice from the jewelweed's succulent stem, which can grow to 5 feet in height, will help relieve the itch of poison ivy. Other common names for the plant include snapweed and touch-me-not (in reference to its seed pods, which pop open when touched), speckled jewels, and weather cock. It has also been called silverweed and shining grass because the bottom part of its leaf will become shiny (or silvery) after being exposed to water.

Just before you would emerge onto Waddles Run Road at 1.25 miles, walk onto the observation platform to look upon Oglebay Falls, which drops about 10 feet over two shelves of rock and into a crescent-shaped basin.

When ready to continue, retrace your steps along the Falls Vista Trail, and return

Oglebay Park

235

to the intersection at 1.5 miles, where you will turn left and walk along the wide bed of the Hardwood Ridge Trail. The observation deck at 1.6 miles overlooks the gorge you just walked out of and presents a rare opportunity. Built upon the lip of the gorge, it is located at the same height as the upper branches of the tree canopy. Instead of looking up, as you usually do, at the life that takes place here, you are on the same level with it. You may now have a close-up look at squirrels running from branch to branch, woodpeckers feeding upon insects, or the hollowed-out home of an owl.

Continuing along the trail, take the steps that descend to the left at 1.7 miles, but avoid the route that descends to the left less than 300 feet later. (It dead-ends in a few hundred feet.) A second set of descending steps at 1.9 miles brings you into a woodlands dominated by sugar maples, the official state tree of West Virginia.

In the spring, the sugar that the tree produced through photosynthesis last summer and stored in the root system begins to rise through the cambium to give leaf buds the energy needed to open and grow. Native Americans taught early settlers how to tap sugar maple trees and harvest the rising sap. An average-sized tree yields approximately 20 to 25 gallons of sap; it takes about 40 gallons of the liquid to make just 1 gallon of maple syrup.

Continuing along the way, another set of steps will return you to the main trail, where a pathway comes in from the left at 2.2 miles. Stay right, and come to another intersection just a few hundred feet later. Beyond this is a short loop trail, so it does not matter if you go left or right.

Can that really be a wolf you hear howling? Can that also be mixed with the chattering of monkeys and maybe the low growl of a black bear? Yes, you may really be hearing those sounds—the Good Zoo is just a few yards up the hill from where you are hiking.

A wooden observation platform overlooks small Hardwood Falls, which drops only a few feet over rocks and may be dry in late summer. Return to the loop trail intersection, retrace your steps to the Hardwood Ridge/ Falls View Trails intersection at 3.1 miles, bear left, cross the footbridge over Schenk Run, and turn left again. Stay left one more time at 3.2 miles, when you come to the route that will take you past the miniature golf course, through the playground, and out of the small tunnel, where you will go by the boat-rental house on the right side of Schenk Lake at 3.4 miles.

To walk a different route than the one you came in on, take the paved trail to the right at the head of the lake at 3.5 miles and ascend. About 200 feet later, stay right again, walking on the right side of the fishing pond. At the head of the pond, bear right along a tree-lined lane, ascending by small tributaries of the pond and lake, and soon enjoy the expanse of the park's manicured slopes. Owls, woodpeckers, ovenbirds, and vireos may have been your companions in the forest, but it may be a sparrow, cardinal, bluebird, or robin that you see in this open area.

Stay right when you come to the next intersection at 3.8 miles. About 200 feet later, turn left along a very gradually ascending route, but less than 300 feet after that make a right, then another right to ascend the first set of steps you walked down on this hike, and return to your car at 3.9 miles.

42

Tomlinson Run State Park

Total distance (circuit): 6.2 miles

Hiking time: 3 hours, 20 minutes

Vertical rise: 800 feet

Maps: USGS 7½' East Liverpool South, OH/WV/PA; park handout map

The Hike at a Glance

0.0	begin on the Laurel Trail
0.9	right onto the White Oak Trail
1.75	end of White Oak Trail
2.5	right onto Laurel Trail
3.5	ford Tomlinson Run
4.0	begin following Beech Trail
4.8	right onto main park road
5.0	left onto another road
5.3	left onto Maple Trail
6.2	end

This is it. This is as far north as you can go to hike on public land in West Virginia and still be in the state. In fact, Tomlinson Run State Park is farther north than Pittsburgh, Pennsylvania and is on the same latitude as Staten Island, New York.

The 1,398-acre park is administratively divided into two areas. Within the larger Activity Area are picnic sites and shelters, a playground, courts for various sports, and miniature golf. Tomlinson Run Lake (rowboat and paddleboat rentals are available during the season) and three smaller fishing ponds attract anglers, while the swimming pool with its 182-foot, figure-eight water slide is popular with children. The campground has electric hook-ups, a dump station, a camp store, laundry facilities, and bathhouses with hot showers.

The focus of the smaller Wilderness Area is Tomlinson Run, which flows to the northwest and empties into the Ohio River less than a mile from the park's boundary. Although it is an easy-moving river, it has carved a gorge into the rolling landscape, whose elevation ranges from 700 feet to 1,200 feet above sea level. During the 1800s, several mills were built along its length to take advantage of the power created by a drop of 100 feet per mile. The forest vegetation that covers this area today appears to be so healthy and profuse that it may be hard to believe that the land had been abused by coal mining, clear-cut timbering, and unsound agricultural practices before it was purchased for the state park in the early 1900s. It is a lesson in what nature

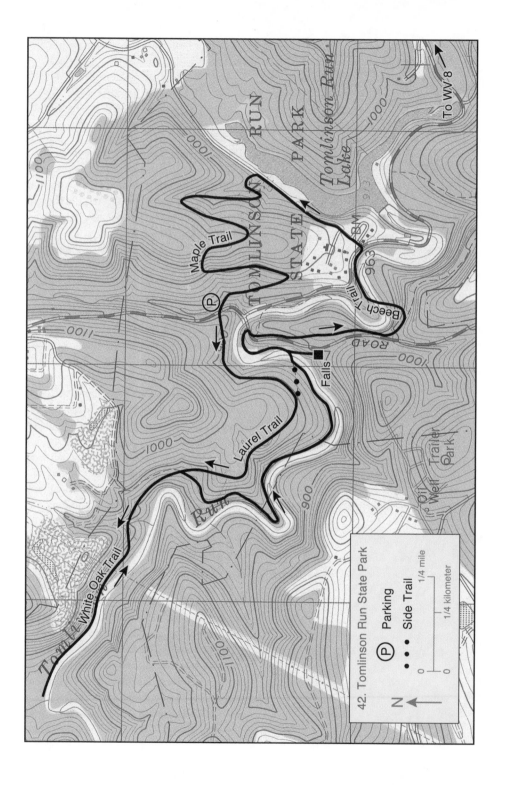

42. Tomlinson Run State Park

Ⓟ Parking

• • • Side Trail

1/4 mile

1/4 kilometer

N

is capable of doing if left alone and permitted to work its magic.

This hike takes you into both areas of the park and consists of two loops. Since your car will be parked in the middle, you could decide to do the loops on two separate occasions if you don't have the time or inclination to do the entire outing all at once. All of the pathways are blazed and signed at trailheads, but you will need to employ one of the most basic elements of backcountry travel—fording a stream—twice. Except in times of very high water, they are easy crossings and good practice for when you may face wider and/or deeper stream crossings.

Animals you may possibly see include deer, turkeys, foxes, beavers, raccoons, squirrels, chipmunks, and rabbits. The flora is just as diverse, with aster, hawkweed, trillium, Solomon's seal, mayflower, violet, goldenrod, club mosses, and hay-scented, sensitive, and other ferns growing in open areas and under the leaf canopy of hickory, maple, beech, hemlock, and locust trees.

The trailhead may be reached from the intersection of WV2 and WV8 just north of New Cumberland. Follow WV8 for almost 4 miles, turn left into the park, and continue for another 2.0 miles to a T-intersection. Turn right onto WV3 (Washing School Road, identified on some maps as Washington Road), and pull into the small parking area on the right in just 0.1 mile.

Cross the road and rise on the blue-blazed Laurel Trail into a woodland of oak, wild cherry, ash, and black birch. Thickets of great rhododendron make up the understory, with mayapple covering the forest floor in early spring. After this short ascent, the trail levels out and runs along shale and sandstone cliffs on the bluff high above Tomlinson Run.

The route coming in from the left at 0.4 mile is another portion of the Laurel Trail.

Stay to the right, and bear right again 200 feet later, where a fainter route comes in from the left and rattlesnake weed rises from the ground. You are walking high above Tomlinson Run, but you can hear it flowing several hundred feet below.

The intersection at 0.9 mile may be unsigned, but this is where Laurel Trail swings left and loops around on itself. You will go that way shortly, but for now, stay to the right on the route you have been following, which becomes the white-blazed White Oak Trail. Within a few feet, you may begin to notice the rock retaining walls on the left side of the road. They were built in the 1930s when this route was the main road through the area. The skill and expertise of the craftsmen who built them is evident in the fact that they still stand, despite being constructed without the use of mortar. The same is true of the rock culvert through which a side stream passes at 1.2 miles. It is still doing its job many decades after it was built.

Descend gradually to walk close to pretty Tomlinson Run, whose opposite bank is a mossy rock cliff undercut by the erosive power of the water. At 1.5 miles is a nice wading pool under the shade of big-leafed sycamore trees. Large rocks are the ideal platforms from which to dangle your feet in the water and watch dragonflies zip close to the surface or observe the many insects visiting the cow parsnips along the bank. Also growing along roadsides; in open meadows, neglected fields, and wastelands; and on the moist ground often found at higher elevations, cow parsnip is one of the largest of the wildflower plants to be found in West Virginia. Not only does it sometimes attain a height of 9–10 feet, it is not unusual for its flower umbels to be close to 12 inches in diameter.

The White Oak Trail officially ends at 1.75 miles, where you come to the confluence of

Built in the 1930s and still doing the job

Tomlinson and White Oak Runs. (You could swing right and follow White Oak Run for 0.2 mile before coming to private property.) It is time to turn around and retrace your steps to the intersection with the Laurel Trail at 2.5 miles. Bear right and descend to Tomlinson Run. Its small cascades, the cliffs rising above you, the quiet of the forest, and one heck of a grand swimming hole at 2.7 miles make this possibly the prettiest spot of the hike.

The trail soon becomes a rough and narrow footpath working its way through rhododendron tunnels, below cliffs, and next to an area of abundant ferns, witch hazel, wild hydrangea, and spicebush. Be alert at 3.0 miles. A fainter trail ascends to the left—you want to stay to the right along the stream, where there is one of the largest colonies of jack-in-the-pulpit that you may ever see.

Be alert again at 3.5 miles. A pathway switchbacks to the left to rejoin the upper portion of the Laurel Trail. You need to keep right and ford Tomlinson Run. It usually involves more than a rock hop but is almost never deep. Just before walking into the Scout Camping Area, make a switchback to the right for a side excursion along an unsigned, but well-used trail. It comes to an end when it overlooks a pretty waterfall in an area where you just would not expect to find one.

Return to the Scout Camping Area, walk through it, and come to WV3 at 4.0 miles. If you have used up your allotted hiking time, or are tired, you can make a left turn and walk 700 feet to your car, saving the rest of this journey for another day.

To continue the hike, cross the pavement and rise along the yellow-blazed Beech Trail. Like the Laurel Trail, this route begins by running along the edge of the escarpment over Tomlinson Run. Wild cherry trees grow above the ferns lining both sides of the trail

as it swings away from the stream. Turn left along WV3 at 4.4 miles, but be alert, as you want to turn left back into the woods less than 300 feet later. Be sure you get back onto the Beech Trail, which runs level for a bit, and not the old road that begins to ascend where it intersects WV3.

Descend into an evergreen grove, ford Tomlinson Run, and ascend. Do not take the faint woods trail to the left; rather, stay to the right, ascend steeply, and turn right onto the paved park road at 4.8 miles. At 5.0 miles, bear left onto the first paved road you come to, avoiding the next paved road to the left a few hundred feet later. As you walk beside 28-acre Tomlinson Run Lake, don't get so distracted by watching people fish for bass, catfish, trout, and bluegill that you forget to be alert at 5.3 miles. Just after passing the boat ramp turnoff on the right of the road, make a sudden left turn, and ascend into the woods on the light green-blazed Maple Trail.

Where you see a thick ground cover of star moss beside the pathway, ascend to the ridgeline at 5.6 miles. The increased amount of sunlight that makes it through the youngest forest you have been in since the beginning of the hike has permitted the sassafras trees to attain proportions usually not seen even in older woodlands. Its leaves may be one of three different shapes—three lobes, two lobes resembling a mitten, or a single lobe. Only one or all three types may be present on any given tree. The sassafras is one of the first trees to change color in the fall, when its leaves become gloriously bright shades of yellow and/or orange, and are sometimes almost pink splotched by small dots of scarlet red. Its dark blue fruits attached to red stalks bring additional hues to the autumnal woods.

Come to a T-intersection at 5.7 miles, descend via switchbacks, and return to your car at 6.2 miles. Other trails in the park, which cover easier terrain, provide additional hiking opportunities.

It doesn't have anything to do with hiking, but for an interesting detour before leaving this area you could take a tour of the Homer Laughlin Factory in nearby Newell. The factory gained nationwide fame in the mid-20th century with its bright, colorful art deco dishes known as Fiestaware, which is currently experiencing a resurgence in popularity.

Western West Virginia

43

Chief Logan State Park

Total distance (circuit): 5.6 miles

Hiking time: 3 hours, 30 minutes

Vertical rise: 1,240 feet

Maps: USGS 7½' Chapmanville; park handout map

The Hike at a Glance

0.7	*views through the vegetation*
2.9	*left onto the Interpretive Nature Trail*
3.8	*left onto the Buffalo Trail*
5.1	*left onto the Cliff Trail*
5.8	*end*

Save this outing for that perfect spring day when the sky is a rich blue and the temperature is cool enough that you don't perspire while hiking, but warm enough that you won't shiver when you take a break. It is at this time of year that the 4,000 acres of Chief Logan State Park become a veritable garden of wildflowers. There are so many species, ranging from the delicate Dutchman's breeches to the 9-foot-tall cow parsnip, that even the most casual of wildflower enthusiasts could spend hours studying and enjoying them. Of particular interest is the Guyandotte beauty, a rare member of the mint family.

Located in the coalfields of southwestern West Virginia, the state park offers a restaurant, campground (with hook-ups and hot showers), picnic areas and shelters, game courts, miniature golf, horseback riding, and a swimming pool with a water slide.

The trailhead may be reached from the intersection of US119 and WV119/90 (Old Logan Road) about midway between Logan and Chapmanville. Follow WV119/90 for 2.0 miles, where it becomes WV10. Continue for an additional 3.0 miles, turn right into the park, and leave your car in the park office parking lot on the right in another 0.3 mile.

Ascend into the woods on the Cliffside Trail, but make a right onto the Backbone Trail in less than 200 feet. Within a few more feet, a steep uphill climb begins along a woods road lined by pawpaw trees. The pawpaw's triangular flowers are green when they first open, but turn to deep red and brown as they grow. Some people say they have a fragrance akin to wine. The 4- to 5-

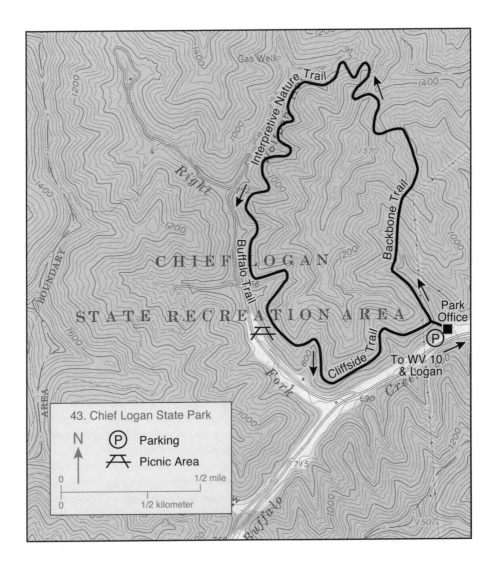

43. Chief Logan State Park

N

(P) Parking

🎪 Picnic Area

0 — 1/2 mile

0 — 1/2 kilometer

inch fruit, which resembles a short, fat banana, follows the same pattern. At first green, it ripens to a purple-brown. Its meat, with the consistency of an overripe banana, was a food source for rural families and is still considered something of a delicacy by many people.

At 0.25 mile, level out for a short distance in an open forest overlooking Bills Branch Hollow. Guyandotte beauty, which blooms in May and June, grows both in the middle and along the edges of the road. The 1-inch flowers, which spring from the axils of the leaves on the upper part of the foot-long stem, are some of the prettiest in the forest. The upper lip is a yellowish white, while the lower lip, with three tiny lobes, has lavender lines running along its length. Although the flower is found from Illinois to Alabama, it never grows in any great numbers and is listed as rare, threatened, or endangered in every state where it occurs. Consider yourself lucky if you see it, as Chief Logan State Park is one of the few places that Guyandotte beauty grows in West Virginia.

Continue the steep ascent, making a couple of switchbacks in quick succession and, starting at about 0.7 mile, passing by breaks in the vegetation that provide views of the jumble of mountains that make up southern West Virginia. Cow parsnip thrives in the sunlight of the forest canopy openings, and baneberry, celandine poppy, and blue cohosh join the floral procession, as you descend for a bit at 1.2 miles and walk along the left side of the ridge. If you were to return here later in the summer, the poppy would still be blooming beside black cohosh and tall meadow rue.

The small, half-inch, starry flowers of the blue cohosh (which can range from a yellowish green to a purplish brown) have six pointed sepals, six hooded glandlike petals, six stamens, and a single pistil. Being so small, they become conspicuous only because they grow in branched clusters. The stamens and pistil mature at different rates, ensuring cross-pollination, while the petals have large nectar glands to attract the bees of early spring. The plant is usually at its most noticeable later in the year when it is adorned by pairs of what appear to be dark blue grapes. These are, in actuality, the seeds that have grown through the fruit wall.

Be alert when you come to the Y-intersection at 1.6 miles. Bear left, and descend into a slightly different environment, where Virginia bluebells, wild ginger, hepatica, and Dutchman's breeches become some of the more dominant flowers and bits of the lake become visible through the vegetation.

By far one of the most enjoyable flowers to come across while hiking, the fragrant Dutchman's breeches favors rocky hillsides (usually the north slope, such as the one you are on), rich woods, and stream banks. Its perfume and unique shape are natural attractants to bumblebees and honeybees. Even though these insects are the main instruments of cross-fertilization for the flower, some are not justly rewarded for their work. The feet of the honeybees pick up the pollen, but their short tongues are unable to reach the nectar. It is believed, however, that the longer proboscis of the bumblebee enables it to enjoy the flower's sweet juices.

With Guyandotte beauty still growing along the route at 2.6 miles, swing around a wide hollow with a spring flowing just below the road. (It may not be running in dry weather.) Be alert at 2.9 miles. You want to make a left turn onto the red-blazed Interpretive Nature Trail, which may be unsigned. (The road you have been following continues straight past a gas well.) Again, this small change in the environment brings you to a new assortment of flowers. In midsummer look for jewelweed and asters, but in the spring the ground will be covered with sweet cicely, Greek valerian, blue-eyed Mary, and lousewort.

Lousewort's common name came into general usage centuries ago, when farmers believed that their livestock would become infested with lice if the animals would happen to graze through a patch of it. In fact, the genus name *Pedicularis* is derived from the Latin word for "louse," *pediculus*. Another common name is wood betony, derived from the Latin *betonica* meaning "herb." Some authorities speculate that this refers to a European herb, which, during the Middle Ages, was believed to have wonderfully strong powers.

Cross a water run at 3.0 miles and swing to the right. After the steep ascents and descents of the Backbone Trail, it is a pleasure to follow this narrow footpath, with its very slight ups and downs. Do not take the trail going to the right immediately after crossing a creek on a footbridge at 3.4 miles; rather, ascend on the route to the left with some nice views of the lake through the vegetation. At 3.8 miles, the Interpretive Nature Trail swings right to a parking area close to the lake. You want to bear left and follow the ascending Buffalo Trail.

Reach the top of the rise at 3.9 miles, and continue by slabbing along the western slope of Backbone Ridge, weaving in and out of several draws. The moist land close to the small water runs contrasts with the drier forests of the descending spur ridges, bringing new flowers, such as mayapple, false Solomon's seal, sweet William, bloodroot, larkspur, and wild geranium, for your perusal.

Because wild geranium is bisexual—meaning its flowers go through both male and female stages—it is unable to self-pollinate. An individual flower only lasts from one to three days, and by the time the female organs have developed to the point that they are ready to be fertilized, the pollen-producing anthers of the male have faded away. Interestingly, when conditions are right, a flower may change from a male to a female in just a matter of a few hours. Since it is so important for the flower to become fertilized as quickly as possible, it is believed that the darker purple lines along its petals help attract and guide insects to the nectar.

The trail to the right at 5.1 miles leads to a picnic area. Bear left and begin following the Cliffside Trail through a forest of beech and buckeye, with jack-in-the-pulpit lining the trail in spring and hawkweed (also known as devil's paintbrush) appearing later in the year. The low rock wall that gave this pathway its name is just above the trail at 5.4 miles, while the draw you pass through at 5.6 miles has a small stream that drops eye-pleasingly along a smooth rock course. Soon you come to the very first intersection you encountered on this hike, turn right, and return to your car at 5.8 miles.

Reasons to linger in the park are many. The Guyandotte Beauty, Lake Shore, Shawnee, and Woodpecker Trails are additional opportunities to see a variety of wildflowers. The park sponsors an annual guided wildflower pilgrimage every April if you want to gain more expertise. In addition, you can learn about the fauna by visiting the wildlife exhibit, with live black bears, bobcats, and other creatures of the forest. The Museum in the Park adds a touch of culture by presenting rotating exhibits of items from the West Virginia State Museum, and an old steam engine is a reminder of the region's coal mining history. To learn about an even earlier history, you could attend a presentation of *The Aracoma Story* in the park's amphitheater. Staged each summer, it is the tragic tale of a Shawnee woman, Aracoma, and her ill-fated love for a captured British soldier, Boling Baker.

44

Beech Fork State Park

Total distance (circuit): 2.9 miles

Hiking time: 1 hour, 40 minutes

Vertical rise: 520 feet

Maps: USGS 7½' Winslow; park handout map

The Hike at a Glance

0.1   bear left at intersection
0.6   intersection with Mary Davis Trail
0.9   figure-eight intersection
1.5   hard left at second intersection with Mary Davis Trail
2.4   return to figure-eight intersection
2.9   end

Whereas Chief Logan State Park (see Hike 43) can be a wildflower lover's springtime paradise, Beech Fork State Park can fill a birdwatcher with excitement year-round. Beech Fork certainly has its fair share of flowers—just a few of them include mayapple, trillium, sweet William, larkspur, live forever, twinleaf, and bloodroot—but it is its wide mix of habitats and environments that attracts such a variety of birds.

Be on the watch for swallows, flickers, hummingbirds, meadowlarks, killdeer, and chickadees in the meadows and mowed areas. Among those you may see in the forest are warblers, owls, thrushes, and woodpeckers. The border areas between woods and fields tend to be favored by kingbirds, thrashers, and sparrows. Floating upon Beech Fork Lake may be mallards, wood ducks, coots, and Canada geese, while the backwater areas and small creeks harbor herons and kingfishers.

Located in the low-lying hills that make up West Virginia's topography less than 10 miles from the Ohio River, Beech Fork State Park occupies 3,144 acres along the upper end of Beech Fork Lake. The 760-acre lake was developed by the U.S. Army Corps of Engineers in the 1970s, primarily as a flood-control measure that would also provide fish and wildlife conservation and recreational opportunities.

Within the park are picnic areas and shelters, game courts, ball fields, a 50-meter swimming pool, and deluxe year-round rental cottages fully equipped with all the amenities you would find in your own home (heating

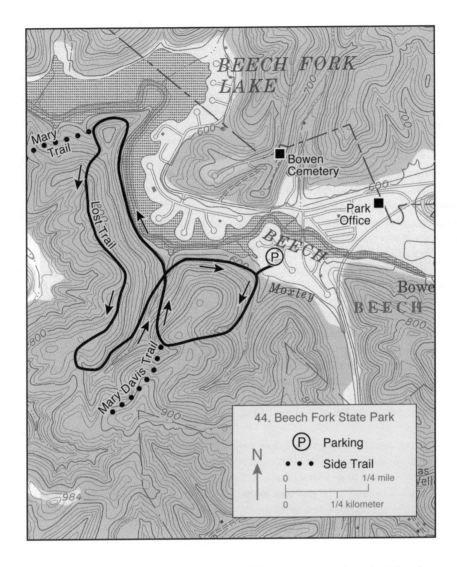

44. Beech Fork State Park

P Parking

• • • Side Trail

N

0   1/4 mile

0   1/4 kilometer

and air conditioning, fireplaces, microwave, telephone, and television). The huge campground, with 275 deluxe sites—80 of which are located on the lakefront—sprawls over several hundred acres and offers full hookups, laundry facilities, modern restrooms, and hot showers. One portion of the campground is open year-round.

There is no doubt that the recreational opportunities on the minds of most of the park's visitors are centered on the lake. Canoes, kayaks, and pedal boats may be rented, and a boat launch is available for those who bring their own watercraft. (Motors are limited to 10 horsepower or less.) The lake is stocked with a variety of warm-water fish on a regular basis, and from a short time before sunrise to the darkening hours of dusk on almost every day of the year, there will be someone, if not many someones, sending a hook and line splashing into the water. Bluegill, channel catfish, tiger musky, saugeye, and largemouth bass are what these folks are hoping to catch.

All this emphasis on the lake means that you may be the only person taking advantage of the park's small network of pathways—except on nice weekends. With its proximity to the population of the greater Huntington area, the park is a lure for local mountain bikers. Although most devotees of the activity I have met have been courteous, you should be prepared to quickly step aside at any moment, as an unannounced biker could go zipping by you.

Take exit 11 off I-64 at Huntington, drive south on WV10 for 3.8 miles, turn right onto Hughes Branch Road (WV43), and come to a major intersection in an additional 3.8 miles. Bear left to stay on WV43, and enter the park 2.0 miles later. Another 1.1 miles brings you to a right turn toward the campground. Just 1.1 miles later, bear left to enter the Moxley Branch Campground, and make the first right turn to leave your car at the bathhouse.

Walk between two campsites, follow the Lost Trail over a footbridge, and keep to the left when you come to an intersection in 0.1 mile. (You will return via the pathway to the right.) At first walking beside a small creek, rise at a rapid rate on an old woods road through a forest of ash, redbud, buckeye, and black walnut. Sadly, black walnut trees are becoming more rare because we humans value the wood so highly. In fact, because this wood now brings such a high price, there have been instances where unscrupulous persons have cut and stolen black walnuts trees from public lands and even have taken them down in someone's front yard.

Swing to the right, and level out a bit at 0.4 mile, where there are some good winter-

time views of the lake. The Mary Davis Trail (used primarily by mountain bikers) goes off to the left at 0.6 mile. Stay right, descend (steeply in spots) to parallel another small creek, and come to the figure-eight intersection at 0.9 mile. Turn left, cross the creek, and take the trail on the right as it runs along the lake. It is here in the shallow water of the creek or lake shoreline that you might spy a kingfisher, great blue heron, or green heron.

Less than half the size of the great blue, the green heron may grow to be about 22 inches in height. Stop and observe if you happen upon one (and it doesn't fly away), and you may be treated to one of the natural world's wonderful little melodramas. Stalking silently through the water by taking exaggerated steps with its bright orange legs, the green heron flicks its tail back and forth and stretches its neck and bill out. Then, taking aim, it strikes in one quick move and pulls a fish out of the water.

At about 1.2 miles, pass through an amazingly large colony of twinleaf that lines the trail for more than 1,000 feet. Soon, black cohosh joins the forest floor vegetation and grows around the rocks that have fallen from the hillside in days long ago. Be alert at 1.5 miles. You need to make a hard left to continue to follow the Lost Trail and ascend; do not take the Mary Davis Trail, which intersects your route at this point.

Reach a low knob populated by oaks at 1.6 miles, descend to a gap, and then ascend, steeply in places. The narrowness of the route here makes it obvious that mountain bikers use it less than other sections of the Lost Trail. Walk along the top of the ridge in a forest of red maple, birch, dogwood, catalpa, and buckeye, listening for the songs of various warblers in the spring. Blackburnian, black-throated green, blue-winged, hooded, yellow-throated, bay-breasted, and black-and-white warblers have been sighted in the park at one time or another.

Of these, the black-and-white warbler may possibly be the easiest one to see. The reason is that, unlike most other warblers that may remain hidden by tree foliage, the black-and-white spends much of its time crawling up and down tree trunks and across lower branches in search of insects. Its high-pitched song of *veesee veesee veesee* has been likened to the sound made by a squeaky wheel. Both male and female warblers are marked with black and white stripes, with the male having a black throat and the female a white one.

Be alert at 2.1 miles. An unmarked trail comes in from the right; you want to bear left and descend (steeply in places) along a woods road. Box turtles are often seen trudging across the terrain here. Return to the figure-eight intersection at 2.4 miles. Turn right, cross the creek, and stay to the left on the trail running along the edge of the lake, where you may get to watch the feeding habits of another bird of the water.

Like other dabbling ducks, only the tail of a mallard is visible above the water as it "up-ends" by sticking its head and body below the surface in search of plants, seeds, and snails. Mallards are the most common ducks in the world, with close to 10 million inhabit-ing North America alone. The male is easily recognized by its shiny green head, chestnut breast, white ring around the throat, and yellow bill. The female is a mottled brown with an orange and black bill. Both have metallic blue bands, known as speculums, on their wings that are offset by bands of white. As with everything in nature, the speculum has a purpose. During the courtship ritual, when the male is trying to attract a female, he will repeatedly dip his bill into the water and follow this with an exaggerated preening of his wings, in which his brilliant blue band is flashed in the eyes of his potential mate.

At 2.7 miles, you will find yourself back at the very first intersection you encountered on the hike. Turn left, cross the footbridge, and return to your car at 2.9 miles.

There are many other hiking opportunities at the park. The 1.0-mile Overlook Trail winds up a long ridge for a view of the campground and other park facilities, and the 0.75-mile Nature Trail is an easy stroll along gentle terrain. Also of interest in the park is the Bowen Cemetery, which you can drive to. A small community once existed here, and of the 163 headstones from the 1800s, the earliest one has a date of 1829. Two Confederate soldiers are buried here, as well as the leg that Mel Ray lost in a train accident.

45

Huntington Museum of Art

Total distance (circuit): 1.6 miles

Hiking time: 30 minutes

Vertical rise: 180 feet

Maps: USGS 7½' Huntington, WV/OH; museum handout map

The Hike at a Glance

0.15 merge onto Tulip Poplar Trail
0.4   ascend steps
0.9   left onto Spicebush Loop Trail
1.3   avoid trail to right
1.6   end

In 1948, years before the urban trails/greenway movement began to attract advocates, the founders of the Huntington Museum of Art resolved that the greater part of its 50 acres would remain in its naturally forested state so that the institution would "enrich the lives of all people." It took a few years, but in 1964, a small trail network was established on the property's western slope. Steps, railings, and wooden bridges blend in well with their surroundings and make it easier to negotiate the pathways' steeper portions. One of the nicest hikes you could take within the limits of any of West Virginia's cities, this is a great place to start a walking/exercise program for yourself or introduce young children to the joys and wonders of the outdoors.

Maintained by museum staff and individual volunteers, the network provides the citizens of Huntington with an easily accessible place in which to recreate in the outdoors. It is short enough that you could easily walk it during your workday lunch break, but it is interesting enough to be worth a drive from some distant place to enjoy its plants, animals, and rejuvenating atmosphere. Despite being located next to an interstate and surrounded by houses, the trails travel through a forest of large oak, poplar, ash, hickory, hackberry, sycamore, chestnut, beech, black locust, and maple that is home to deer, squirrels, chipmunks, turtles, woodpeckers, and other creatures. In spring, the unfolding fronds of a variety of ferns are joined on the forest floor by mayapple, trillium, sweet cicely, and jack-in-the-pulpit.

Take exit 8 off I-64 at Huntington, drive

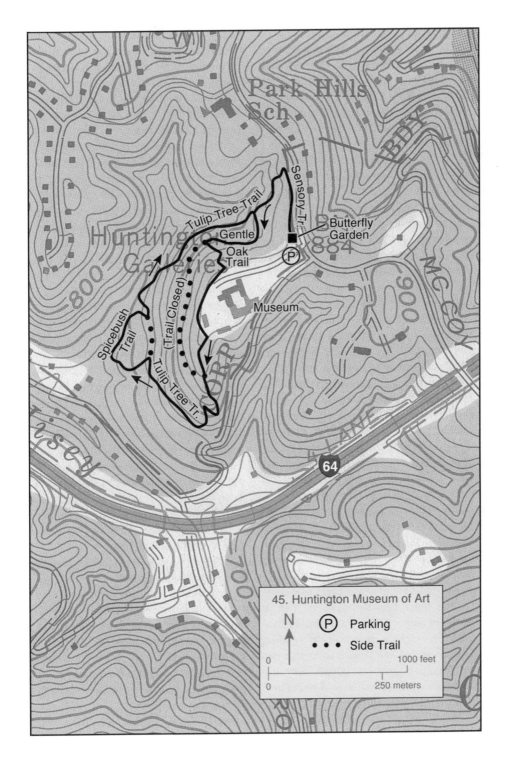

Park Hills Sch.

BDY

Tulip Tree Trail

Sensory Tr.

Gentle

Butterfly
Garden

Huntington
Galleries

Oak
Trail

884

P

800

(Trail Closed)

Spicebush
Trail

Museum

900

MCCOY

Tulip Tree Tr.

CORP

64

LANE

700

sey

45. Huntington Museum of Art

N

P Parking

••• Side Trail

0   1000 feet

0   250 meters

north on WV527 for 0.1 mile, and turn right on Miller Road (WV54/1). Come to an intersection in another 0.9 mile, bear left onto McCullogh Road (still WV54/1), turn left onto McCoy Road 0.6 mile later, make an immediate left into the museum grounds, and park next to the entrance for the Steelman Butterfly Garden.

Walk through the garden and onto the paved and accessible Teubert Foundation Sensory Trail, designed to provide blind persons with an outdoors experience. Three stations, one each for smell, touch, and hearing, are accompanied with signage and images created by wildlife artist Chuck Ripper. At 0.15 mile, pass through a gate and onto the Tulip Tree Trail, which reaches an intersection in just a few hundred feet.

Bear left and ascend on the Gentle Oak Trail, contouring the hillside to ascend a set of steps at 0.4 mile, walk behind the museum buildings, and turn to descend into a deep forest along another section of the Tulip Tree Trail. Pileated woodpeckers are often heard above the sound of the interstate. Often mistaken for poison ivy, even though it has five leaves and not three, Virginia creeper covers much of the ground and climbs onto tree trunks, while American ipecac, a member of the rose family, is part of the understory.

Also known as Indian physic, American ipecac was listed as a laxative and emetic in the *United States Pharmacopoeia* for more than four decades. The drug, which is made from the plant's roots, still has limited commercial value, but at only 2 cents to 4 cents a pound, there is surely not much of an incentive to gather it. The plant (and its flowers) very closely resemble a relative, Bowman's root, but American ipecac has large, jagged stipules (small leafy appendages attached to the main leaf stems) lacking on the Bowman's root.

At 0.65 mile, descend steps along the Tulip Tree Trail, named for the many towering tulip poplar trees along its route. Attaining heights of 80 feet to over 100 feet, the nearly smooth, ashy-gray bark of a young tulip poplar becomes thicker and develops interlacing deep furrows as the tree ages. Its shiny, hairless, dark green leaves emerge folded but open up to an unmistakable square shape that measures 3 to 6 inches long and wide. Its name comes from the large tulip-shaped flowers that grow high on the upper limbs in early June. As summer progresses, they fall off the trees, and you will see dozens of them decorating the brown and gray soil of the trail.

Descend into a ravine, walk past mayapple, and use rock steps to pass through a cleft between two boulders. Be sure to not take the unauthorized trail to the right at 0.8 mile, where the Tulip Tree Trail makes a switchback to the left. About 200 feet later, merge onto a dirt service road lined by large oak trees. To lengthen the hike by a few hundred feet, turn left onto the Spicebush Loop Trail at 0.9 mile. (Those not wanting to take this little loop may continue to the right and rejoin this description at the 1.1 milepoint.) Because it cannot tolerate direct sunlight, you will not see Solomon's seal growing along the pathway in springtime until the leaf canopy has begun to develop. Spicebush, which may grow up to 15 feet high, can easily be seen throughout the year.

The very small, star-shaped, yellow flowers of the spicebush bloom in March or April, before the aromatic leaves appear. Native Americans and early settlers made a tea from the leaves and frayed the ends of young twigs to use as toothbrushes or add to cooking pots to season meat. The bright red fruits that ripen from July into September can be dried and crushed and used as a substitute for allspice.

At 1.0 mile, swing right and ascend,

Tulip Tree Trail

One of the things you may be privileged to enjoy is the *kik kik kik* call of a pileated woodpecker or the similar-sounding *wik wik wik* call of another woodpecker, the common flicker. Although they will enlarge cavities in trees to make nests, flickers are the only woodpeckers in the United States that feed on the ground, searching for larvae and ants. A flicker's tongue is somewhat like that of an anteater's—long and covered with a sticky substance. One thrust into an anthill nets the woodpecker dozens of tasty morsels, and it has been estimated that a flicker may consume as many as 3,000 ants in a single meal.

Black cohosh is part of the understory where the trail passes by a small amphitheater. Avoid the trail to the right at 1.3 mile, climb a set of steps, cross three small bridges, and turn left upon returning to the first intersection you had encountered on the hike. Retrace your steps along the Teubert Foundation Sensory Trail through the butterfly garden, and return to your car at 1.6 miles.

Do not drive away without making at least a short visit to the art museum. This is the largest such facility in the state, so once you get inside and see what it has to offer, you may be tempted to spend quite a bit of time. It is easy for minutes to slip away while you look over exhibits of Appalachian folk art, 19th- and 20th-century American and European paintings, glass produced primarily in the Ohio Valley, Islamic prayer rugs, Georgian silver, sculptures, and more. Also, be sure to take in the C. Fred Edwards Conservatory. It is the only plant conservatory in the state and has year-round displays of palms, shrubs, and herbs.

There is no fee to walk the trails and no admission fee on Tuesday for the museum, which is open every day of the week except Monday.

maybe stopping to sit on the benches that provide a spot to watch Fitzpatrick's Branch babble down its creek bed. Continue on your way, return to the Tulip Tree Trail at 1.1 mile, and turn left to arrive at an observation deck overlooking the creek. The deck was built in memory of Othel Rogers, and a plaque invites you to "rest and enjoy the beauty of the forest all around you, just as my mother did."

46

Kanawha State Forest

Total distance (circuit): 11.1 miles

Hiking time: 6 hours, 30 minutes

Vertical rise: 1,940 feet

Maps: USGS 7½' Charleston West; USGS 7½' Racine; state forest handout map

The Hike at a Glance

1.2   view of Polly Hollow
1.3   left onto Wildcat Ridge Trail
2.0   begin following Pine Ridge Trail
2.9   intersection with Dunlop Trail
3.9   left onto Rocky Ridge Trail
5.3   begin following Logtown Trail
6.1   left onto dirt road
8.4   left onto Teaberry Rock Trail
9.6   left onto Davis Creek Trail
10.8 begin following Spotted Salamander Trail
11.1 end

Being so close to the large population of the greater Charleston area, Kanawha State Forest has come to be viewed by its neighbors as more akin to a regional or municipal park than the typical state forest. Because amenities often associated with such facilities are quite absent in this portion of West Virginia, the state forest is a magnet for those looking for outdoor recreation. Contained within its 9,300 acres are picnic grounds and shelters, a swimming pool, several children's playgrounds, and a shooting range. A developed campground provides a modern bathhouse with hot showers, laundry facilities, and electric and water hook-ups, with a separate dumping station. (Backcountry camping is not permitted.)

Almost all of these facilities are located within the narrow valley created by Davis Creek, which leaves the rest of the state forest undeveloped—except for a system of fire and gas well roads. These roads are for authorized vehicles only, so traffic is basically nonexistent, and the routes can be used in conjunction with more than 25 miles of trails to create some very long and adventurous loop hikes. The terrain is steep and rugged, but most ascents on this hike are moderate with just a few short, steep sections. All of the pathways are blazed and signed at trailheads and are often in a better state of repair and maintenance than those found in other state forests.

Whereas Chief Logan State Park (see Hike 43) can be a wildflower lover's springtime paradise, and Beech Fork State Park (see Hike 44) can fill a birdwatcher with ex-

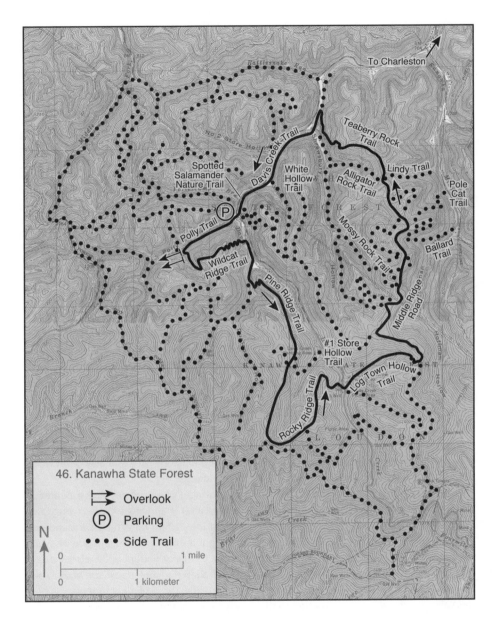

Map labels (as they appear on the map):

Rattlesnake
To Charleston
No. 2 Store Hollow
Teaberry Rock Trail
Davis Creek Trail
Spotted Salamander Nature Trail
White Hollow Trail
Alligator Rock Trail
Lindy Trail
Pole Cat Trail
(P) Parking
Mossy Rock Trail
Ballard Trail
Polly Trail
Wildcat Ridge Trail
Pine Ridge Trail
Middle Ridge Road
KANAWHA STATE FOREST
#1 Store Hollow Trail
Log Town Hollow Trail
Rocky Ridge Trail
LOUDON
Branch
Davis Creek
Briar
Creek
FOREST BOUNDARY

46. Kanawha State Forest

→ Overlook
(P) Parking
•••• Side Trail

N

0   1 mile
0   1 kilometer

citement, Kanawha State Forest has such an abundance and variety of flora and fauna that it is beginning to garner international acclaim. In fact, some birdwatchers maintain that more birds may be seen at Kanawha State Forest than at any other place in the state. So many species of wood warblers have been identified (at least 19) that it is now attracting birdwatchers from other countries. Also within the forest boundaries are just about every other type of wildlife found in the state, including deer, bobcats, foxes, coyotes, black bear, rabbits, chipmunks, squirrels, mice, voles, raccoons, muskrats, opossums, groundhogs, snakes, turtles, salamanders, lizards, skinks, frogs, toads, and bats.

More than 1,000 species of flora have been identified here. All of the cove hardwoods—including basswood, cherry, beech, maple, and poplar—grow here and intermingle with trees, such as the tamarack, more often associated with forests farther north. Of all of its natural wonders, it may be the state forest's wildflowers that attract the most attention and visitors. More than 20 species of wild orchids have been seen, and springtime bursts forth with bluets, hepatica, mayapple, bloodroot, trillium, spring beauty, lady's slippers, trout lily, and more. Wintergreen, rattlesnake plantain, jewelweed, Indian pipe, and joe-pye weed appear during the warmest months of the year, while goldenrod, asters, and other composites persist into the cool temperatures of autumn.

Take exit 58A off I-64 in Charleston, drive south on US119, turn left onto Oakwood Road in 1.0 mile, and make a right onto Bridge Road in another mile. Keep straight, driving onto Louden Heights Road 0.4 mile later. Make a right onto Connell Road in an additional 0.2 mile, and negotiate a hard left turn onto Kanawha State Forest Drive 2.2 miles later. Another 2.5 miles brings you into the state forest. Continue for an additional 2.4 miles to a small parking area on the right side of the road, where a sign identifies Polly Hollow. Do not block the gate.

Walk past the gate, take the trail to the right, rock-hop the creek, and walk left through the grass to come to the red-blazed Polly Trail, which you quickly ascend beside false Solomon's seal, mayapple, and jack-in-the-pulpit. Bear right at the loop trail intersection and walk on the pleasant sidehill trail above the creek. Jewelweed joins the vegetation growing under oak, beech, and cucumber magnolia trees.

As you hike, you may see a couple of reminders of coal mining days. Around the turn of the 20th century, six mines operated on what is now state forest land, and the area had a community of more than 130 homes, three schools, three churches, two stores, and a post office. One of the schools and one of the churches were located close to the mouth of the hollow where you left your car. At one time, most of the land and mines were owned by Anheuser-Busch. (Yes, it's the same corporation that now brews Budweiser, Busch, and Michelob beers.) The company also operated an iron ore smelter, brick factory, sawmill, and several other small facilities.

Walk almost level with the creek in a small hemlock grove at 0.4 mile, but be alert at 0.5 mile. Stay left on the main trail; do not go to the right onto the service road, for soon your route swings away from it and begins to rise to the left of another stream. At 0.8 mile, pass by a large boulder perched atop another one, with a tree growing out from the crack between them, and soon walk below several sandstone cliffs that may cover wood rat middens.

Looking unlike most people's expectation of what a rat is and more like an overgrown mouse, the eastern wood rat has a round face with light brown fur above and grayish white below. Its bushy, flattened, 7-inch tail is also bicolored. Since their tracks are hard to distinguish from those of other rodents, the best way to discover whether wood rats are in the area is to search for their bulky nests—piles of sticks and debris in a bush or cave or a large pile of sticks almost 4 feet in height up against a tree. Since these are the "pack rats" of legend, their nests may also contain all manner of debris, such as a hiker's missing pocketknife or a buckle chewed off a backpack.

Polly Trail

Be alert again at 1.2 miles, as the trail swings right between large rocks and ascends to a pleasant, but limited view of Polly Hollow and surrounding hillsides.

The Polly Trail comes to an end on top of the knob at 1.3 miles. Turn left onto the blue-blazed Wildcat Ridge Trail, part of the Mary Draper Ingles Trail, and descend.

Mrs. Ingles and several members of her family living near Radford, Virginia, were kidnapped by Shawnee Indians in 1755. Forced to travel west to the Native Americans' village near present-day Portsmouth, Ohio, Mary made a daring 45-day, 840-mile escape back to Virginia. When completed, the Mary Draper Ingles Trail will trace the approximate route of her escape. A great read, *Follow the River* by James Alexander Thom is an historical novel based upon her experiences.

To help prevent erosion, stay on the main route and do not cut the switchbacks, as some mountain bikers have evidently done. Break out of the woods at 1.9 miles, and turn right through a picnic area, but be alert just 500 feet later. At the edge of an open meadow (formerly a baseball field), turn right onto a service road, soon following the yellow-blazed Pine Ridge Trail as you reenter the woods and ascend steeply beside rattlesnake weed.

Switchback onto the ridgeline with sassafras trees and good winter views of the Davis Creek Valley, staying left when the Dunlop Trail comes in from the right at 2.9 miles. The #1 Store Hollow Trail, so named because one of the community stores was once located there, descends to the left at 3.2 miles. Stay right, but less than 600 feet later, turn left onto a dirt road, soon ascending through a forest of tulip poplar trees. Be alert again at 3.9 miles. Turn left onto the road, which, hopefully, will be signed as leading to the Rocky Ridge Trail. Walk past two gas wells at 4.25 miles, and continue on a route, once again, signed as leading to the Rocky Ridge Trail. Expect this to be very overgrown if you are here in summer.

Turn left onto the blue-blazed Rocky Ridge Trail at 4.4 miles, and ascend for a short distance before leveling out and then descending. Walk onto an old railroad grade at 5.0 miles before dropping down to the main forest road and crossing it diagonally to the left. Follow the paved road into the picnic area, taking the left fork as it goes by restrooms and picnic shelters #4 and #3. Shelter #4 was built by the Civilian Conservation Corps (CCC) in the 1930s and is constructed with wormy chestnut logs that were cut on site. The men of the CCC also removed old houses and coal mining tipples and constructed roads and many of the structures that are still in use today.

Beyond the last shelter at 5.3 miles, reenter the woods on the yellow-blazed Logtown Hollow Trail, named for the several log houses that once stood here. One of the pleasures of hiking in the woods, especially early in the morning, is the birdsong serenades. Dozens of songs and calls bounce off the walls of this narrow defile in the mountains, and you may hear the *weet weet weet weet tsee tsee* of a yellow warbler or the *tidly tidly tidly tidly* of a Blackburnian warbler. Also listen for the *weesee weesee weesee* of the black-and-white warbler and the *tory tory tory tory* of the Kentucky warbler.

Gradually ascend beside—and sometimes in—the creek in a forest that is so lush with vegetation that it almost feels like a rainforest of cucumber magnolia trees, bloodroot, jack-in-the-pulpit, and wild ginger. At 5.5 miles, a miniature waterfall with a drop of just a few feet enhances the beauty of this hollow's green moss-covered rocks. Adding to the appeal of the forest floor are blue-bead lily, rosy twisted stalk, mayapple, and Solomon's seal. Also watch out for the thick growths of poison ivy and stinging nettle.

The ascent quickens at 5.8 miles, but switchbacks take you over the steepest terrain just before you turn left onto dirt Middle Ridge Road at 6.1 miles. Keep right when you come to the Y-intersection at 6.6 miles, and stay right again when a fainter woods road comes in from the left at 6.9 miles. Within the next mile, the Middle Ridge Trail, which is a part of the Mary Draper Ingles Trail and built by volunteers primarily as a mountain biking trail, will weave across the road a number of times. Stay on the road, bypassing the Mossy Rock Trail descending to the left at 7.4 miles, the Polecat and Ballard Trails dropping to the right at 7.7 miles, the Lindy Trail going off the right at 8.2 miles, and the Alligator Trail coming in from the left a few feet later.

Be alert at 8.4 miles. Just as the main dirt road swings to the right, bear left onto the Teaberry Rock Trail, a footpath marked with orange blazes that gradually descends a spur ridge with winter views. At 8.75 miles, switchback right onto sidehill trail; do not continue straight or go to the left. In summer, you will soon hear the screams and shouts of children playing in the swimming pool. After a series of switchbacks, do not descend left to the woods road below you, as it seems you should do at 9.3 miles. Rather, stay on the orange-blazed route, which is now along an old railroad grade running through hemlocks high above Davis Creek.

At 9.6 miles, descend and turn left onto the Davis Creek Trail as it parallels the waterway upstream. There is a great wading pool in the creek where the trail crosses a service road at 9.8 miles. Just be mindful that snapping turtles live in the same water you

may choose to put your feet in. Take the wooden bridge over a tributary of the creek at 9.9 miles, walk through the picnic area in front of the swimming pool, cross the paved picnic area road, and reenter the woods on the Davis Creek Trail. There is another nice wading pool at 10.1 miles, just after the trail merges onto an old railroad grade for a short distance.

You can see a picnic area across the stream as you walk beside a rock overhang—whose underside may be dotted with dozens of spider webs—at 10.4 miles. If you look carefully you may see orb, funnel, and dome webs, each spun by a different type of spider hoping to catch insects that visit the hundreds of jewelweed blossoms growing in the moist ground next to the creek.

The blue-blazed White Hollow Trail goes off to the left at 10.6 miles. Stay right, cross a footbridge over Davis Creek at 10.7 miles, and turn left onto the main park road beside Copperhead Rock, so named because it resembles the snake's head. At 10.8 miles, reenter the woods to the left on the Spotted Salamander Nature Trail (handicapped accessible), with interpretive signs on the area's natural history. Walk beside joe-pye weed, boneset, and goldenrod, staying to the right when you come to the loop trail intersection at 10.8 miles. The vernal wetlands along this pathway are home to spotted, four-toed, and marbled salamanders, as well as a variety of frogs and toads, including gray tree frogs and American toads. Green frogs may let out a distinctive *c'tung* as they jump out of the way of your advancing footsteps.

As the trail starts to loop back on itself at 11.0 miles, step over the wire handrail, cross the paved main park road, and return to your car at 11.1 miles.

47

Coonskin Park

Total distance (circuit): 1.1 miles

Hiking time: 30 minutes

Vertical rise: 100 feet

Maps: USGS 7½' Big Chimney; park handout map

The Hike at a Glance

0.1	first intersection
0.25	cross small water run
0.4	avoid trail to the left
0.5	cross two tributaries
0.8	walk behind waterfall
0.9	turn right
1.1	end

The setting for Coonskin Park's Nature Trail is so enchanting that it was featured in a full-color, multipage article in *Wonderful West Virginia* magazine. Winding along a pathway that clings to the hillside of a deeply shaded ravine, the trail passes through a lush forest of mixed hardwood and hemlock trees, runs under interesting sandstone rock formations and overhangs, comes into contact with a small brook, and is lined by dozens of ferns and scores of springtime wildflowers. The temperature is usually a few degrees cooler than surrounding areas, thanks to the lush forest canopy blocking much of the sunlight. Those same leaves make this a colorful walk in the fall, and icicles clinging to the rock overhangs turn the ravine into a sparkling wonderland in winter. Its short length and many little delights make it a good choice for families with children—just be aware that the pathway is narrow and can be slippery in places.

The park is a gift that the people of Kanawha County gave to themselves by passing a $200,000 bond levy in 1948. It may have the distinction of being the only park in the state, and possibly the entire country, that was built in just two days. With more than a million dollars' worth of equipment, materials, and labor donated to the effort, two lakes, an access road, picnic shelters, comfort stations, and a dance pavilion were built on June 27 and 28, 1950, in what some spectators described as lightning-fast construction speed.

Through the years, the park has continued to develop and now has so many offerings that appeal to so many people that

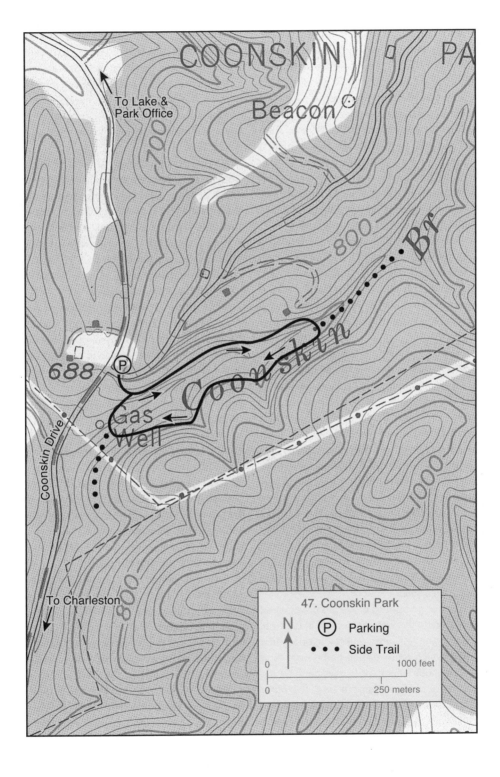

COONSKIN PA

Beacon

To Lake &
Park Office

688

Gas
Well

Coonskin Br

Coonskin Drive

To Charleston

47. Coonskin Park

N

Ⓟ Parking

• • • Side Trail

0   1000 feet

0   250 meters

it sometimes hosts several thousand visitors on a single weekend. Within an easy 15-minute drive of downtown Charleston are picnic areas and shelters, a handicapped-accessible 18-hole golf course, a swimming pool, concessions, game courts and playing fields, children's playgrounds, miniature golf, a skate park, a fitness trail, fishing, a canoe/boat ramp, bicycle and pedal boat rentals, and even a wedding garden. A 2,000-seat soccer stadium and modern amphitheater attract crowds for games, live music concerts, and other special events.

The park may be reached from exit 99 off I-64 in Charleston. Drive WV114 North (Greenbrier Road) for 2.6 miles, turn left onto Coonskin Drive (WV51/2), enter the park in an additional 0.8 mile, and leave your car in the large parking area on the right in another 0.5 mile.

Cross the road to the upper picnic area, and enter the woods on the signed Nature Trail, descending into a deep hollow of poplar, beech, maple, and hemlocks that tower over both Solomon's seal and false Solomon's seal. Distinguishing false Solomon's seal from Solomon's seal is best accomplished at either flowering or fruit-bearing time. The Solomon's seal's little bell-shaped flowers hang down from the stem, while the tiny, starred blossoms of false Solomon's seal extend from the end of the stem. Later in the year, Solomon's seal's fruit is a dark blue—almost black—berry, easily differentiated from the red berries of false Solomon's seal.

Do not go right to cross the creek when you come to the first intersection at 0.1 mile. Stay to the left, and walk by slippery elm trees, which receive their name from their mucilaginous inner bark. In days gone by, the bark was peeled from the tree, the outer layer discarded, and the inner layer used as a wound dressing that helped reduce inflammation. Native Americans used the bark as food, while children often chewed it to relieve the pain of a sore throat. However, please refrain from trying this. Not only would it harm the tree, but slippery elms are having a hard enough time trying to survive the effects of Dutch elm disease, to which they are highly susceptible.

Cross a small water run at 0.25 mile and walk under a rock overhang, where a few drops of water may drip on you. You are almost level with the creek at 0.3 mile, where you walk next to another rock face and into an almost neon-green, moss-covered grotto. Wild ginger pops out of the ground in early spring, close to where you need to avoid the trail coming in from the left at 0.4 mile.

Wild ginger is not related to the ginger you purchase in the supermarket to add to Asian dishes. Yet, its rhizome does have a similar taste and has been used as a substitute flavoring. Early settlers made a sweet treat by cutting up the rootstocks and cooking them for several days in syrupy sugar water. The candied roots would then keep for long periods of time and could be carried into the field to provide a refreshing snack.

At 0.5 mile, cross the two small tributaries that make up the main creek, and follow the pathway as it begins to circle back toward the point of origin. The abandoned fire ring and tiny amphitheater located between the two small streams were used by YMCA day campers in the mid-20th century.

Bird enthusiasts have sighted dozens of species in the park, and within this forest you may see or hear warblers, tanagers, thrushes, orioles, and vireos. While many birds are most active in the early morning hours, the red-eyed vireo sings all day as it searches for insects on the undersurfaces of leaves and in the cracks of tree bark. Roger Tory Peterson, possibly America's most famous naturalist, says its song is made

Nature Trail

up of short, abrupt phrases that resemble those of the robin, are separated by pauses, and are repeated as many as 40 times a minute. One of the most common and abundant birds in the eastern United States and Canada during the warmer months (it winters in northern South America), the red-eyed vireo is about the size of a sparrow, olive-brown on top, white underneath, and has black and white stripes above its eyes.

The waterfall does not have a very large flow and can even be dry much of the year, but there is something about being able to walk into the crescent-shaped grotto and behind flowing water at 0.8 mile that brings a certain amount of delight and satisfaction to both children and adults. Growing close to the waterfall, the leaves of the mayapple can brush up against your legs without doing any harm, yet be careful of those of the stinging nettle and poison ivy. It may be 48 hours or more before you experience any reaction to touching poison ivy, but brushing up against the stinging nettle will give its tiny, stiff hairs an opportunity to scratch your skin and deposit an irritant that may itch immediately—and probably for the rest of the day. One experience of this kind will, no doubt, keep you on the watch for it.

Be very alert at 0.9 mile. Unless a sign has been placed here, it will be very easy to miss the descending right turn you want to take to complete this hike. (If you go straight, you could end up on other trails or on the main park road.) The swamp milkweed that grows close to the footbridge you used to cross the creek at 1.0 mile is more often found in swamps and along shorelines than in the deciduous forest. The plant's genus name *Asclepias* comes from the Greek god of medicine, Asklepios, as it has been used to treat a number of sicknesses. Its fiber is so strong that it has been woven into twine.

The outing comes to an end when you return to the first intersection you encountered on the hike, turn left, and return to your automobile at 1.1 miles.

Within a few years of the turn of the 21st century, a dedicated group of volunteers put the final touches on upgrading, signing, and making official a network of trails that had existed informally for decades. The pathways take visitors through some of the more isolated portions of the park, close to its boundary line, into several picnic areas, and down to the park office. For a perfectly level walk, the Elk River Trail parallels its namesake waterway for close to a mile. Check at the park office for more information if you have the desire to hike more than just the described Nature Trail.

48

North Bend Rail-Trail

Total distance (one way): 22.9 miles

Hiking time: 11 hours

Vertical rise: 200 feet

Maps: USGS 7½' Pennsboro; USGS 7½' Ellenboro; USGS 7½' Harrisville; USGS 7½' Cairo; USGS 7½' Petroleum

The Hike at a Glance

1.0	Tunnel #8
1.6	pass under old US50
4.6	convenience store in Ellenboro
4.7	overpass of WV16 and Dairy Queen
5.9	pass under US50
7.7	Tunnel #10
9.4	Tunnel #12
9.8	Tunnel #13 and turnoff to North Bend State Park
10.2	Cornwallis
13.0	Cairo
15.7	Silver Run Road
16.2	Tunnel #19
20.2	Petroleum
22.9	end

Never underestimate the power of a group of citizens banding together to achieve a common goal, as the North Bend Rail-Trail is the result of one man's vision and hard work and many people's collaborative efforts. After the CSX Corporation abandoned its rail line between Clarksburg and Parkersburg, Dick Bias dedicated himself to the development of a rail-trail. Upon establishing the North Bend Rails to Trails Foundation, he led negotiations with CSX to purchase the corridor and is credited with raising the majority of the $350,000 that funded the initial phase of the project.

The line was built in the 1850s as the Northwestern Virginia Railroad and was soon incorporated into the Baltimore and Ohio Railroad's main line that stretched westward to St. Louis. More than 30 bridges and 12 tunnels were constructed to enable the line to pass through the hills and rolling terrain of western West Virginia. Used for both freight and passengers, the line serviced the region's booming oil and gas industry and helped establish many of the small towns that still exist. The number of passengers began to decline in the 1950s as Americans became enamored of the automobile to supply their transportation needs, while the freight train made its final run on this line in 1984.

Today, the North Bend Rail-Trail is a part of the West Virginia state park system and runs 72 miles from I-77 at Parkersburg to Wolf Summit in Harrison County. (Plans call for it to eventually connect Parkersburg and Clarksburg.) The 22.9-mile stretch described

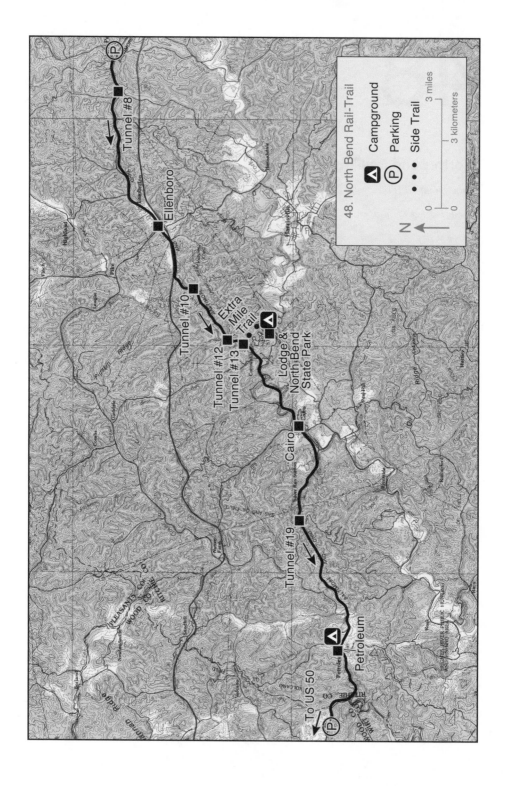

48. North Bend Rail-Trail

▲ Campground
Ⓟ Parking
••• Side Trail

N

0 ____ 3 miles
0 ____ 3 kilometers

Tunnel #8

Ellenboro

Tunnel #10

Extra
Mile
Trail

Tunnel #12

Tunnel #13

Lodge &
North Bend
State Park

Cairo

Tunnel #19

Petroleum

To US 50

below was chosen because it contains some of the rail-trail's most scenic sections, passing through small communities, into five historic tunnels (bring a flashlight), and over a number of bridges, while providing options for sightseeing, dining, lodging, or camping (in designated sites) without venturing far from the trail.

Like the Greenbrier River Trail (see Hike 17), the North Bend Rail-Trail is a great place to introduce friends to the joys of outdoor walking without subjecting them to harsh or isolated terrain. The pathway has barely perceptible little ups and downs, picnic areas, and vault toilets located at convenient intervals, and road crossings are frequent if the need for help should arise. Be aware that the only water sources are from businesses close to the trail, so carry plenty and fill up whenever the opportunity presents itself.

This is a one-way hike, so a car shuttle will be necessary. From the intersection of US50 and I-77 at Parkersburg, drive US50 East for 12 miles, turn right onto WV5, go another 2.7 miles, and bear right onto WV28. Follow this route's many twists and turns for 4.0 miles to make a left turn onto dirt WV7, where you come to the trail crossing in just a short distance. Leave one car on the pullout next to the trail (making sure not to block it or the gate), and drive the other car back to US50. Continue eastward for approximately 20 miles, turn left onto WV74, and follow it less than 2.0 miles into Pennsboro and the parking lot beside the restored B&O Depot.

The hike begins by walking westward on the North Bend Rail-Trail. The tracks were once four wide in Pennsboro, a community established in the early 1800s. At one time, it was a boomtown that produced timber, tobacco products, and glass. The many abandoned brick buildings you see close to the trail were hotels, groceries, and other businesses. Soon after the town fades away, the trail passes through 588-foot Tunnel #8 at 1.0 mile. If this is the first tunnel you have ever walked through, it may appear a bit ominous and intimidating at first. Water drips from the rocks above, and it gets darker as you enter, but as it curves to the right you—literally—get to see the light at the end of the tunnel.

Green frogs inhabit the small, cattail-lined ditch next to the trail as it passes under old US50 at 1.6 miles. The green frog is somewhat misnamed as it can be green, reddish brown, or brown—but it always has a small patch of green on its upper lip. Its call, which may be the only thing that alerts you to its presence, is a low, explosive, twangy *c'tung*. They often let out a high-pitched *squeenk* when startled and jumping for safety.

Small homes dot the rural countryside where the trail crosses gravel roads at 2.4 miles and 2.9 miles. A convenience store in the small town of Ellenboro is located next to the trail at 4.6 miles. The trail's overpass of WV16 at 4.7 miles is the steepest grade you will encounter on the entire hike. (A few feet to the left is a Dairy Queen, which you may want to consider patronizing. Unless you take the 2.0-mile round-trip side journey to North Bend State Park, it is the last source for water until Cairo, more than 8 miles away.) In some places, the landscape closes in on the trail where the railroad bed has been cut through rock. These narrow spots are always more shaded than the rest of the trail, and you will feel a drop in temperature as soon as you enter them. Some of them were actually tunnels at one time but were "opened up" for safety reasons.

After passing under US50 at 5.9 miles, the trail swings away from the four-lane highway, and birdsongs and the sound of running water in Hushers Run replace the whine of 18-wheeler truck tires. The length of Tunnel #10, at 7.7 miles, is in dispute; one source

Tunnel #12

says it's 337 feet long, while another says it's 377 feet long. It is the only tunnel on the trail that is cut through solid sandstone, meaning it does not need any additional bracing. Also known as the Dick Bias Tunnel, it honors the memory of the trail's originator, who passed away in 1995. Tunnel #12, located at 9.4 miles, is 577 feet long and will lead you to the largest wetland on the trail between Ellenboro and North Bend State Park.

Many of these wet areas were created when the construction of the railroad grade prevented the normal flow of water. Once called "black ponds" because they collected the oil, soot, cinders, and creosote from the railroad, they are now home to turtles, snakes, fish, herons, and other water-loving creatures.

After hiking 9.8 miles from Pennsboro, you will walk through 353-foot long Tunnel #13, built in 1868 and lined by brick and masonry. On its far side is the turnoff for North Bend State Park. This is about halfway through the hike, which makes it a convenient place to spend the night in either the campground or lodge. (Call 304-643-2931 to make reservations.) If this is what you decide to do, follow the park's Extra Mile Trail to the campground (the lodge is a short distance beyond it) and add a little more than 2.0 miles to the overall length of this hike.

Continuing on the rail-trail, pass through the small community of Cornwallis at 10.2 miles. Now just a cluster of modest homes, it was an oil and gas boomtown in the late 1800s, with numerous stores, churches, a school, and warehouses for the freight that passed through it. Beyond the community, the trail goes by a number of black pools, whose surrounding tree trunks have been gnawed by the resident beavers. The high walls of the cut at 12.3 miles are what remain of Tunnel #18, which was 965 feet long before its top was removed.

The brown concrete building at 13.0 miles was once a marble factory that produced thousands of the little glass orbs daily. It now marks your entrance into the largest town of the hike, and the place you will want to linger for a while.

Cairo (say CARE-oh or the locals will immediately peg you as an outsider) was established in 1821, and began to thrive when the railroad arrived in 1856. Timber was the first economic engine, but growth really began with the discovery of oil and gas in the late 1800s. Three hotels, a bank (still standing to the left of the rail-trail), a newspaper, hardware and mercantile stores, and even an opera house all prospered here at one time.

Points of interest for the rail-trail hiker of today include a bike shop (with a small grocery section for snacks and drinks), a restaurant, and a couple of gift shops with West Virginia arts and crafts. Built around 1900, but now closed, the R. C. Marshall Hardware had become something of a tourist attraction, as it retained its original tin ceilings, rolling ladders, and vintage showcases. It specialized in items from the turn of the 20th century and did not carry any electric appliances or products made with plastic. It is interesting to stop by the post office, with its early-20th-century interior. Again, be sure to pick up water somewhere in town, as there are no sources on the rest of the hike.

The most used portion of the rail-trail is between North Bend State Park and Cairo, so the number of people you will encounter diminishes as you follow the trail across the North Fork of the Hughes River. This is by far the quietest section of the hike, and houses become few and far between as you pass through deciduous forests and rural countryside. Cross Silver Run Road at 15.7 miles, and, at 16.2 miles, enter the longest tunnel of the hike, the 1,376-foot Silver Run Tunnel (Tunnel #19). Walking through the darkness, you may not really want to hear the story of the Ghost of Silver Run. Local legend states that the shadowy figure of a young woman dressed in a flowing white gown occasionally appears to those traveling through the tunnel. One account says she was struck by a passing train many years ago, while another version holds that she disappeared one night while riding the train to meet her beau in Parkersburg.

The clapboard farmhouse at 16.6 miles was built in the late 1800s, when agriculture played a more important role in West Virginia. Yet, the agrarian life has not faded away completely, as evidenced by the cows you hear mooing in the field a short distance later. The trail makes several crossings of Goose Creek before coming into Petroleum at 20.2 miles. Now just a few houses, it is another one of the towns that have diminished from their heyday. However, today it is the only place on this hike where you are permitted to camp. A small shelter and vault toilet mark the spot.

Leaving Petroleum, you will cross four bridges over Goose Creek that were built between 1907 and 1911 before crossing a gravel road at 22.2 miles. The next gravel road crossing, at 22.9 miles, brings the hike to a close.

49

Mountwood Park

Total distance (circuit): 3.7 miles

Hiking time: 2 hours

Vertical rise: 360 feet

Maps: USGS 7½' Petroleum; park hand-out map

The Hike at a Glance

0.9   Four Corners
1.6   Stiles Mansion ruins
2.0   ruins of caretaker's house
2.6   left onto Haystack Trail
3.2   footbridge over small ravine
3.7   end

Sometimes, a lack of money can be a good thing. Especially for those of us who like our parks more on the natural side. Due to funding cutbacks, many of the expansive outdoor recreational facilities originally proposed for Mountwood Park in the 1970s were never built. This is not to say that there is a lack of activities to engage in. A launch is available for those who bring their own boat to the 50-acre lake, decks and platforms provide barrier-free access for fishing for trout and bass, and a marina rents paddleboats, canoes, johnboats, and kayaks. Miniature golf, game courts, ball fields, and a disc-golf course cater to the competitive minded. Picnic shelters and more than 200 tables enable families to enjoy outdoor gatherings. A campground, located on a disjunct portion of the park just a short distance away, has full hook-ups, modern restrooms, and hot showers.

It may sound like a lot, but all of these activities and facilities are located on a relatively small portion of the park, leaving the rest of the 2,600 acres undisturbed. Around the turn of the 21st century, a dedicated group of local mountain bikers worked with officials to rehabilitate and expand the park's network of trails, creating some of the most environmentally sound pathways I have ever seen volunteers build. Sidehill sections are banked and shored up correctly, switchbacks are long and wide, and extremely steep sections are kept to a minimum. Their superb construction should keep the routes in good shape for years to come.

On rolling topography located less than 20 miles from the Ohio River, this hike starts

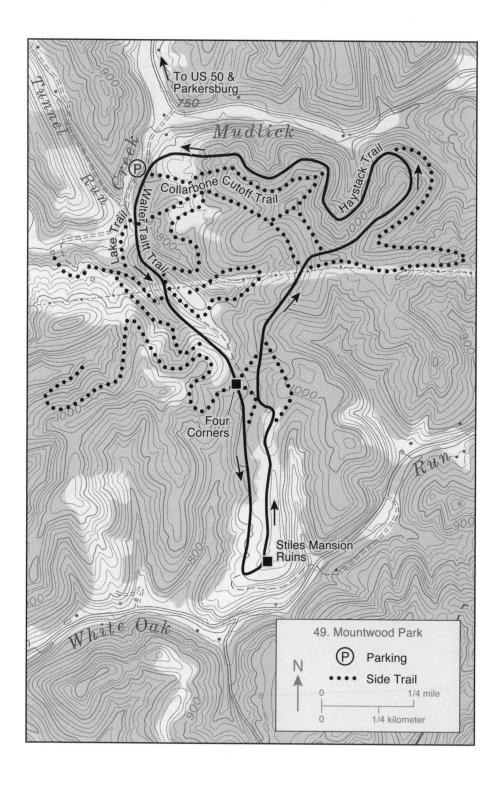

To US 50 &
Parkersburg

Tunnel Run

Creek

Mudlick

Collarbone Cutoff Trail

Haystack Trail

Lake Trail

Walter Taitt Trail

Four
Corners

Stiles Mansion
Ruins

White Oak

Run

49. Mountwood Park

Ⓟ Parking

•••• Side Trail

| 0 | 1/4 mile |

| 0 | 1/4 kilometer |

N

with an initial short, quick rise from the lake but continues with just minor changes in elevation before gradually descending back to the starting point. In addition to being a walk through deciduous forestland populated by squirrels, rabbits, foxes, chipmunks, and turkeys, it can be a lesson in the history of the region's oil and natural gas industry.

Mountwood Park may be reached by taking exit 176 off I-77 at Parkersburg, driving east on US50 for 12.0 miles, and turning right onto Volcano Road (WV5) to immediately enter the park. Drive for another 0.7 mile, make a right turn onto the road for the marina, and continue through the parking lot and onto the small roadway signed for FISH-ING, HIKING, AND BOATING. Park on the right, across from the trail, shortly before the road comes to an end.

Walk into the woods, ascend on the Walter Taitt Trail, and stay right at the first intersection in less than 250 feet. The wide pathway you are following was once a major county road, connecting the town of Volcano to other parts of the state. Located near the park's southeastern border, Volcano is now just a few houses on a hillside, but in its prime it had a population of more than 8,000, with numerous stores, hotels, saloons, warehouses, churches, two schools, an opera house, and its own newspaper. Like other towns in the region, its fortunes rose and fell with the discovery and then near depletion of one of the richest oil and natural gas fields in the country.

The Lake Trail goes off to the right at 0.1 mile. Stay left and ascend gradually along the graveled route. A mountain bike trail comes in from the left at 0.4 mile. Stay to the right on the main route, and pass under power lines whose cleared right-of-way looks onto a deep ravine populated with buckeye, tulip poplar trees, and red maple trees. The red maple is well named, as it adds splashes of red to the forest throughout much of the year. Its springtime red-and-yellow male flowers and deep-crimson female flowers soon develop into two-winged, scarlet seed pods, while its broad green leaves are attached to branches by dark red stems in the summer. In fall, the red maple leaves are well known for their fiery reds and oranges.

Descend to pass through a gap, a pine plantation, and—although nothing is now visible—the homesite of Jim Shock, who worked for the local natural gas company. Rise to a spot known as the Four Corners intersection at 0.9 mile. Forsake routes going left and right, continue straight on the main route, and descend past many beech and a few catalpa trees. With large, heart-shaped leaves, the catalpa is the northernmost representative of a tropical family of plants that includes close to 700 species of trees, shrubs, and vines. Not native to West Virginia, it was well known in the mid-20th century to many country boys, who would sneak behind the barn to smoke one of its long, cigarlike fruits. They are not a very tasty smoke, but they do add character to the forest by dangling like pendants on long stems months after the leaves have fallen off the trees.

The rock wall to the left of the trail at 1.2 miles was used to hold dirt and level the field, making it easier to maintain it as farmland in the early 1900s. The farmer and his crops and livestock are no longer here, and grapevines now grow over the trees and other vegetation that have taken over the meadow. Come to a T-intersection at 1.5 miles. To the right it is a few hundred yards to WV28.

Bear left and reach the ruins of the Stiles Mansion at 1.6 miles. The huge house, known as Thornhill, was built in the shape of a Maltese cross in 1874 by William Cooper Stiles. As you walk around its foundation, overgrown by honeysuckle and other

Ruins of the Stiles Mansion

vegetation, you can get only a small idea of how large it was. With three stories and 25 rooms, it contained Wood County's first bathtub and was adorned by a rambling porch reached by steep stone steps. Stiles was born in Philadelphia, Pennsylvania, and was one of the first and most successful of the investors and operators in the oil fields of the area.

Continue past the homesite on a grassy woods road, bypassing a narrow trail that comes in from the left in about 100 feet. Stay on the main route and come to a Y-intersection. Go left and swing around the pit of the old cistern. The woods road comes to an end at 1.75 miles. Take the narrow footpath signed as leading to the caretaker's house foundation, and enjoy easy walking along the flat ridgetop you are now traversing. The crumbling foundation of the caretaker's house at 2.0 miles shows that it, too, was built in the shape of a Maltese cross.

Just beyond this is a shortcut trail to the left leading back to Four Corners. You want to stay right along the ridgeline, swinging left as you join a woods road at 2.1 miles, and descend for a short distance. At 2.3 miles, stay to the right at the top of a knob (left goes back to the Walter Taitt Trail), pass under power lines at 2.5 miles, and be sure to continue to the left, not to the right downhill. Be alert at 2.6 miles. Do not continue to the right, but make a hard left onto the narrower Haystack Trail. Squawroot and jack-in-the-pulpit are part of the vegetation growing on this northwest-facing slope.

Many people think that the green, white, or purple sheath with a hood (the pulpit), which surrounds and covers "Jack," is the plant's flower. Actually, the sheath is just a leaf bract, and in order to see the diminutive flowers, you need to lift up the hood and look inside to see them clustered around Jack's base. Insects are drawn into the sheath, known as a spathe, to reach the flower's pollen on the floor of the spathe. Once there, they find that the only escape is through a tiny hole where the two sides of the spathe meet. Often an insect is not small enough to slip through or strong enough to muscle its way out and dies, entombed in the flower.

Swing around the head of a hollow on a well-designed sidehill trail at 2.8 miles, cross several small water runs, and begin a gradual descent. The footbridge at 3.2 miles crosses a small ravine, whose stream emerges from a small cave below a rock above the trail, and you will know you are getting close to the end of the hike when the lake and marina become visible through the vegetation at 3.4 miles. It has to have been a long, long time since the old hay harvester beside the trail at 3.5 miles was last used. Not only is it heavily rusted, but trees and vegetation are growing through it. The Collarbone Cutoff Trail comes in from the left at 3.6 miles. Stay to the right, and make another right a few feet later onto the Walter Taitt Trail, returning to your car at 3.7 miles.

If you started your hike early in the morning, there are probably several more hours of daylight left. My advice about what to do with them? Don't go home yet. Take a look at the park handout map, figure out another circuit hike, and go walk some of the other many miles of trails.

50

Middle Island/Ohio River

Total distance (circuit): 2.25 miles

Hiking time: 1 hour

Vertical rise: 10 feet

Maps: USGS 7½' Raven Rock

The Hike at a Glance

0.3   bench
0.5   loop trail intersection
0.9   wildlife blind
1.1   left onto dirt road
1.5   break in vegetation with view
        of river
2.25 end

The story of the National Wildlife Refuge System is a lesson to skeptics who don't believe that one person can make a difference.

Not long after arriving in the United States from his native Germany, Paul Kroegel moved to Florida in 1881 and became alarmed that plume hunters were causing a rapid decline in the population of pelicans on a coastal island. He expressed his concern to others, going so far as to contact President Theodore Roosevelt.

Roosevelt, who helped instigate a worldwide movement of protecting lands and wildlife through the establishment of dozens of national parks, monuments, and forests, created another mechanism for reaching the same goal by pronouncing Florida's Pelican Island the country's first wildlife refuge in 1903. By the time his presidency came to an end in 1909, Roosevelt had signed 51 executive orders to establish more.

From the frigid tundra of Alaska to a small atoll of the Samoan Archipelago in the South Pacific, the National Wildlife Refuge System, administered by the Department of Interior's U.S. Fish and Wildlife Service (USFWS), has grown to include more than 500 refuges in all 50 states and U.S. territories. With more than 95 million acres, the system contains more land than our national park system.

Established in 1990, the Ohio River Islands National Wildlife Refuge currently consists of more than 20 islands and several mainland tracts in Pennsylvania, West Virginia, and Kentucky. The refuge helps protect, restore, and enhance habitat for wildlife native to the river's floodplain. Close to 200

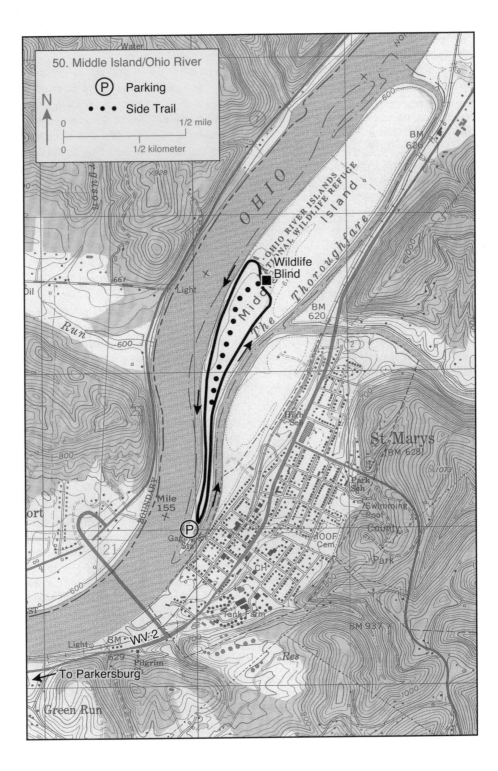

50. Middle Island/Ohio River

Ⓟ Parking

••• Side Trail

N

0 ————————— 1/2 mile

0 ————————— 1/2 kilometer

Wildlife
Blind

OHIO

OHIO RIVER ISLANDS
NATIONAL WILDLIFE REFUGE

Island

The Thoroughfare

BM
626

BM
620

St. Marys
(BM 628)

Mile
155

Park
Sch

Swimming
Pool

County

High
Sch

IOOF
Cem

Park

CH

Tank Farm

Gage
Sta

BM 937

WV 2

Light   BM
629   Pilgrim

To Parkersburg

Res

Green Run

species of birds use refuge lands and surrounding waters, including warblers, bald eagles, ospreys, and a variety of ducks and other waterfowl. Deer, squirrels, raccoons, opossums, groundhogs, cottontail rabbits, foxes, frogs, toads, and snakes are frequently seen, and muskrats and beavers swim along the water's edge. Smallmouth and largemouth bass, white bass, and catfish are just a few of the scores of species of fish found in refuge waters, as well as more than 40 species of freshwater mussels.

Unbeknownst to many people, the Ohio River (up to the high-water mark on its western shore) is part of West Virginia, which enables Middle Island to be included in a hiking guide to the state. The 240-acre island is one of only two in the refuge that are currently accessible by automobile. With easy walking, a nature trail takes visitors through several different types of vegetative cover and wildlife habitats. The island is the perfect spot to bring city-bound children who have never been delighted by a rabbit hopping from the underbrush, the cry of an osprey flying overhead with a fish grasped in its talons, or the bark of a red fox calling out to its young.

To reach Middle Island, take exit 179 off I-77 (north of Parkersburg), drive on WV2 North for 16.5 miles, turn left onto George Street in St. Mary's, continue to the end of the street, and go over the bridge to the parking area on Middle Island.

Start the outing by following the trail across the road from the parking area. Ever since the island was purchased in 1995, the USFWS has pursued a policy of allowing the island to reforest itself, as well as actively planting native trees to encourage a diversity of habitat. Many of the open areas will gradually progress from meadow plants to pioneer trees to, eventually, a climax woodland of hardwoods. In the open areas, expect to

see many composite flowers, blackberry, milkweed, and grasses.

A bench at 0.3 mile provides a rest area, and if you pay attention here or in other places along the hike, you might see somewhat circular patches of disturbed vegetation that may indicate a deer slept in the spot within the last day or two. Stay to the right when you come to a loop trail intersection at 0.5 mile. This open area, dotted by tall milkweed plants, permits you to see the mountains of Ohio on the far side of the river. To aid in reforestation, the USFWS has planted a number of trees tolerant to flooding, including silver maple, cottonwood, sycamore, black willow, red elm, green ash, hackberry, and river birch.

With a range extending farther south than that of any of the other birches, the river birch, also known as red birch, has a tendency to fork at its base, with several trunks leaning outward and providing shade along the river bank. Its seeds ripen in May and June, when rivers are typically running at their highest. Borne upon the currents, the seeds travel to some distant shore, germinate in its muddy soil, and send up shoots within a few short weeks.

Pass by another bench at 0.7 mile, and come to the wildlife blind overlooking the seasonal wetland at 0.9 mile. Mallards, wood ducks, and Canada geese are some of the most common waterfowl seen here, while buffleheads, mergansers, and scaups are frequent winter visitors. Scaups are the only ducks in North America to have a broad white stripe on the trailing edges of their wings. Of the two species that occur on the continent, it is most likely you will see the lesser scaup, as the greater scaup is usually confined along the coast and in northern parts of the United States and Canada. About the only way to tell the two species apart is that the male greater scaup's head is

Ohio River

a glossy green, as opposed to the male lesser scaup's glossy purple.

You have an option when you are ready to leave the blind. You could make a hard left onto the footpath and follow it back to the loop trail intersection, where a right turn will bring you back to your car. However, because it allows you to walk a little longer and also enjoy views of the Ohio River, I'm suggesting you take the handicapped-accessible trail, walk past maintenance buildings, and turn left onto the main island dirt road at 1.1 miles. (You could make a right at this point and walk another mile on the road to the end of the island and then backtrack to this point, adding about 2 miles to the length of this hike.)

Although purple loosestrife is certainly a pretty purple flower that grows along the road and in the fields, it is an invasive plant that spreads so aggressively that it replaces native vegetation and destroys important wetlands. Among the other plants invading the island are Japanese knotweed and mile-a-minute, a spiny vine that climbs 10 to 20 feet into trees, often smothering native shrubs and robbing sunlight from herbaceous plants. Two other plants that are not native to North America, day lily and mullein, sprout up along the edges of the narrow woodlands between the road and the river.

If lucky, you may hear the *zweet zweet zweet zweet zweet zweet* song of prothonotary warblers, which are fond of wet, wooded areas. Their bright, golden-orange heads and chests make them easy to spot against the forest's dark foliage. Arriving from the south around April, they are the only eastern warblers to nest in cavities. Amazingly, the young are capable of swimming, certainly an important skill when born close to a river.

A break in the vegetation at 1.5 miles provides the best view of the Ohio River you will have on the hike. Looking at the deep, rolling water, it is hard to imagine that it was just a shallow stream not much more than a foot deep when settlers first appeared along its the banks. As early as 1825, the U.S. Army Corps of Engineers began dredging sandbars and removing snags. The first dam was completed in 1885, and today there are 20 dams that maintain a minimum 12-foot-deep channel for navigation. No longer a free-flowing, shallow river, the Ohio is now a series of slow-moving lakes, some of which are close to 100 miles long and 50 feet deep. The river carries about 25 percent of the country's total inland waterway traffic, with an annual freight of close to 150 million tons.

The short trail to the left at 1.7 miles provides access to the loop trail and the rest of the nature trail, if you decide you have had enough of walking the road. However, if you stay along the road, you may get to see a raccoon rob a muskrat's cache of shellfish to include in its omnivorous diet. At the turn of the 20th century, it is said that the Ohio River basin was paved with hundreds of thousands of freshwater mussels. While impoundments, siltation, channelization, and pollution have taken their toll, the native mussels now face a major threat from the introduced zebra mussel. Attaching themselves in such great numbers, the zebras deny native mussels the ability to feed or respire.

The reproductive process of the native mussels is a complex and fascinating one. Males release sperm into the water, which is taken in by females as they respire. The eggs are fertilized and develop into larvae, known as glochida, in the females' gills. When released, the glochida must attach themselves to the gills or fins of specific fish species, where they grow into juvenile mussels and drop off to complete their lives on the riverbed.

The hike comes to an end at 2.25 miles, returning to the parking area where your car is ready to whisk you away to your next exploration of West Virginia's natural wonders.

Happy trails.

Suggested Reading and Field Guides

Adams, Kevin, and Marty Casstevens. *Wildflowers of the Southern Appalachians: How to Photograph and Identify Them.* Winston-Salem, NC: John F. Blair Publisher, 1996.

Adkins, Leonard M. *The Appalachian Trail: A Visitor's Companion.* Birmingham, AL: Menasha Ridge Press, 2000.

———.*50 Hikes in Maryland: Walks, Hikes, and Backpacks from the Allegheny Plateau to the Atlantic Ocean.* Woodstock, VT: Countryman Press, 2007.

———.*50 Hikes in Northern Virginia: Walks, Hikes, and Backpacks from the Allegheny Mountains to the Chesapeake Bay.* Woodstock, VT: Countryman Press, 2006.

———.*West Virginia Explorer's Guide.* Woodstock, VT: Countryman Press, 2011.

———.*Wildflowers of the Appalachian Trail.* Birmingham, AL: Menasha Ridge Press, 2000.

Brill, David. *As Far as the Eye Can See: Reflections of an Appalachian Trail Hiker.* Harpers Ferry, WV: Appalachian Trail Conservancy, 2004.

Brooks, Maurice. *The Appalachians.* Morgantown, WV: Seneca Books, 1995.

Burn, Barbara. *North American Trees.* Avenel, NJ: Gramercy Books, 1992.

Busch, Phyllis. *Wildflowers and the Stories Behind Their Names.* New York: Charles Scribner's Sons, 1977.

Byrd, Nathan, editor. *A Forester's Guide to Observing Animal Use of Forest Habitat in the South.* Atlanta, GA: U.S. Department of Agriculture, Forest Service, 1981.

Chambers, Kenneth A. *A County-Lover's Guide to Wildlife: Mammals, Amphibians, and Reptiles of the Northeastern United States.* Baltimore, MD: Johns Hopkins University Press, 1979.

Dana, William S. *How to Know the Wildflowers.* Boston: Houghton Mifflin, 1991.

Eastman, John. *The Book of Forest and Thicket: Trees, Shrubs, and Wildflowers of Eastern North America.* Mechanicsburg, PA: Stackpole Books, 1992.

Giardina, Denise. *Storming Heaven.* New York, NY: Ivy Books, 1991.

Grimm, William and John Kartesz. *The Illustrated Book of Trees: The Comprehensive Field Guide to More than 250 Trees in Eastern North America.* Mechanicsburg, PA: Stackpole Books, 2001.

———.*The Illustrated Book of Wildflowers and Shrubs: The Comprehensive Guide to more than 1,300 Plants in Eastern America.* Mechanicsburg, PA: Stackpole Books, 1993.

Johnson, Hugh. *Hugh Johnson's Encyclopedia of Trees.* New York: Portland House, 1990.

Murie, Olaus J. *A Field Guide to Animal Tracks.* Boston: Houghton Mifflin, 2005.

Peterson, Roger Tory. *A Field Guide to the Birds of Eastern and Central North America.* Boston: Houghton Mifflin, 2002.

Peterson, Roger T. and McKenny, Margaret. *A Field Guide to Wildflowers of Northeastern and North-Central North America.* Boston: Houghton Mifflin, 2002.

Petrides, George A. *A Field Guide to Trees and Shrubs.* Boston: Houghton Mifflin, 1988.

Reid, Fiona. *Field Guide to Mammals of North America.* Boston: Houghton Mifflin, 2006.

Stokes, Donald W. *The Natural History of Wild Shrubs and Vines: Eastern and Central North America.* New York: Harper and Row, 1981.

Thomas, Vaughn, editor. *Appalachian Trail Guide to Southwest Virginia.* Harpers Ferry, WV: Appalachian Trail Conference, 1994.

Williams, John Alexander. *West Virginia: A History.* Morgantown, WV: WV University Press, 2003.

Addresses

Hike 1:
Harpers Ferry National Historical Park
P.O. Box 65
Harpers Ferry, WV 25425
304-535-6029
www.nps.gov/hafe

Hike 2:
Cacapon Resort State Park
818 Cacapon Lodge Drive
Berkeley Springs, WV 25411
304-258-1022
www.cacaponresort.com

Hike 3:
Lee Ranger District
95 Railroad Avenue
Edinburg, VA 22824
540-984-4101
www.southernregion.fs.fed.us/gwj

Hike 4:
Lost River State Park
321 Park Drive
Mathias, WV 26812
304-897-5372
www.lostriversp.com

Hikes 5, 7, 8, 9, and 10:
Potomac Ranger District
HC 59, Box 240
Petersburg, WV 26847
304-257-4488
www.fs.usda.gov/mnf

Hike 6:
Seneca Rocks Discovery Center
P.O. Box 13
Seneca Rocks, WV 26884
304-567-2827
www.fs.usda.gov/mnf

Hike 11:
Canaan Valley Resort and Conference
Center
230 Main Lodge Road
Davis, WV 26260
304-866-4121
www.canaanresort.com

Hike 12:
Blackwater Falls State Park
1584 Blackwater Lodge Road
P.O. Drawer 490
Davis, WV 26260
304-259-5216
www.blackwaterfalls.com

Hike 13:
Cheat Ranger District
P.O. Box 368
Parsons, WV 26287
304-478-3251
www.fs.usda.gov/mnf

Hikes 14, 15, and 16:
Greenbrier Ranger District
P.O. Box 67
Bartow, WV 24920
304-456-3335
www.fs.usda.gov/mnf

Hike 17:
Greenbrier River Trail
HC 82, Box 252
Marlinton, WV 24954
304-799-7416
www.greenbrierrailtrailstatepark.com

Hikes 18 and 22:
Marlinton Ranger District
P.O. Box 210
Marlinton, WV 24954-0210
304-779-4334
www.fs.usda.gov/mnf

Hikes 19, 20, and 21:
Gauley Ranger District
932 North Fork Cherry Road
Richwood, WV 26261
304-846-2695
www.fs.usda.gov/mnf

Hikes 23 and 24:
Droop Mountain Battlefield State Park
HC 64, Box 189
Hillsboro, WV 24946
304-653-4254
www.droopmountainbattlefield.com
www.beartownstatepark.com

Hikes 25 and 26:
White Sulphur Springs Ranger District
410 East Main Street
White Sulphur Springs, WV 24986
304-536-2144
www.fs.usda.gov/mnf

Hike 27:
Greenbrier State Forest
HC 30 Box 154
Caldwell, WV 24925-9709
304-536-1944
www.greenbriersf.com

Hike 28:
Appalachian Trail Conservancy
799 Washington Street
 P.O. Box 807
Harpers Ferry, WV 25425-0807
304-535-6331
www.appalachiantrail.org

Hikes 29 and 30:
Pipestem Resort State Park
Route 20, Box 150
Pipestem, WV 25979
304-466-1800
www.pipestemresort.com

Hike 31:
Bluestone State Park
HC 78, Box 3
Hinton, WV 25951

304-466-2805
www.bluestonesp.com

Hikes 32 and 33:
New River Gorge National River
P. O. Box 246
Glen Jean, WV 25846
304-763-3715
www.nps.gov/neri

Hike 34:
Twin Falls State Park
Route 97, Box 667
Mullens, WV 25882
304-294-4000
www.twinfallsresort.com

Hike 35:
Panther Wildlife Management Area
HC 63, Box 923
Panther, WV 24872
304-938-2252
www.pantherstateforest.com

Hike 36:
Carnifex Ferry Battlefield State Park
1194 Carnifex Ferry Road
Summersville, WV 26651
304-872-0825
www.carnifexferrybattlefieldstatepark.com

Hike 37:
Cedar Creek State Park
2947 Cedar Creek Road
Glenville, WV 26351
304-462-7158
www.cedarcreeksp.com

Hike 38:
Stonewall Resort State Park
940 Resort Drive
Roanoke, WV 26447
304-269-7400
www.stonewallresort.com

Hike 39:
Lewis Wetzel Wildlife Management Area
HC 62, Box 8
Jacksonburg, WV 26377
304-889-3497
www.wvdnr.gov/hunting/D1WMAareas
.shtm

Hike 40:
Coopers Rock State Forest
61 County Line Drive
Bruceton Mills, WV 26525
304-594-1561
www.coopersrockstateforest.com

Hike 41:
Oglebay Park
465 Lodge Drive
Wheeling, WV 26003
304-243-4000
www.oglebay-resort.com
or
Oglebay Institute
Schrader Environmental Education
Center
The Burton Center
Wheeling, WV 26003
304-242-6855
www.oionline.com

Hike 42:
Tomlinson Run State Park
84 Osage Road
P. O. Box 97
New Manchester, WV 26056
304-564-3651
www.tomlinsonrunsp.com

Hike 43:
Chief Logan State Park
376 Little Buffalo Creek Road
Logan, WV 25601
304-792-7125
www.chiefloganstatepark.com

Hike 44:
Beech Fork State Park
5601 Long Branch Road

Barboursville, WV 25504
304-528-5794
www.beechforksp.com

Hike 45:
Huntington Museum of Art
2033 McCoy Road
Huntington, WV 25701
304-529-2701
www.hmoa.org

Hike 46:
Kanawha State Forest
7500 State Forest Drive
Route 2, Box 285
Charleston, WV 25314
304-558-3500
www.kanawhastateforest.com

Hike 47:
Coonskin Park
2000 Coonskin Drive
Charleston, WV 25311
304-341-8000
www.kcprc.com/coonskin_park.htm

Hike 48:
North Bend Rail-Trail
Route 1, Box 221
Cairo, WV 26337
304-643-2931
www.wvparks.com/northbendrailtrail

Hike 49:
Mountwood Park
1014 Volcano Road
Waverly, WV 26184
304-679-3611
www.mountwoodpark.org

Hike 50:
Ohio River Islands National Wildlife
Refuge
3983 Waverly Road
Williamstown, WV 26187
304-375-2923
www.fws.gov/northeast/ohioriverislands

Become a West Virginia Trail Master

Become a recognized West Virginia Trail Master by hiking every one of the *50 Hikes in West Virginia*. Simply keep a record of the date of each of your hikes and write a report (it doesn't need to be more than one or two sentences) for each trail, providing your feelings about the hike, its condition, and if anything has changed since this book was published. In return, receive the suitable-for-framing West Virginia Trail Master certificate of recognition. Join a very elite club—as of the publication of this book, the author, Leonard M. Adkins, is the only person to have reported having done all of the hikes. Send reports to habitualhiker@verizon.net.

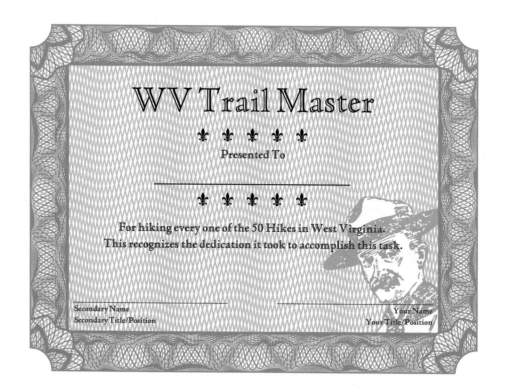

WV Trail Master

✣ ✣ ✣ ✣ ✣

Presented To

_____

✣ ✣ ✣ ✣ ✣

For hiking every one of the 50 Hikes in West Virginia.
This recognizes the dedication it took to accomplish this task.

Secondary Name
Secondary Title/Position

Your Name
Your Title/Position